Oscillations of Literary Theory

SUNY series, Transforming Subjects: Psychoanalysis, Culture, and Studies in Education

---

Deborah P. Britzman, editor

Oscillations of Literary Theory

The Paranoid Imperative and Queer Reparative

A. C. Facundo

SUNY PRESS

Cover art: *Vanishing Point* by A. C. Facundo, oil on canvas, 16" × 20", 2015

Published by
STATE UNIVERSITY OF NEW YORK PRESS
Albany

Printed in the United States of America

For information, contact
State University of New York Press
www.sunypress.edu

Production, Laurie D. Searl
Marketing, Anne M. Valentine

Library of Congress Cataloging-in-Publication Data

Names: Facundo, A. C., 1985– author.
Title: Oscillations of literary theory : the paranoid imperative and queer reparative / A. C. Facundo.
Description: Albany : State University of New York Press, 2016. | Series: SUNY series, transforming subjects: psychoanalysis, culture, and studies in education | Includes bibliographical references and index.
Identifiers: LCCN 2016007707 (print) | LCCN 2016029030 (ebook) | ISBN 9781438463094 (hardcover : alk. paper) | ISBN 9781438463087 (pbk. : alk paper) | ISBN 9781438463100 (e-book)
Subjects: LCSH: Literature, Modern—Psychological aspects. | Psychoanalysis and literature. | Literature, Modern—20th century—History and criticism. | Paranoia in literature. | Homosexuality in literature.
Classification: LCC PN56.P92 F35 2016 (print) | LCC PN56.P92 (ebook) | DDC 809/.04—dc23
LC record available at https://lccn.loc.gov/2016007707

10 9 8 7 6 5 4 3 2 1

For Margo

Contents

Acknowledgments

A constellation of individual and institutional support has made it possible for me to complete this project. I thank the Social Sciences and Humanities Research Council of Canada (SSHRC) for investing in my research throughout the several stages of its development, of which this book is a product. Because institutional intelligibility is so vital to a project of this magnitude, I am grateful to the English Departments at York University and University at Buffalo (SUNY), as well as UB's Center for the Study of Psychoanalysis and Culture, for providing me with library and technology resources, as well as vibrant academic communities that allowed my ideas to flourish. I thank members of ACCUTE (Association of Canadian College and University Teachers of English) for providing a collegial venue to present my ideas annually and receive feedback as this project took shape.

I feel privileged to work with several scholars whose conceptual and practical insights were integral both to the development of my thinking and to the publication of my writing. I thank Tim Dean in his capacity as postdoctoral mentor for his incisive perception, attentive guidance, and detailed feedback, as well as for giving me the opportunity to work with him. I am indebted to Deborah Britzman, who has helped me create new paths of inquiry and reinvigorated my capacity to ask new questions. As the series editor, Deborah has been the driving force behind the publication of this book, and I thank her sincerely for believing in my work. I thank my editor, Beth Bouloukos, for showing interest in my writing, for taking the time and effort to see this project through, and for working with me so generously. I give thanks to Laurie Searl, Anne Valentine, and the marketing and production department at SUNY Press for the collaborative support. I also thank the anonymous reviewers who communicated to me through SUNY Press to provide feedback that was necessary to the book's completion. As a doctoral supervisor and dear friend, Terry Goldie has been a consistent source of clear thinking and grounded perspective in his editorial and conceptual feedback. The rigor with which Thomas Loebel treated my writing was indispensable to my thinking, and I am grateful to him. I suspect that I have not let on to either Terry or Thomas how much I've appreciated (and relied on) their constant support. I am grateful for my conversations with Adam Phillips, who inspired the final stages of the manuscript and the rewriting of the Introduction.

I thank my colleagues and peer readers who devoted a significant amount of time and energy providing feedback on early drafts of the manuscript. Bernice Neal has read multiple versions since its inception and saw its evolution with staggering enthusiasm. Jared Morrow and Thom Bryce-McQuinn enriched the dialogical aspects of the book with their generous readings. I offer my thanks to Steven Bruhm, who provided thorough and extensive conceptual and editorial feedback for the purposes of publication.

Many members of the larger academic community enlivened my thinking, ultimately to the benefit of this book. These thinkers include Hannele Kivinen, Robin Morden, Kristen Ames, Duncan Clegg, Kate Siklosi, Richard Welch, Dani Spinosa, Navneet Alang, Denise Handlarski, Jonathan Vandor, Aparna Tarc, Lisa Farley, Daena Crosby, Natalie Samson, Sorouja Moll, Karen MacFarlane, Craig Patterson, Smaro Kamboureli, Clive Thomson, and Lynn Weinlos. I also thank John Englar and the staff at Jet Fuel Coffee Shop, for providing a neighborhood office space, for caffeinating this project, and for the familial consistency that added structure to my work day.

I thank my parents, Lucille and Ramon Facundo, whose abundant and unconditional support allowed me to thrive. Thanks to my brother, Mark Facundo, whose sense of humor provided a kind of support that no one else could replicate. I thank the rest of my large family for teaching me how familial consistency enables me to work and think.

Margo Gouley was a most generous and exacting reader. I trust Margo for incisive observations and reliable suggestions, and I owe the clarity of my thought to her. As my companion in difficult thinking, Margo has shared with me a joy that I had not previously known. With love, I thank her.

Introduction

Queering Omniscience

Myths of decline are myths of progress inverted.

—Adam Phillips, *Missing Out,* 113

An attachment to catastrophe offers an unexpected degree of comfort. At best, catastrophe provides an alibi for letting go of desire and of the wish. At worst, catastrophe allows an escape from the difficult vulnerability that can accompany the pleasure of surprise and the surprises of pleasure. Such attachment, in other words, offers a life structured by anticipation and certainty. Catastrophe allows an insistence on no future; but the certainty of that insistence mirrors the certainty in any mythical future that it would deny.

A variety of postwar fiction (1945 onward), however, invites readers to entertain inescapable catastrophes. This book illustrates how such catastrophes provoke a desire for omniscience, either in the characters or the reader. Indeed, one way to cope with implacable catastrophe is to gain omniscience over it: to read it thoroughly and repeatedly in order to gain, at the very least, interpretive mastery. While a relationship to omniscience varies among subjects, omniscience is consistently an elusive object of desire; in critical practice, however, omniscience is vital in its promise to "see" what others cannot. As a perennial question for literary studies, omniscience functions in narrative to motivate characters and propel the action. The desire for omniscience—that is, for certainty—can serve as a point of, not arrival, but entry into thinking. Omniscience changes from an aim to part of a technique to which one submits only provisionally. Because of the aesthetic distance omniscience affords, it is irreconcilable with intimacy, yet both omniscience and intimacy are necessary to the process of creative thinking. In the literature that I address here, I explore how the reader can inherit this desire for omniscience: its promise mediates a relationship to the text, while its inevitable failure initiates creative thinking and an elaboration of intimacy.

Adam Phillips suggests that certainty about an undesirable condition can enable and justify escape. He contends that the urge to "get out" of a situation might be "unduly omniscient" (*Missing Out* 113). The *OED* defines omniscience as "an attribute of God, or of a person: the fact, state, or quality of having infinite knowledge." Another definition is less absolute: "the fact, state, or quality of having, or claiming to have, great knowledge." The *OED* defines omniscience also in relation to literary theory "as an attribute of the author or a third-person narrator: a full and complete knowledge concerning all the events of a narrative, and the private motives, thoughts, etc., of all the characters." Associated with both infinity and claims to greatness, with both inner and outer worlds, with both belonging to the author or narrator but shared with the reader, omniscience becomes a slippery signifier in that it exists only through a claim, elusive object, or myth (God). In psychoanalysis, omniscience is the basis of curiosity, but because it remains elusive, especially as it structures narrative, it becomes more closely associated with frustration.

In psychoanalytic terms, omniscience is a defense that stems from the phantasy of omnipotence.[1] In such phantasy the subject inhabits a paranoid position that is necessary but insufficient to difficult thinking. Paranoia involves a projection of knowledge into a reality that the subject can only ever approximate rather than fix with certainty. With literature, difficult thinking becomes difficult reading because the text provides a site for phantasies to play out. This book argues that, in the particular process of reading fiction, catastrophe becomes not an obstacle but a condition for the surprise of intimacy and pleasure. Fiction is where phantasy is drawn out at length, and its slow unfolding is mimetic of the extensive search for meaning in subjectivity, a search that is not necessarily fulfilled in its completion. In fiction, then, phantasy allows readers to enjoy in subjectivity less a point of arrival than an elastic relationship to longing. The process of reading that I propose fosters such longing in a way that one could describe as erotic. In my queer approach to omniscience, I show how the reader can "know" a text in the biblical sense, so to speak. Indeed, in light of the psychoanalytic notion of the unconscious, what comes into question is the idea of carnal "knowledge" about a body or text—whatever one prefers to read at any given moment.

The lure and subsequent failure of omniscience is a literary, aesthetic, political, theoretical, and critical problem. Queer theory comes into play because, over the past few decades, its focus has shifted from thinking about sexual preference and non-normative sex acts within the socio-political realm to thinking more abstractly about object relations. This book makes a timely call to consider what the last few decades have learned about queer sex in relation to the aesthetic and literary artifact. Reading facilitates attachments to objects, attachments that are as varied, provisional, and interrelated as those that mediate human relationships: love, hate, indifference, projection, aggression, mastery, scopophilia, epistemophilia, eroticism, guilt, care, surprise, hurt, and betrayal. In offering one resolution to the question of subjectivity, this book demonstrates that being queer has less to do with identity than a particular way of attaching to objects, and that literature elaborates such attachments.

Attachments can be queer because sometimes they are difficult to articulate. In the socio-political realm, critique works to detach from dominant narratives, but for what new attachments remain ambiguous. In the epigraph that opens my introduction, Phillips alludes to the critique against the post-Enlightenment myth of progress, a critique that emerges perhaps most famously in Walter Benjamin's essay, "Theses on the Philosophy of History." Benjamin invokes Paul Klee's painting, *Angelus Novus*, to imagine an Angel of History who faces the past: "Where we perceive a chain of events, he sees one single catastrophe which keeps piling wreckage upon wreckage . . . [A] storm irresistibly propels him into the future to which his back is turned, while the pile of debris before him grows skyward. This storm is what we call progress" ("Theses" 257–58). Benjamin's metaphor is so aesthetically striking that the Angel resonates in the critical imaginary more soundly than its character foil, Benjamin's preferred protagonist, the historical materialist.[2] The latter, more preferable protagonist "remains in control of his powers, *man* enough to blast open the continuum of history" (262, emphasis added). This "manly" hero rummages adeptly through the shattered discards in the wreckage that the Angel can only wish to make whole again. But the Angel has lost control of its wings and cannot close them. Already the Angel seems more conducive to identification in its ungendered relationship to, not history, but longing. For Benjamin, the Angel is not "man enough" and is thus the problematic character. But the juxtaposition between Angel and heroic "man" of historical materialism exemplifies the condition of any character foil: one half cannot exist without the other, and together they formulate a central enigma of the text.

Given the implications of Phillips's claim, the negation of progress that the metaphor of the Angel induces is a repression and displacement of myth, in this case, the myth of omniscience. The Angel is elevated, and sees from an omniscient point of view, while the historical materialist gains a more immediate relationship with the discards of history. Whereas one enjoys a sense of visual mastery, the other enjoys a tactile one. In both cases, omniscience is an object of desire, whether diachronically across the movement of history, or synchronically in any single moment of history. An attachment to catastrophe suggests an attachment to omniscience. Criticism that repudiates myths of ideal life requires a kind of thinking that is more difficult than a negation of progress. The difficult task for subjectivity is not to insist on disaster but to let go of omniscience after having articulated its phantasy. Whether from the position of the Angel or the historical materialist, phantasy plays a role for the engagement with the wreckage of society to "make whole what has been smashed" ("Theses" 257). As the Angel laments, the twentieth-century struggle with the totality of progress has exacerbated the difficulty of fostering intimacy with the other. The mourning of omniscience is where intimacy begins.

Catastrophe ignites anxiety about thinking, giving us pause on how to think, on where we can think in safety, or on whether we can think in the first place. Since Michel Foucault's *History of Sexuality, Volume 1: An Introduction,* queer theory has been negotiating the capacity to think about sex within the discursive totality of sexuality. The crisis of queer theory, which I describe below, parallels the crises of the humanities, of the university, and in psychoanalysis about the discursive resistances against it. On another level, Julia Kristeva's essay, "Thinking in Dark Times," considers the "crisis of civilization" as a whole (15). She updates Benjamin and Theodor Adorno's paranoia about Enlightenment to question the possibility of thinking in the "dark times" that she identifies as the current, war-torn, technologically saturated society. She questions the value of intellectual work in the twenty-first century, "its place in the world today and its future . . . in a world subject to the automatization of minds by technology" ("Dark Times" 13). She reminds her readers of the "failure of rationalist humanism in twentieth-century totalitarianism" and its potential to reemerge in the current milieu ("Dark Times" 15). Kristeva expresses urgent concern about the new "malady of ideality," which she defines as an ideological imposition of ideal (commodified, sanitized) life on young people, and what Lauren Berlant alternatively names "cruel optimism."[3] The image of ideal life squelches epistemophilia, the polymorphously perverse desire to know, such that belief replaces curiosity ("Dark Times" 18). The inevitable dissatisfaction with belief, unlike the dissatisfaction that follows curiosity, leads people of younger generations to religious fundamentalism and addictions that threaten organic creativity.

An anxiety about the capacity to think underlies Kristeva's concerns about the malady of ideality, adolescent nihilism, technology-based addictions, and ideological fundamentalism. I add that such anxiety knows unconsciously that a twenty-first-century "televisual civilization" ("Dark Times" 16) in crisis will change the theoretical structure of psychic reality in the discourse of psychoanalysis in ways that no one can anticipate. Kristeva's anxieties bespeak epistemological and methodological problems in addition to clinical ones. Her critique of the myth of progress risks conflating technology with catastrophe and authoritarianism.[4] While anxiety circulates in the humanities about the dissolution of curiosity in favor of doctrinaire belief, fiction reminds us that reading practices can blur the difference between curiosity and belief in the very moment of interpretation. Literary reading thinks through the point at which one tips into the other.

In each scene—queer theory, the humanities, academia, a totalized technological society—struggle and frustration play out, but the insistence on catastrophe as an absolute condition marks an incapacity to tolerate such frustration. In light of frustration and its many forms, this book examines what it means to "let go" and what kinds of things we can let go of, culminating in the last chapter's analysis of the wish, "never let me go." We can let go of objects, such as a person, a discourse, an outmoded method, a line of inquiry, or more broadly, the academic institution itself and the investment in education. Conversely, we can let go of the necessary phantasies that structure relationships to such objects in order to arrive at what Leo Bersani calls "new relationality," or "a new way of being present to another person" (*Intimacies* 4). Both kinds of letting go are related; yet, while the former plays out at the level of the social, the latter is more solitary, even though it remains intersubjective.

Because this book thinks about the paranoid position as necessary but insufficient to difficult thinking, the analyses of novels in my chapters imagine dire, indeed catastrophic, manifestations of paranoia that emerge from formations of totality. The inconvenient problem with the ultimate breeding ground of paranoia—authoritarian society, the closed system of capital or of discourse—is that the subject cannot "let go" of it, because once totality can be posited, no "outside" exists. Kristeva, as well as Benjamin, Adorno, and Max Horkheimer, follow Sigmund Freud in negotiating totality. Unlike Freud, who found an "outside" by fleeing from Vienna to Britain to escape the Nazis, the writers in my book who contemplate totality consider a cultural sphere saturated by authoritarian aesthetics. Because my thinking moves from the social to the psychical, this book explores the paranoid attachment to omniscience less as a condition of proto-authoritarian subjectivity than as an entry-point to difficult reading. Subjection to political and social totalities is very much an aesthetic concern.[5] In the socio-political scene of catastrophe, the question is not only about the human capacity for violence, but also, perhaps more importantly, the possibility for and degree of human intimacy. While schools of thought like the Frankfurt School and queer theory work through the politicized relationship between collective human existence and totalized systems, literature works to reanimate human relations.

Now, as philosophical and literary thought marks a shift from the linguistic turn to what W.J.T. Mitchel in *Picture Theory* (1994) calls the "pictorial turn" (11), a shift that seeks visual supplements to the written signifier, the stakes of reading in the twenty-first century affect this persistent question of subjectivity.[6] During the linguistic turn, the tenuous relationship between text and "meaning" transformed the politics of representation and drew attention to the materiality of the signifier. Now, a question arises as to what happens to the way readers consume texts when human perception is mediated by an over-investment in images. Reading practices affect the capacity to think within totalized systems. My book's central question hinges on reconciling how human desire is both a linchpin of unethical acts and a catalyst for an ethical regard of the other. This question implies another: what kind of creative thinking would come after the necessary and valued practice of critical thinking? How does art allow the self to negotiate ideological complicity while realizing a creative, sexualized life? For me, queer is an aesthetic question, playing out at the level of the signifier, and so a problem of reading. In queer theory, thinking finds its rhythmic momentum in the revitalizing potentials of sexuality.

The question of subjectivity—of what to do with it aside from romanticizing its rupture and disarticulation—often becomes reduced to a question of identity politics, which itself risks static thinking because of its attachment to critique. Whether we should undo or affirm identity is a reductive dilemma that, for example, queers have trouble letting go of, understandably due to the politics of representation, equity, and rights at stake, as well as the role that identity has played in gay and lesbian political activism. The concept of identity is reductive because its roots are in the ego, that ever-leaky and inflatable thing, and (indeed, like the blow-up doll) fun only under favorable circumstances and awkward when caught out of context. While the ego will remain (as will identity), its integrity and assurance ought not to be at stake. The project of articulating the self should be capable of flux, divested from the illusory assurance of stable ego-identifications.

My entrance into queer theory, then, stems from the framework of Holocaust Studies, specifically theories on totalitarianism. Yet I depart from such fields in my focus on the psychical rather than the social. In this book, I slow my thinking to consider at length what pleasures and pains can happen in the very solitary relationship between reader and text. Social implications are embedded in rethinking the way phantasies of certainty and identification mediate between self and other. Because I want to focus on the solitary relationship with texts as a way of seeing phantasies through to their completion and loss, I posit a reading subject. The "reader" that this book invokes is different from Gerald Prince's concept of the narratee, which he defines as the fictional character whom the narrator addresses (Prince 7), because of my reader's historical specificity. Other literary theorists use other signifiers to indicate the reading subject, such as Roland Barthes's simple and elegant interchange of first- and second-person pronouns in *The Pleasure of the Text*, or D.A. Miller's use of first-person singular and plural in his queer close readings of film.[7] This present book returns to the term "reader" to posit a speaking subject who is embedded in a queer, psychoanalytic context of the twenty-first century. This hypothetical reader helps me dramatize the theory of reading I call the paranoid imperative and queer reparative, as the reader luxuriates in an erotic relation to the text.

I maintain that omniscience is still useful, if only because in the process of psychoanalytic development, desire for it is unavoidable when its promise initiates thinking. However, omniscience in the context of this book no longer serves as the final object of desire, as implied in the practice of critique, but as part of a technique that remains provisional in the processes of reading and thinking. Omniscience constitutes the "paranoid imperative" in the kind of reading I propose, and the analysis of the fiction in the chapters imagines how omniscience in totality can enthrall the reader.

The "queer reparative" opens up to pleasure and surprise in the text. Surprise is specific in this context to the moment when the detour through the paranoid imperative articulates a phantasy of omniscience only in order to mourn it. At this stage, narratives of certainty and anticipatory relations give way to narratives of intimacy, vulnerability, and longing. On the completion of a reading, as each chapter will show, one mourns the traversal of phantasy's contours in the text. My full investigation of the queer reparative necessitates the various interpretions of literature in each chapter. A kind of reading that submits to such oscillations learns from the discourse of queer theory and its struggles with institutional intelligibility.

In a general sense, "queer" designates a category of sexuality, more often than not an illicit one; however, its place in the humanities is confusing when one considers how "queer" facilitates critical thought. The work of queer theory is multifaceted, and it is often contradictory in both method and agenda within and among its various projects. At times, queer theory attempts to find the sexual in the nonsexual, and so its objects of inquiry and their analytical outcomes end up becoming decidedly "unsexy,"[8] albeit productively so. At other times, queer theory critiques identitarian logic, paradoxically for a political agenda in service of the marginalized other.[9] Such contradictions and noncommittal practices reproduce the very indeterminacy inherent to its name that scholars both celebrate and condemn. As we settle into the second decade of the twenty-first century, queer subjectivity has experienced more than a century of discursive emergence and transformation only to arrive at what seems, presently, like a crisis. The indeterminacy of what queer refers to today often provokes a preoccupation with queer theory's potential death, the major difficulty of its work. Anxiety about queer theory's death concerns the fear that it has lost its capacity to bring about social change; to disrupt heteronormative logic; to free itself from complicity with dominant discourse; to defend against its label as the Americanization of academia; or to secure its canonical position in academic disciplines. Paradoxically, as a result, queer theory retains its sense of political and epistemological urgency in its ongoing development. The difficulties within the field serve as points of active discussion. Gaps, impasses, and contradictions in queer discourse perpetuate its movement forward.

The discursive existence of queer is multivalent. As an object of inquiry, queer theory reflects on its institutional status, develops its theoretical scope, and traces its histories of emergence.[10] As a method, queer theory offers a way of reading cultural paradigms that challenges dominant preconceptions of gender and sexuality.[11] As either object or method, queer analysis employs two rhetorical strategies. On the one hand, according to Janet Halley and Andrew Parker in their volume, *After Sex: On Writing Since Queer Theory* (2011), the "anti-social" negative strategy works to undo identity categories, even to the point of "political and psychic dysphoria" (9). This "anti-social" turn was explicated in the *PMLA*'s 2006 roundtable discussion, "The Antisocial Thesis in Queer Theory," and retroactively characterizes its keystone text, Lee Edelman's *No Future: Queer Theory and the Death Drive* (2004). On the other hand, a turn to the "reparative" borrows from the Kleinian vocabulary of reparation and is grounded in Eve Sedgwick's work, but this turn moves away from psychoanalysis toward the lived experience of political and public life. The reparative turn, associated with more positive modes of thought, has thus far become synonymous with the turn to affect, in contradistinction to the vocabulary of the drives that is more closely associated with the anti-social thesis. Although borrowing from Melanie Klein, Sedgwick moves away emphatically from the drives toward theories of affect. Her turn to affect leads queer theorists to a field ultimately separate from psychoanalysis, even though the notion of affect does appear in Freud's writings, particularly *Inhibitions, Symptoms, and Anxiety* (1926). The two theoretical trends that Halley and Parker identify are more than different approaches. I mark the "anti-social" and reparative approaches as a central split in queer theory that contributes to a crisis of academic inertia but also offers fertile grounds for examination.

The recent conflict within queer theory between two camps, the anti-social and the reparative, is symptomatic of the difficulties in thinking through queer as it becomes academically institutionalized. At the end of her life, Sedgwick wanted to move away from what she calls "paranoid reading" toward reparative reading practices. Unlike Halley and Parker, and rather following Sedgwick, this book articulates the central split in Kleinian terms: what I call the paranoid imperative and queer reparative. The general move away from detailed discussions of psychoanalysis coincides with the turn to affect, a move that is in the spirit of carrying queer theory forward after Sedgwick but that displaces, for better or worse, its theoretical basis.

Sedgwick's last collection of essays published while she was still alive, *Touching Feeling* (2003), investigates the habitual practices of critical theory surrounding the paranoid imperative. The latter is marked by a certain epistemophilia and skepticism: "A disturbingly large amount of theory seems explicitly to undertake the proliferation of only one affect, or maybe two . . . sublimity, self-shattering, *jouissance*, suspicion, abjection, knowingness, horror . . . or righteous indignation" (146). Sedgwick draws from Klein's conception of the paranoid-schizoid position, whereby the ego's relation to objects involves such negative affects as envy, hatred, anxiety. Paranoid reading practices are pervasive in critical thinking, from Marxist exposures and critiques of false consciousness, to anti-colonial practices, to feminist critique, to queer theory, all of which speak for marginalized groups. The epistemophilic valence of paranoia assumes that if one exposes the mechanisms of oppression, then omniscient knowledge about how the world works would become available for possession.

The paranoid imperative is especially salient in queer theory, since, as Sedgwick reminds her readers, Freud's essay on paranoia links it to a latent same-sex desire. In his metapsychological essay "On Paranoia" Freud describes the paranoid subject as he undergoes the process of regression, repression, projection, and aggression in relation to his own desires for the same sex. Sedgwick writes: "If paranoia reflects the *repression* of same-sex desire . . . then paranoia is a uniquely privileged site for illuminating not homosexuality itself . . . but rather precisely the mechanisms of homophobic and heterosexist enforcement against it" (*Touching Feeling* 126, emphasis in original). In this sense, paranoia lends itself productively, perhaps ideally, to queer reading practices.

Unidirectional and future-oriented, paranoia develops a complex relation to the past and future since it "requires that bad news be always already known" (*Touching Feeling* 130). The anticipatory mode of paranoia is understandable as a resistance to heterosexist politics. Marked by such positive affects as love, joy, and pleasure, the Kleinian depressive position for Sedgwick facilitates the ethical possibilities in reparative practices. In contradistinction to the paranoid-schizoid position, the depressive position emerges "in the form of a guilty, empathetic view of the other as at once good, damaged, integral, and requiring and eliciting love and care" (*Touching Feeling* 137). *Touching Feeling* proposes that queerness let go of negative affects and instrumental drives toward a kind of queer reparation.

Symptomatically, Sedgwick's chapter "Paranoid Reading and Reparative Reading" devotes most of its pages to a critique of the paranoid imperative (a critique of critique), because the vocabularies of the reparative have yet to develop in subsequent scholarship. The reparative turn in critical theory for which Sedgwick calls has so far focused on affect studies.[12] Various theorists, including Sedgwick, have aligned the "reparative" with *tentative*, *contradictory*, fleeting feelings of love, mourning, guilt, and gratitude, in contradistinction to the psychic depth of the drives. Sedgwick thus calls for a vocabulary of affect in place of the drives. The recourse to affect theory might have something to do with a difficult paradox that queer theorists since Sedgwick neglect to consider: in psychoanalytic terms, the depressive position is the basis for reparative practices but has aggressive and destructive drives as intimate prerequisites.

Sedgwick's posthumous collection of essays, *The Weather in Proust* (2011), elucidates the violence and aggression in the Kleinian subject that manifests through "endogenous anxiety." In this work, Sedgwick almost returns to the notion of the death drive, but the term itself remains repressed in the text:

> Instead of the undifferentiatedly blind, pleasure-seeking drives of the Freudian infant, which encounter no check but the origi-

> nally external ones of prohibition or lack, the Kleinian infant experiences a greed whose aggressive and envious component is already perceived as posing a terrible threat both to her desired objects and to herself . . . It is against this endogenous dread that the primary defence mechanisms are first mobilized—the splitting, the omnipotence, the violent projection and introjection. (*Weather* 132)

In attempt to differentiate Freud from Klein, Sedgwick describes the Kleinian subject in a way that nonetheless resonates with Freud's description of the death-driven monad in *Beyond the Pleasure Principle*, which my Chapter 1 discusses at length. For Sedgwick, the Freudian subject is an unequivocally paranoid one. According to Sedgwick, Freud contends that omnipotence is an object of desire, whereas Klein asserts that omnipotence is a source of danger, something to both fear and wish. Omnipotence fosters an aggressive and envious greed in the subject that potentiates her dissolution as well as the dissolution of her loved ones.

Sedgwick prioritizes Klein over Freud because the latter's binary logic of the drives excludes middle terms. For example, Freud posits an ambivalence between omnipotence and powerlessness: two positions that become polarized in attachments to catastrophe. Sedgwick's reading of Klein opens up a less absolute theory of subjectivity: "The sense that power is a form of relationality that deals in, for example, negotiations . . . the middle ranges of agency—the notion that you can be relatively empowered or disempowered without annihilating someone else or being annihilated . . . is a great mitigation of that endogenous anxiety" (*Weather* 130). This passage reinforces why Sedgwick prefers the tentative flux of affect over the binary modes of the drives. My book agrees with the arrival at agency through this middle term, negotiation, as a rigorous strategy that keeps the phantasies of omnipotence and powerlessness in dynamic balance. But I differ methodologically from Sedgwick in my proposal that neither ambivalence toward omnipotence nor arrival at negotiation is foreclosed in Freud. I would go as far as to argue that the oscillations of the drives are what make phantasies of omnipotence and frictions of negotiation erotic. The eroticism of both phantasy and friction transfers from a relation of the body to one of textual aesthetics.

The "reparative" has become a bit of a trend in literary criticism while lacking a solid definition. In her reflection on Sedgwick's work, Heather Love's essay, "Truth and Consequences: On Paranoid Reading and Reparative Reading," begins to address productively the duality between paranoid and reparative. Initially, Love defines the paranoid and the reparative clearly. On the one hand, paranoid "is described as *rigid, grim, single-minded, self-defeating, circular, reductive, hypervigilant, scouringly thorough, contemptuous, sneering, risk-averse, cruel, monopolistic,* and *terrible*" ("Truth" 237). On the other hand, reparation "is on the side of *multiplicity, surprise, rich divergence, consolation, creativity,* and *love*" ("Truth" 237). The difficulty of incorporating such reparative characteristics into a theory of reading remains my task at hand. Love makes insightful observations that Sedgwick's essay is both reparative and paranoid despite its call toward more reparative practices: "[Sedgwick's] essay itself is not only reparative—it is paranoid" ("Truth" 238). Indeed, Love's treatment of Sedgwick's work resonates very strongly with my approach to the paranoid imperative and queer reparative. Her "own reading of Sedgwick's essay vacillates between a schizoid-paranoid mode and a reparative mode. What the essay argues, and what it performs, is the impossibility of choosing between them" (238–39). In addition to submitting to this hermeneutical vascillation, Love challenges the paranoid assumption that the arrival at truth involves a disavowal of affect and, following Sedgwick, incorporates affect into her methodology.

Psychoanalytically speaking, paranoid and reparative reading share an interdependent relation. Heather Love differentiates paranoid from reparative reading and likewise acknowledges that both are mutually necessary, yet the reasons why and how remain to be explored thoroughly. Love states, "so many of us feel compelled to answer Sedgwick's call to reparation, which cracks us out of academic business as usual and promises good things both for Sedgwick and for us. But I also think we need to answer the call to paranoia and aggression" ("Truth" 239). My working through responds to both Sedgwick and Love, but by sticking to the drives, I also shift the methodology in order to explore the operation behind the paranoid and the reparative. My methodology details the mechanism of the drives to prove why oscillation is necessary. When readers endorse the reparative but are unsure as to how to practice it beyond its theorization, I respond that it has to do with a paranoid detour and proliferation of phantasy for, ultimately, mourning. Following a reevaluation of the drives and of binding, my reading of Sedgwick acknowledges that negativity and aggression are the basis of psychic life—that thinking is impossible without aggression.

While in her last works, Sedgwick and her adherents turn to affect, my book remains at the psychoanalytic level of the drives. In Freud's most speculative terms, then, the paranoid-reparative conceptual split is a representation of the conflict and negotiation between the death drive and the life drive. Because the reparative turn is coextensive with the turn away from psychoanalysis, the former has neglected to define its terms clearly, and the reparative has become an empty signifier defined by negation: not the anti-social, not psychoanalysis, not the drive, not negative, not paranoid. I want to provide the psychoanalytic explication of the reparative to show its inextricable bind with the paranoid position, not only in Klein's work but also, more importantly, in the genealogy of the drives as they inform twentieth-century literary and critical theory. The reparative turn encourages a turn away from psychoanalysis because the paranoid anti-social position privileges the concept of the death drive as the dominant force that mediates social relations. From Horkheimer and Adorno to Jacques Derrida, Jacques Lacan, and Jean Laplanche, major psychoanalytic thinkers have maintained the dominance of the death drive. In their application of the death drive in literary and critical theory, then, Edelman and Judith Butler follow a tradition. My own return to the drives in a queer theoretical context differs from Edelman's well-known employment of the death drive. A clearer understanding of the reparative necessitates a reminder that Freud speaks of *two* drives.

Provisionally, the death drive refers to an unconscious tendency toward death, which manifests in life as a tendency toward static modes of being or toward destruction and rupture. As this book explores, the death drive has figured heavily in contradictory ways for critical theory, both in thinking through the irrevocability of totalitarian subjectivation and the desire for radical emancipation. While such psychoanalysts as Freud and Klein would argue that the death drive is primary, and while the death drive is conceptually rich, it is always bound up with the life drive, which has been largely neglected as a concept. The life drive's cathectic weakness, as well as its provisional and biological status, is firmly established in theoretical texts.[13] The life drive is worth analyzing because it complicates the death drive conceptually. The life drive describes both the imperative for biological survival and, as this book will argue, the drive for the life of thinking and the constant search for revitalizing modes of signification.

The paranoid imperative, in which the death drive dominates, and queer reparative, in which the life drive dominates, constitute the central dynamic of my book. I want to explore the precarious position of sex and sexuality between these two drives. At times, analyses in the book may seem to perpetuate the dichotomization of the drives, but such moments rather emphasize the symptomatic tendency of psychic splitting, the attraction of one drive over the other and the value judgments that may ensue, even though the drives operate together necessarily through ongoing dialectical tensions. The dominance of one drive over the other is a fleeting moment in a continual oscillation, which manifests in narration. Such blended interplay of the drives operates in the novels that each chapter addresses. The paranoid imperative and queer reparative characterize the difficult relationship between reader and text.

The paranoid-reparative split in queer theory comes out of an effort to think through the crisis of social totality that Horkheimer and Adorno introduce and that queer theorists since Foucault have developed. Butler's major works, *Gender Trouble* (1990), *Bodies That Matter* (1993), and *Undoing Gender* (2006), play a central role in a theory of negativity that associates queerness with radical disarticulation.[14] Bersani, Tim Dean and Teresa de Lauretis are among those whose work in the 1980s, 1990s, and early 2000s associated queerness with the death drive, and Edelman's *No Future* explicates the link in a forceful polemic.[15] *Touching Feeling* marks a turn in queer theory toward life, positive conceptions of love, and the Kleinian concept of reparation. "Life," however, is a loaded term, especially in North America's current political climate, which sees a morbid attachment to the idea of "life" in the anti-choice movement and in the debates surrounding end-of-life care and physician-assisted death. In light of these circumstances, the anti-social stance of queer theory maintains political urgency.

Terms like "reparative" and "life"—signifiers that figure heavily in my book—are more closely associated in the popular imaginary with conservative activism in prolife action and the homophobic violence of "reparative therapy." Indeed, in their book, *Sex, Or The Unbearable*, Berlant and Edelman pick up on the potentially problematic resonances of the reparative, namely "the wrongheadedness of any reparative politics that turns being undone into a symptom of an illness or a measure of injustice" (*Sex* 7). In other words, a reparative investment in the positive risks a potential endorsement of reactionary values perpetuated by "cruel optimism." The polarization of language across the political spectrum is antithetical to the project of literary analysis, which prevents the reification of language and allows us, in psychoanalytic terms, the power of redescription. In *Weather in Proust*, Sedgwick addresses the potential polarization between "reparative" and "ill" by reminding her reader that reparation comes out of the depressive position. The distinction between depression and reparation is precarious and requires difficult working through. Far from the negation of the negative, reparation emerges provisionally, perhaps against the odds in a totalized world, out of the risks one takes in thinking. Berlant and Edelman do question the split between the anti-social thesis and the reparative thesis, considering whether one can be both at any given moment, but they do not pursue this line of inquiry. Unlike the reparative turn toward more positive hermeneutics, Berlant and Edelman's book holds onto the anti-social thesis while turning toward affect. In turn, I think through the reparative while holding onto the drives. Like Kristeva, Berlant and Edelman work through the emergence of closed systems in the twentieth century by describing the "negative" strategy as "psychic and social incoherences . . . that trouble any totality or fixity of identity" (*Sex* vii–viii). Through negativity, they arrive at the intimate encounter with the other as an experience of nonsovereignty. My analyses re-appropriate "life" and "reparative" in an effort to imagine alternative strategies to what Berlant and Edelman describe as "negativity."

The question of intimacy is at the crux of both sides of the paranoid/reparative split in queer theory. Unlike scholars such as Mari Ruti, who suggests in *A World of Fragile Things* that relationality and autonomy are not mutually exclusive, Berlant and Edelman imply in their book that relationality undermines phantasies of autonomy and self-control: "negativity disturbs the presumption of sovereignty by way of 'an encounter,' specifically, an encounter with the estrangement and intimacy of being in relation" (viii). Their thinking through is a working through of what they call "Panoptimism" (3), a life of biopolitical surveillance that regulates normativity and that disavows catastrophe through the myth of progress. Berlant and Edelman arrive at intimacy through their investment in "undoing": "whatever our definitions of 'sex,' this meant turning to the distinctive undoing within it—an undoing that we don't see identically but that we recognize as undoing our own as well as the other's understanding of it" (7). In other words, they make sex unbearable, at least in its conceptualization. Ultimately, Berlant and Edelman's investments raise the question: what is queer "undoing" doing? My first chapter returns to Freud in order to investigate "undoing" as a metaphor in twentieth-century critical thought. I shift away from the term "undoing" to specify how this metaphor develops. Rather, I reframe the drives according to "binding" and "unbinding."[16]

The life drive that I want to explore focuses on the life of the signifier. D.W. Winnicott's concept of the transitional object marks the beginning of signification, as the child employs an object to stand in for an absence and to mediate between the ego and the external world.[17] Indeed, this moment affords material survival—life—yet it also works through the desire for omniscience that is subject to the death drive. If literature is a transitional object in the death-driven landscape of socio-political totality and stagnated thought, then literary narrative is a necessary component to creative contemporary life. In literary reading, the oscillation between the paranoid imperative and queer reparative play out the tensions between the drives in a way that counters the acting out against material life in a catastrophized world.

The split between paranoid and reparative positions in queer theory manifests in different ways. A question arises as to whether the term "queer" can serve as a point of identification at all. The tension between queer and identity politics involves, for example, the (mis)appropriations of queer subjectivity by popular culture, appropriations that subtend queer theory's capacity to disrupt heteronormativity because of queer's susceptibility to commodification. Part of the difficulty in reconciling queer with identity politics indicates a gendering in queer theory.[18] The difficulty with gender emerges in Erica Rand's essay "After Sex?!," a critique of queer theory as a domain of the white, middle-class, male academic. While critiquing the conditions of marginalized subjectivity, she argues, queer theory disavows its own position of privilege within the academic realm.

The task of articulating queer theory in a globalized context rubs up against identity again as it intersects with the politics of race and nation. Case studies of queer praxis, activism, and theory emerge from Australia and New Zealand, across the European and Asian continents as well as North America, considering queer in relation to racialized, Chicana/o, indigenous, and European subjectivity. Queer theory has been predominantly characterized outside of the States as an Anglo–North American discourse, but other international regions have contributed to the field. Some essay collections point out queer theory's imperial or colonial tendencies across disciplines and national borders as part of the Americanization of the global academy.[19] While *Queer in Europe* focuses predominantly on case studies of place-based queer politics, its general premise takes Derrida's imperative to maintain a distinctively European way of thinking in order to resist the Americanization of academia. Queer theory would then seem like Derrida's unwanted bastard child, since a lot of the groundbreaking work in the United States, such as Butler's *Bodies that Matter* and Edelman's *Homographesis* (1994), depends heavily on deconstruction. Downing and Gillet describe "queer" accordingly as the strange offspring of Continental Philosophy and Anglo-American direct action. An irreconcilable split in investments between identity politics and undoing identity characterizes queer theory.

As a result of the preoccupation with identity politics, this central institutional split has perpetuated a resistance to (or perhaps a repeated recognition and disavowal of) psychoanalysis. Despite Dean and Christopher Lane's edited volume *Homosexuality and Psychoanalysis* (2001), which brings together the once antagonistic positions of psychoanalysis and Foucauldian analysis, the presence of the former in queer theory is steadily decreasing, especially since Sedgwick's death. Dean and Bersani are major figures who continue to insist on the link between psychoanalysis and queer theory, but resistance to psychoanalysis persists.[20] Although considerations of, for example, queer temporalities implicate the psychoanalytic notion of *Nachträglichkeit* (deferred action) to characterize queerness as a temporal lag, such studies prefer Foucault's archeological critique to challenge traditional practices of historiography.[21] Queer temporality undermines the distinction of past, present, future, and plays with belatedness, anticipation, and temporal foreclosure; in other words, it queers any sense of temporal linearity. In other fields, the inextricable bind between burgeoning trans discourses and medical discourses, as well as the ongoing project to denaturalize discursive formations of gender and sexuality, has recently facilitated active engagements with scientific discourses as opposed to psychoanalysis.[22]

The preoccupation with language and the logic of signification still underpins much queer analysis.[23] Engagements with language are turning away, however, from psychoanalytic considerations toward other issues, such as the translations of queer into languages other than Anglo-American English,[24] as well as theories of poststructuralism and deconstruction in textual and digital media. Indeed, queer theory increasingly tends to follow a decidedly Foucauldian lens over a Freudian one. Any consideration of queer theory and psychoanalysis this century has resorted almost exclusively to Lacan, including Dean's *Beyond Sexuality* and Edelman's *No Future*. In the turn to affect theory, Ann Cvetkovich and Berlant extend Sedgwick's desire to move away from the binary model of the drives to consider the polyvalent, contingent, sensuous promises of affect theory, what Berlant calls a "disorganized" intelligence ("Starved" 81). For Cvetkovich, who has been fueling *The Public Feelings Project* in the U.S. since 2001 as a response to 9/11, "affect" provides a model to work through public traumas in order to maintain a critical stance to U.S. policymaking ("Public Feelings" 170). Psychoanalysis allows me to identify more precisely this split between negative anti-social and positive reparative practices as having less to do with identity than with a struggle to signify and thus a struggle to read and think. Through psychoanalysis, this book revises the conflict in queer theory from one between undoing identity and identity politics to one between a resistance and an imperative to signify.[25]

In light of all these recent concerns, my interest is to theorize the effects of holding together the split between death and life. The book continues Sedgwick's project of locating the reparative in queer practices, but while she favors affect, I work through the theoretical compulsions of the death drive in order to reimagine the concept of the life drive. The conceptions of queerness and the drives provide the vocabulary to read contemporary fiction that is concerned with the breakdown of its own coherence. The selected texts for Chapters 2 through 5 confront the vanishing point of textual intelligibility and the subject's sense of self, whether that subject is a character within the narrative or the reader. The novels of this study are preoccupied with themes of love, desire, and death. The drives operate, then, on the levels of thematic content and form—that is, the process of reading. While in these texts I can identify, provisionally, an amorphous queer quality, my approach analyzes the ways in which the reading process itself becomes queer.

The book does not list exhaustively which queer theorist of recent years belongs to each side of the conceptual split between death and life. Rather, I offer a narrative that shows the ways in which this split develops, so as to implicate both aesthetics and psychoanalysis. My close readings that articulate and hold together this split set out to prove the central argument that queer emerges not from sexual identity but from an ongoing response to totality, whether located socially or psychically. Unlike other studies of queer emergence, such as Heather Love's *Feeling Backward* (2007), mine does not trace the history of nonheteronormative identities.[26] Indeed, many nuanced queer theories nonetheless find case studies of queer identity in literary characters or figures, such as Sedgwick's *Epistemology of the Closet* (1990), de Lauretis's *Freud's Drive*, and Hall's *Reading Sexualities.* Dean concludes in *Beyond Sexuality* that Edelman and Butler are invested in gay male and lesbian egos, in spite of their theoretical acrobatics to undo identity. Dean employs psychoanalysis to get beyond identity, and I now follow suit. My investment focuses on aesthetic forms, as literary texts become self-conscious of the reading processes that bring them into dialogic existence.

Queer practices emerge from negotiating the threat of political and cultural totality. Such totality depends on the psychical defense of splitting and perpetuates dominant power relations in closed systems. In creative life, splitting is necessary but must remain provisional. The group of literary texts that I work with is an unlikely collection, in contrast to a style of scholarship that locates the seeds of gay, lesbian, or trans identity in a marginalized character to produce a basis for queer literature proper, such as the case with Radclyffe Hall's *The Well of Loneliness* (1928). The history that my first chapter narrates is organized around the themes of totality and the breakdown of the reading process. Trouble ensues when reading seeks something excessive to mimesis, implicating the process of the reader's identification with, not characters, but the struggle to signify in the text itself.

In literary studies, the emergence of new reading practices is an ongoing phenomenon.[27] Like Sedgwick's turn away from paranoid critique, Rita Felski's *Limits of Critique* (2015) theorizes what she calls "post-critical reading," while Stephen Best and Sharon Marcus's article introduce "surface reading." Given their suspicion of suspicion, these works, either directly or indirectly, reject (a misreading of) psychoanalysis based on its application in the humanities that was common up until the late 1990s, in which psychoanalysis was heavily associated with "hidden depths," "unconscious contents," and "symptomatic reading."[28] Chapter 2 celebrates the parody of such dogmatic applications in Nabokov's *Lolita* and contrasts an alternative implication of psychoanalysis. My treatment of psychoanalysis understands the unconscious not as hidden in "depths," not as a repressed "content" or "meaning" which can be accessed through a "symptom," but something that unfolds in plain sight between self and other through the formal aspects of language—an unfolding that is the prerequisite to relational intimacy. For me, the implication of psychoanalysis hinges less on the symptom than on the work of mourning. As my analyses will show, my reading practice stretches beyond symptomatic reading through a process that mourns—that lets go of—the "meanings" that textual "symptoms" might produce.

Literary reading practices that interest me in particular are ones that synthesize reading and sexuality. In his article, "Hitchcock's Hidden Pictures," D.A. Miller introduces his practice of "Too Close Reading" as a "perverse" form of the close reading practices that were established in the postwar period. Like other queer theorists who consider "unlimited intimacies" (Dean), Miller insists on the "too close." The close reader, in this case, would consent to an "undue intimacy" with the author-text (Miller 127). This relation is built on intricate textual details in order to see in relief a shadowy, shady alternative universe to the one that is explicated, in this case, onscreen. Similar to Edelman's insistence on the death drive, Miller's "Too Close Reading" measures "a text's drive to futility" (127). While my theory of reading engages a kind of sexual intimacy, I want to reconsider the role of mediation, so that the "too close" of "unlimited intimacy" becomes not the aim but a resting point in a constant undulation, so that the reader develops a paradoxical relation to restraint and flexibility, so that the process of reading becomes a play of aesthetic distance and affective closeness.

Perhaps most akin to the literary theory I develop is Roland Barthes's *Pleasure of the Text*, a prominent work that conceptualizes the relationship between erotic pleasure and the literary text. His theory of reading resonates strongly with mine, yet whereas his *Pleasure of the Text* is more conducive to theories of deconstruction, my book is invested in the psychoanalytic valences of pleasure in the text. Barthes posits a dialectic in *Pleasure of the Text* between pleasure and bliss that parallels the difference Freud establishes between pleasure and beyond pleasure. He argues that in Sade's work, "the language is redistributed. Now, *such redistribution is always achieved by cutting.* Two edges are created: an obedient, conformist, plagiarizing edge . . . and *another edge*, mobile, blank . . . the place where the death of language is glimpsed" (*Pleasure* 6, emphases in original). Barthes associates the rupture of language with a split in the text. For Barthes, pleasure contains while bliss undoes, even though, paradoxically, the pleasure of the text is always-already unsettling. Barthes figures the dialectic of pleasure and bliss as a contrast, a chiaroscuro, a split or slit of the garment that invites the reader's engagement.

The way Barthes relates the two concepts of pleasure and bliss, however, differs from the paranoid imperative and queer reparative. For Barthes, bliss is a conceptual vanishing point, a hermeneutical pinnacle in the text that exceeds language: "pleasure can be expressed in words, bliss cannot" (*Pleasure* 21). Bliss is unpredictable, untimely. Associated with jouissance, bliss according to Barthes resonates more closely with the ways in which the anti-social branch of queer theory engages the death drive. Bliss is not only a perversion but the "extreme of perversion" (*Pleasure* 52); it marks an undoing or a rupture. As Gallop maintains, "Barthes's 'perverse' carries many of the meanings of our contemporary 'queer'" ("Precocious *Jousisance*" 571).[29] Like queer, the text of bliss marks disturbances in normative adjustment.

Barthes also polarizes pleasure and desire. He associates the latter with (Lacanian) psychoanalysis, characterizing pornographic books as "books of Desire, not of Pleasure. Or, more mischievously, they represent Pleasure *as seen by psychoanalysis*. A like meaning says, in both instances, that *the whole thing is very disappointing*" (*Pleasure* 58, emphases in original). Whereas psychoanalysis is associated here with theories of desire or lack, I want to return to Freud's prioritization of sexuality as a difficult concept that cannot be defined simply in negative terms. I think about erotic pleasure through psychoanalysis, which includes but is not limited to desire. I follow Bersani in rethinking pleasure in psychoanalysis not as economic homeostasis but as an erotic, stimulating, exciting, surprising experience. The erotic relation to the text that I want to think through questions the hermeneutical endpoint of "bliss" or "jouissance" or the "beyond the pleasure principle" of the death drive. I ask the question: how do we return to our "selves" in language once we have come undone through it? The close readings of the fiction have various answers to this question, such as (re)mediation or narrative transference with the reader, concepts that the chapters explore in detail. As my chapters illustrate, the elaboration of the self-in-love (with body or text) has to do with how one works through the wish for immediacy, for escape, or for omniscience.

At times, Barthes is quite literal in his analogy between reading and sex. The act of reading becomes a response to the text's animating desire: "The text you write must prove to me *that it desires me*" (*Pleasure* 6, emphasis in original). In the book's closing sentence, Barthes speaks of orgasm in relation to bliss: the text "comes: that is bliss" (*Pleasure* 67). And so the orgasm ends the book. My slow, close readings of theory and fiction resist a literalizing analogy to sex, but in relation to Barthes one ought to be approximated here. If Barthes's theory of reading culminates in what is analogous to a precocious or delayed orgasm, to bliss, then my reading ponders the foreplay that begins again immediately after a long orgasm happens. In this sense, literary reading is structured not by a single disruption of meaning, not by the absolute instance of perversion, not by (in terms of queer theory) the little death of the death drive that undoes futurity, but rather by a cumulative ebb and flow of erotic persistence, by a potentially infinite drama of rupture and regathering.

My book's aim is twofold. By working through the conceptual split between paranoid and reparative approaches, I develop queer theory as an object of inquiry and as a method. The execution of a queer method, however, extends beyond the field into the project of reading, which implicates two other fields of psychoanalysis and literary studies. One of the motivations behind this thesis is more general in nature, but no less urgent and timely than the ongoing call to think about sexuality. I appeal for the survival—nay, the proliferation—of literary studies. The appeal is certainly not a new one, as the defense for the cultural value of artistic mimesis traces back to Aristotle, but it bears repeating in the theory of reading this book develops. Regardless of how the model of the psyche will potentially change and how the methods of psychoanalysis will adapt, the pleasure of deferral in lengthy engagements with texts must endure. The imperative of making the time and space to read at length, or more ambitiously to "close read," especially given Kristeva's and Berlant's anxiety about the threat to curiosity in contemporary culture, has political, psychical, and sexual implications. Textual deferral comes in many forms, including conscious, conceptual, interrelational, and narrative deferral, all of which "cruel optimism" tends to circumvent.

My book returns to a sustained, intimate, and vulnerable relationship with words and images that is sensitive to desire. I follow Deborah Britzman's call for a difficult, slow, and solitary learning in the experience of reading. Britzman's last chapter in *After-Education* (2003) explores the loneliness in education, which makes reparative thinking possible: "A particular kind of loneliness is made from contact with the incoherent, with that which remains inexplicable, even as this relation to the unknown can threaten to disorganize what has, one hopes, already been settled in the compromise of a signification" (152). What follows phantasy for Britzman, then, is not reality but loneliness and feelings of remorse and mourning, processes that enable the subject to think while encountering the unknown. This opportunity for difficult thinking arises in the process of reading.

The first chapter of this book narrates the theoretical development of the drives, demonstrating how the rather large question of subjectivity involves the relationship between thinking and reading, and how this general question funnels into the work of queer theory. I redefine life and death in psychoanalysis by unpacking the conflation between what I identify as the economic and dynamic formations of the drive. This chapter presents a story that requires a careful working through of difficult, malleable concepts. These soft concepts evolve in contradictory ways through different stages of inquiry in the twentieth century and explain why ambivalence about subjectivity—whether and how to keep or undo or redo or discard it—has been prevalent. The story brings together a number of paradoxes that have yielded divergent modes of thinking, producing a narrative about a pattern of critical thinking that encounters a conceptual limit and the desire to breach it. The chapter opens with a close reading of Freud's *Beyond the Pleasure Principle* in order to think through the ways in which literary reading can return to pleasure.

Psychoanalytic scholarship lacks a definitive explanation of binding, and much of its theoretical employment in Freud's work is either implied or general, a problem that my reading of Freud aims to resolve. My untangling of the conflation between the economic and dynamic binding explains how the death drive can play a role in critical theory as both complicit in authoritarian society and instrumental to radical queer politics. As I demonstrate in the following chapter, economic binding speaks to a desire for containment, control, stillness, homeostatic constancy. Since these conditions serve as barometers for survival, economic binding is a necessary component of psychical life. But this type of binding becomes subject to the death drive when the aim overshoots from survival to inorganic calm. Metaphorically speaking, inorganic calm describes a type of subjection within a social system, a static being that stifles the self. The transition from mere survival to death marks a moment of dynamic unbinding, in which silence takes over acts of signification. Conversely, dynamic binding becomes activated when the subject introjects her love objects into the system of language and divests from the phantasy of static ideals, both of what the object is and of how the self relates to it. The subject can then let go of the projective phantasies of her love objects and catalyze a transition from death driven stasis to a thriving creativity at the level of signification, a creativity that divests from narratives of certainty.

As Chapter 1 discovers through close reading, the two different conceptions of economic and dynamic binding do not simply mark a revision of Freud's thought. My first chapter proves that the two types of binding have an inverse relationship to one another. Economic binding often operates in tandem with dynamic unbinding, while economic unbinding constitutes a dynamic binding. The former describes a psychic process in which the death drive dominates, while the latter marks the influence of the life drive. Both processes are necessary, and necessarily dialectical, for the aesthetic elaboration of the self. These two types of binding account for the ambivalence in literary hermeneutics about containment and rupture, critique and celebration, affirmation and undoing.

The first chapter also addresses the suspicion that reparative reading and positivity encourage a potentially reactionary return to ideal life, a return that marks an occlusion of oppressive power networks. Horkheimer and Adorno's critique of totalitarianism in *Dialectic of Enlightenment* remains a major text that implicates the economical metaphor of Freud's drive into the social sphere. They expose the direct relationship between conscious Reason and ideological complicity. Horkheimer and Adorno's conceptual relationship to the death drive becomes the model for the paranoid imperative that makes possible the queer reparative. Given their contribution, the inescapability of Enlightenment allows me to posit totality. In my theoretical genealogy, the Frankfurt School comprises the roots of the anti-social thesis in queer theory. In order for the reparative to avoid reactionary idealizations, it ought to align more closely and dangerously with depression in the Kleinian depressive position, taking the detour into paranoia and indulging its phantasies.

The subsequent chapters investigate four contemporary novels, all of which have death-driven narratives, spanning the postwar period and leading into the visual turn. These novels present a kind of totality, and thus speak to the anxiety about the emergence of authoritarianism in the twentieth century. As a predecessor to the authors I address here, Franz Kafka's work blends paranoia and longing. As unwilling authoritarian subjects, the figures of Joseph K. in *The Trial* and Gregor Samsa in *The Metamorphosis* haunt my book as foils to the characters whom I address in my analyses. The question of implacable desire within authoritarian contexts, with which Kafka leaves his readers in paranoid cynicism, calls for the queer reparative. Part of my intervention in queer theory involves the analysis of non-gay authors, with the exception of the fourth chapter. My analyses reinforce my argument that queer extends beyond LGBT identity categories to the ongoing project of kneading plasticity into thinking. Each novel represents different manifestations of systematized knowledge and its necessary failures, thus elucidating the economic binding of melancholia and the dynamic binding of mourning. Chapters 2 and 3 explore the dominance of the paranoid imperative in the process of reading. Chapter 2 focuses on Vladimir Nabokov's *Lolita,* in which epistemological failure involves the humorous frustration in projective identifications and the sticky trouble with reified knowledge. Humbert's desire for omniscience manifests in his extensive knowledge about the discourse of sexuality. In *Lolita,* the reader and each character become subject to the process of splitting as the contagion of epistemophilia becomes a death drive.

Chapter 3 reads Mark Danielewski's *House of Leaves* to explore the dissatisfaction with written signification and a melancholic attachment to the dead referent, as the desire to gain omniscience becomes increasingly desperate and epistemological failures proliferate accordingly. In Chapter 3, conceptual failure results in horror and operates through scopophilia, which allows me to situate the text within the framework of the queer gothic. Danielewski's novel illustrates how the death drive can gain momentum through language, at points where language fails. I introduce the term "visual literalization" to designate the refusal of signification and a melancholic attachment to lost objects.

As both Chapter 3 and 4 prove, the process of mourning is possible through what Katherine Hayles calls "narrative remediation," a term that describes a retelling of narrative through different media—newspaper clippings and film and journal entries. Chapter 4 examines Timothy Findley's *The Wars* as a narrative critique of proto-authoritarianism. In *The Wars*, technology and political totality combine on the World War I battlefield. Discourses of nation, civilization, and gender decimate precarious life. The life drive emerges through narrative, which redeems precarious life through the relation between the reader and narrator. The novel's queer temporalities and failed identification emphasize the disjuncture between text and reader. Reparative work becomes possible as narrative disjuncture allows the subject to let go of the desire for omniscience that, on a large scale, underpins war.

The fifth and final chapter articulates the process of mourning in Kazuo Ishiguro's *Never Let Me Go*, a novel that presents a totalitarian society in which Enlightenment has gone awry. The novel's conclusion reflects on the role of visual literalization after the self has arrived at conceptual failure. Kathy narrates the Kleinian transition from symbolization to signification. Through the process of mourning, Kathy's narrative lets go of a world of part objects in order to love. Once the death drive leads the characters to their point of conceptual failure, the life drive renews their attachments through the life of the signifier. While earlier chapters articulate how *Lolita* and *House of Leaves* perform an undoing of subjectivity, the last two chapters introduce the ways in which an unraveled, death-driven subjectivity potentiates a return of the self. In all four novels, the characters and reader experience frustration in the face of supposedly complete knowledge, a polished knowledge whose gloss renders thought slippery, attractive, impenetrable, and yet deeply flawed. Such gloss points to a conceptual vanishing point that marks epistemological failure.

The narrative of theory that I draw in the first chapter parallels the process of reading in the subsequent chapters. Both the characters in the novels and the reader are faced with the task of figuring out what to bind and unbind, how to do so, and whether to do so with words or actions, in order to negotiate a subjectivity into which the self becomes interpellated. The mode of textual engagement reevaluates the subject's relationship to knowledge and anxiety. An intimate relationship with failure counters the "malady of ideality" that Kristeva repudiates in contemporary digital culture and the universe of the television ("Dark Times" 18). All four novels I explore present a kind of labyrinth as a representation of subject formation, resonating with Jorge Luis Borges and Kafka: *Lolita* immerses the reader in a labyrinth of discourses on sexuality; *House of Leaves* confronts the reader with the labyrinth of the unconscious, whose structure resides in the signifier; *The Wars* presents the labyrinth of history's failures in the archive; and *Never Let Me Go* implies a labyrinthian negotiation of the projected intentions of the big Other and of figuring out what exactly one ought to learn in the repeated encounter with conceptual dead ends. In each context, the consumption of objects becomes fraught and the reader leaves the universe of ideality for a search for intelligibility, in which anticipatory stances are rendered impotent. The passive consumptions of ego-affirmations, which constitute the maladies of ideality, are no longer at play. Queer reading replaces belief in ideal life and catalyzes a return of curiosity, of the epistemophilia that fuels sublimation for unexpected relations to unfold within totalized systems.

Each chapter searches for the reason behind the fascination with destruction and catastrophe. One outcome is that when a character faces a destructive force, it emerges through language—more specifically, through too much of it. Humbert's sadism comes through his logorrhea. The horror that threatens the reader and the characters in *House of Leaves* is a verbal acuity that operates like a contagion. Moreover, the language that moves like free-flowing cathexis in *House of Leaves* is far from reified. Visual and written documentation in *The Wars* becomes associated with the shot of a gun, in which recognition is coextensive with destruction. Throughout *Never Let Me Go*, as the clones grow up, verbal divulgence of phantasies and the awkward attempts at communication often lead to further alienation and the release of aggression. The stage on which the paranoid imperative and queer reparation play out is, I assert, necessarily literary.

My book considers the reader's engaged and activating—but not necessarily active in the dominant self-positing sense—relationship to the text. In this scene of reading, the desire for omniscience becomes the lure that engages the reader, but the promise of such mastery gives way to an experience of the oscillation between the two drives of life and death. In simplistic and provisional terms, think of the cliché, to "lose oneself" in a book. Such a reading process can affect the trajectory of queer theory. In the process of reading, the sexual is separated from static ego-identifications, and the reader experiences something other than "having sex" with an object, something that can still be called an erotic experience but that enmeshes the active subject in an ego-divested, pleasurable relation with the text.

In his recent review, "No Sex Please, We're American," Dean laments the "critical squeamishness about sex" in Queer Studies in the United States ("No Sex" 615). He observes, "Queer Studies, like the broader lesbian and gay political movements to which it bears a complex relationship, has won institutional respectability by strategically distancing itself from the messiness of the erotic. Academic high-mindedness easily edges out attention to bodily desire" ("No Sex" 616). In Queer Studies, "sex" became the operative word due to, as Dean reiterates, the "germinal" idea that circulated for decades through various articulations that "*sex undermines identity*" ("No Sex" 619, emphasis in original). Insofar as "identity" implies a fixed knowledge about the self which is defined against a fixed knowledge about the world, I would add to Dean's reminder that sex undermines narratives of certainty.

In conversation with such psychoanalytic theorists as Bersani and Freud, my first chapter does address the conceptualization of "sex," but more as a theoretical problem than a politicized answer. Although positioning itself as an intervention in queer theory (as well as psychoanalysis and literary studies), my book is not about sex, strictly speaking. That is, my analyses focus on neither explicit representations of sex nor queer identities. Nor do they reiterate the now-fraught political urgency in Queer Studies behind having queer sex. But what I hope to show is that somehow, indirectly, my reading practice can influence the enjoyment of erotic relations—with texts, human bodies, or human minds. My analyses of theory and fiction enjoy close reading as a kind of slow touching. Like physical touch, reading offers an inimitable pleasure when it is done as slowly as possible, with variation in rhythm of course. The imagined reader that I posit responds to and activates the text through implacable attention to surface and depth, detail, dips, texture, rhythm, repetition, return, and ultimately, through the "technique" that I develop, the undulating give-and-take between phantasy, longing, omniscience, knowledge, loss, reparation, and linguistic mediation. In other words, an intimate and pleasurable "carnal knowledge" of the text emerges through oscillations between the paranoid imperative and queer reparative.

CHAPTER ONE

The Death Drive and the Life Drive Revisited

> The monument of psychoanalysis must be traversed—not bypassed—like the fine thoroughfares of a very large city, across which we can play, dream, etc.: a fiction.
>
> —Roland Barthes, *The Pleasure of the Text,* 58

I. "To Push" the Drives: Sigmund Freud's Productive Speculations

Contrary to debates in queer theory explored in my introduction, the paranoid and the reparative are not manifestations of drive and affect. Rather, they are expressions of the conflict between the life and death drives. This chapter formulates a theory of the life drive and explores the historical attraction of the death drive in critical theory. My story of the drives underpins the readings in the subsequent chapters. As the story goes, Freud theorizes the drives in 1920. In doing so, he confuses two types of binding: economic and dynamic. Both definitions of binding, which I detail below, are at play in both the death drive and the life drive, but this point is not yet clear when Freud was writing. Because the economic definition of binding lends itself more readily to metaphors of cultural critique, Horkheimer and Adorno and then queer theory's paranoid imperative employ the economic metaphor. The Frankfurt School theorists attribute extreme economic binding of Enlightenment to the death drive. Conversely, queer theorists associate economic *un*binding (undoing) with the death drive. As my analysis will explicate, Bersani unwittingly reintroduces the dynamic mode of binding in his theorization of how the sexual operates in artistic representation. Bersani implies that the self-shattering effects of art necessitate the life drives of signification. Jacqueline Rose and Winnicott each discuss the creative potentials for epistemological crisis, suggesting that the economic unbinding of reified narratives of certainty is bound up with the dynamic binding of signification: that is, the production of new associative links and an intimate engagement with discursive modes. Sedgwick introduces a reparative reading practice as an alternative to the paranoid critique that dominated queer theory. But the reparative turn itself resulted in a split, a crisis of knowledge within the field, a crisis that Rose identifies as the grounds for creative thinking.[1]

My book's own reparative project reconciles the push of the drives with their reparative sublimation into aesthetic forms. This current chapter sorts out the roles that economic and dynamic binding play in processes of thinking and reading; the book explains queer theory's attraction to negativity and offers the possibility of life-driven futurity through engagements with language. The attachments that unfold out of queer reading are akin to the movement of love.

Freud's *Beyond the Pleasure Principle* (1920) constitutes the theoretical basis of the book. I return to this text repeatedly due, ironically, to a fascination with the concept of the repetition compulsion and the myriad effects it holds for psychic reality. My reading of Freud is less a search for the ontology of the drives than a perusal of strange moments and apparent contradictions in his dialectical thinking process, which works through the opposition of the life drive and the death drive. These contradictions ripple throughout the historical employment and development of the drives up to the time of queer theory. Although Freud reconciles the concepts of binding and unbinding in relation to the drives more decidedly in later works such as *An Outline of Psychoanalysis* (1940) and *Civilization and Its Discontents* (1930), his thinking in *Beyond the Pleasure Principle* introduces slippages that lend themselves to the theorization of queer as it becomes defined in terms of the drives. My reading proves two seemingly contradictory claims: the death drive involves binding *and* unbinding; the life drive involves binding *and* unbinding. In order for these claims to make sense together, I will explain what I identify as two types of binding.

Freud opens *Beyond* with the economic factor of the psyche as his main concern; that is, he thinks about how the psyche manages quantities of excitation that it receives from the external world and from within. By the conclusion, he veers reluctantly from his economic model. Freud begins his book with a review of the two principles of mental functioning: the pleasure principle and the reality principle. He defines pleasure in economic, quantitative terms as a diminution of excitation and unpleasure as an increase in excitation. Counterintuitive to the twenty-first-century reader, Freud defines pleasure in negative terms, as an avoidance of pain, or the maintenance of net quantity of energy in an organism. Whereas he distinguishes these two principles quite definitively in his earlier 1911 essay, "Formulations on the Two Principles of Psychic Functioning," the pleasure and reality principles become more closely linked in *Beyond* as both serve to satisfy a principle of constancy, in which the organism seeks cathectic homeostasis. The reality principle involves the compulsion to repeat unpleasurable experiences as an adaptive measure, when the organism exposes itself to agitating stimuli in order to gain an active position toward mastery and desensitization.[2]

Because Freud speculates about more primal psychical functions than the pleasure principle, he does not focus on the speaking subject in this text but rather turns to unicellular and multicellular organisms. For the organism's survival, Freud ventures, protection becomes more vital to survival than the reception of stimuli. Freud asserts that the mere purpose of reception to stimuli is to "discover the direction and nature of the external stimuli" (*BPP SE* 31). By extrapolation, the whole of human experience is reduced to direction and degree of danger. In order to maintain homeostasis and gain pleasure, the organism attempts to transform mobile energy, or free-flowing cathexis, to quiescent or bound energy. Stimuli from the external world arrive in the form of subdued samples in small quantities, highly mediated by the organism's defense mechanisms. The receptive cortical layer, which he calls the perceptual conscious (Pcpt-Cs), develops a shield that is "baked through" with external stimuli such that it undergoes a permanent structural modification: "its outermost surface ceases to have the structure proper to living matter, becomes to some degree inorganic, and thenceforward functions as a special envelope or membrane resistant to stimuli . . . By its death, the outer layer has saved all the deeper ones from a similar fate" (*BPP SE* 30).[3] The integration of death into the structure of the organism is necessary for the prolongation of life.

Freud counters his initial observations about the principle of constancy by discussing patients who suffer from traumatic neurosis and whose dreams contain a wish to repeat unpleasure that has been forgotten and repressed. He explores another effect of the compulsion to repeat that contradicts the purpose of the "Fort-da" game,[4] when the compulsion overrides the pleasure principle and produces a repetition that cannot possibly yield a net gain of pleasure. Freud remarks on the unconscious character of this compulsion: "We are much more impressed by cases where the subject appears to have a *passive* experience, over which he has no influence, but in which he meets with a repetition of the same fatality" (*BPP SE* 24, emphasis in original). The cortical shield that protects the receptive elements of the conscious system defends against the external world only. Those unpleasurable excitations that arise endogenously from the unconscious during a compulsive repetition of repressed traumas encounter no protective defense system. The best that the organism can do in this case is to externalize the endogenous stimuli through projection and defend against it as if it originated from the outside, a measure that does not ultimately prevent a repeated experience of the trauma.

The unconscious repetition of traumatic experiences threatens the organism's structure with unbound energy. Such potential threat allows Freud to posit a primal self-destructive tendency. Freud postulates a conservative element in the drives, that the drives tend toward an earlier, inorganic state: "If we are to take it as a truth that knows no exception that everything living dies for *internal* reasons—becomes inorganic once again—then we shall be compelled to say that '*the aim of all life is death*'" (45–46, emphases in original). The condition of this sentence is strange given its radical and absolute conclusion: *all* life aims toward death. His readers cannot "take it as truth that knows no exception" that living organisms die for internal reasons as opposed to external ones. He rather implies that, left to its own devices in an ideal environment, the living organism will die due to a failure of its own metabolism. The organism strives toward reproducing such ideal environments by avoiding the dangers of the outside world so as to die in its own way. The compulsion to repeat acquires this radical function to return to an inanimate state, from the inside out, not vice versa. The more organically complex the species, the more complicated the detours developed toward the aim of death.

In this moment, the death drive takes precedence and becomes the theoretical seed for the twentieth-century question of subjectivity. A question of what "death" signifies emerges here and runs throughout this book. In attempting to establish a science through his image of a unicellular organism, Freud creates a conceptually transportable metaphor. While the death drive sends Horkheimer and Adorno into despair because it is what secures our totalitarian subjection, Edelman regards the death drive as a cause for celebration because it is the only thing that saves us from totality. Despite the defensive measure the organism takes to ensure survival, it aims for death. In dystopian literature such as Kafka's, the death drive is not simply about a singular desire to die, but also about how our ultimate aim for death potentially manifests in a horrific way of life. By implication, totalized ideological subjectivity, capable of genocide, is a necessary condition of human existence. An extension of Horkheimer and Adorno's fixation is that our death drive is what dooms us to totalitarian subjectivity, resulting in the Holocaust and the culture industry, or more presently, biopolitics in cybernetic monopolies. In such a world, "love" or the life of the signifier are mere "detours" to the ultimate aim of, in Kafka's words, "not death, alas, but the eternal torments of dying" (*Diaries* 302). What is history if not the latter?[5]

On an economic level, the unconscious compulsion to repeat traumatic neuroses involves a contradictory desire to sabotage the mastery of the ego, to break through its baked-through structure. Freud undermines his grandson's cultural accomplishment of developing the capacity to tolerate the absence of the love object through symbolization in his "Fort-da" game. With the introduction of the death drive, "the theoretical importance of the [drives] of self-preservation, of self-assertion and of mastery greatly diminishes. They are component [drives] whose function it is to assure that the organism shall follow its own path to death" (*BPP SE* 47). The drive to die in one's own fashion takes precedence as the final endpoint over the accomplishments of civilization.

Since Freud's speculative text, *Beyond the Pleasure Principle*, the death drive has assumed many forms, some contradictory, both in critical theory and in the broader cultural sphere. Confusion arises from Freud's different conceptualizations of binding and unbinding. Generally, binding is associated with life-giving functions—all-inclusive synthesizing, a bringing together—while unbinding signifies a kind of destruction—taking apart, splitting, or separating. But these associations were not always the case, especially in *Beyond*. Jean Laplanche and J.B. Pontalis differentiate between the *economic* type of binding "long-recognized that correlates to the ego and secondary processes" and another, I would say, *dynamic* type, "closer to the laws governing unconscious desire and organization of phantasy—the laws . . . of the primary process—where the free energy itself . . . is not a massive discharge of excitation but rather an energy which flows along chains of ideas and implies associative 'links'" (Laplanche and Pontalis 51–52). In the latter sense, binding describes the linking together of ideas, the synthesizing conditions of thought processes, repairing, mourning, and letting go: life-giving functions. *Unbinding* in the dynamic sense would mark a melancholic attachment to lost objects, as well as the breakdown of thought: a tendency toward destruction and the function of the death drive.[6] Arguably, Freud's *economic* employment of binding and unbinding in *Beyond the Pleasure Principle* contradicts the *dynamic* definition of binding on which he settles in his later work and which Melanie Klein takes up in her theorization of psychic positions.[7] I argue that these two types of binding, as well as the confusion arising from their conflation, produces compelling effects for thinking through the drives.

The structure of the ego in *Beyond* adheres to the economic model of binding, for the most part. Because the drives emerge from unconscious, primary processes, "The impulses arising from the [drives] do not belong to the type of *bound* nervous processes but of *freely mobile* processes which press towards discharge" (*BPP SE* 40, emphases in original). Unbound, free-flowing energy produces unpleasure in the organism. Working within the structures of the protective cortical layer, binding manages energy and prevents an influx "analogous to a traumatic neurosis" (*BPP SE* 41). Under the forces of the pleasure principle in the service of survival, the psyche transforms free-flowing energy into bound energy by processing excitation through psychic facilitations, or neuronic pathways that direct the cathectic flow.

While the compulsion to repeat can lead to either binding as protection from the outside or unbinding as a desire to sabotage from the inside, the link between binding and the drives is ambiguous. The "daemonic" unbinding force emerging from within is what interests Freud and what ultimately leads him to speculate about the death drive. In his later works, Freud reinforces this initial association between unbinding and the death drive.[8] The way Freud initially theorizes the death drive in economic terms leads him to a central contradiction, because he uses the pleasure principle as his departure point. Although he later departs from his speculative ambivalence in this text, certain moments beg for reconsideration in order to think about their effects. If the pleasure principle aims to keep the amount of excitation as low as possible, then the principle's function "thus described would be concerned with the most universal endeavor of all living substance—namely to return to the quiescence of the inorganic world" (*BPP SE* 76). The phrasing of this last clause causes a proliferative ambiguity in Freud's thinking. When describing different forms of energy, Freud uses the signifier "quiescent" (*ruhender*) synonymously with the signifier "bound" (*gebunden*). In this moment, Freud reaffirms that economic binding is in the service of the death drive.

In this case, the work of binding, if taken to its extreme completion uninterrupted by the shattering effects of life, necessarily leads to the complete "quiescence" of the inorganic world. The death drive is not linked to unbinding here, as Laplanche and Pontalis conclude, but rather the opposite, the epitome of the bound psychic state, an ever-spreading work of absolute silence and the gradual cessation of free-flowing cathexis. Death occurs in the event that the baked-through structures of the protective cortical layer extend throughout the organism to maximize inorganic calm. In this case, binding would constitute a complete structural reification. The work of binding in this moment is not antithetical to the death drive but is rather in its service. Binding's operation to ensure life acquires a deceptive appearance.

A major difference between the drives is their relation to internal perception, and this difference contributes to the problematics of binding. Freud draws some telling conclusions about the drives that also potentiate confusion:

> the life [drives] have so much more contact with our internal perception—emerging as *breakers of the peace* and constantly producing tensions whose release is felt as pleasure—while the death [drives] seem to do their work unobtrusively. The pleasure principle seems actually to serve the death [drives]. It is true that it keeps watch upon stimuli from without, which are regarded as dangers by both kinds of [drives]; but it is more especially on guard against increases of stimulation from within, which would make the task of living more difficult. (*BPP SE* 77, emphasis added).[9]

The death drive operates stealthily. Insofar as perception works on qualitative and quantitative differences in rhythms of stimuli, the subject cannot perceive its workings since the death drive remains consistent with the principle of constancy. That the death drive is quiet is also anti-intuitive, whether conceived of in its politically destructive manifestation in connection with the Third Reich or in its emancipatory romanticization in connection with avant-garde art.

The life drive, on the other hand, is out and proud, so to speak, disturbing the peace as the only drive that the subject can readily perceive. The endogenous unbinding threat that initially leads Freud to speculate about the death drive becomes, by his conclusion, attributed to those life forces opposing the death drive. Freud's suggested description of the death drive as a "daemonic force" is also tenuous. The pleasure principle defends against the life drive, those "increases of stimulation from within" that push toward life but which, in doing so, make "living more difficult." Earlier in the text, Freud indicates that the compulsion to repeat plainly exhibits the character of the drives and, "when they act *in opposition to the pleasure principle*, give the appearance of some *'daemonic' force* at work" (*BPP SE* 41, emphasis added). If the pleasure principle is, as Freud concludes, in the service of the death drive, and if it guards initially against a "daemonic" force, then that "daemonic" force stems not from the death drive but from the life drive, that breaker of peace. In *Beyond*'s economic model, contrary to Freud's initial observations about the endogenous unbound energy of traumatic neuroses, the life drive unbinds and the death drive binds, and contrary to Freud's expectations, the "daemonic" drive refers to the former.

Perhaps the passage above indicates a change of mind, but more generally it suggests the difficulty of differentiating clearly between the drives in Freud's thinking. The contradictions throughout this specific text make it unclear which drive is the instigator of subversion and tension. Because the life drive tends to be neglected conceptually, the contradictions that arise have less to do with the opposition of the life and death drives than the oppositional theoretical developments of the death drive.

Related to the problematics of binding, the difficulty in *Beyond the Pleasure Principle* also lies in the two-fold task of articulating the sex drive as the major opposing force to the death drive, while maintaining the primacy of the latter. First, Freud defers accounting for the contradiction between the sex drive and the conservative or regressive characteristic of the drives: "There may be [other drives] which push forward towards progress and the production of new forms. This argument must certainly not be overlooked, and it will be taken into account at a later stage" (*BPP SE* 44). He concedes that the sex drive pushes toward greater unities through reproduction, and such unities offer a promise of ever-unfolding differences. But Freud maintains in *Beyond* that the drives seek an eternal return by "circuitous paths" to an "old state of things" (*BPP SE* 45). He claims that the conservative drives appropriate every modification of organic living matter, such that change and progress are mere deceptions of difference. As the "termination of individual development" (*BPP SE* 56) death can also signify a psychical stasis that results from biological reproduction (in which the capacity for change and growth is passed onto the offspring). Death can refer also to cultural conditions, to inhibitions in both creativity and the proliferation of difference within the self. This moment in the text echoes Freud's discussion of the monad's protective barrier in his previous chapter: the measures that afford more life ultimately fall in the service of the death drive.

While Freud cannot dichotomize the two drives, he must redefine them such that they do not become homogenized. Sexuality becomes associated with the life drive in Laplanche's clarification of the murky relationship between drive and instinct, two signifiers that are conflated in the translation of Freud's oeuvre from German to English in the Strachey *Standard Edition*. Laplanche claims that the words *Trieb* and *Instinkt* share the same root word, to push, but they diverge in their impetus, aim, object, and source (Laplanche 10). The *anaclitic* character of the drive differentiates it from instinct: that is, the drive's development out of what Freud calls "propping" distinguishes it from biological instinct. Laplanche notes: "The phenomenon Freud describes is a leaning *of the drive*, the fact that emergent sexuality attaches itself to and is propped upon another process which is both similar and profoundly divergent: the sexual drive is propped upon a nonsexual, vital function" (16, emphasis in original). The drive props itself on and eventually becomes independent from the instinct.

As instinct develops into drive, the object and source become less specific, more varied, and the human animal necessarily becomes a sexualized subject full of potential variations. The subject replaces the lost object, the breast, with other objects, not only to nourish but also to satisfy the drive's aim of release in tension through a widening array of sources and impetuses. The source disperses from digestive organs to any erotogenic departure point, which as Laplanche points out, includes any human organ or human activity, such as intellectual labor or mechanical stimulation in general. He states: "What is perverted is still the instinct, but it is as a vital function that it is perverted *by* sexuality . . . The drive properly speaking, in the only sense faithful to Freud's discovery, *is* sexuality" (Laplanche 23, emphasis in original). The sexual satisfaction from "sensual sucking" of the breast and the desire subsequent to nourishment develop a qualitatively different urge "to push" *beside* the biologically pushing necessity of feeding. The drives develop as displacements of biological imperatives, and thus become themselves agents of displacement, deferral, binding, and unbinding. The function of the drive resembles that of the signifier. Coming out of but independent from biological instincts, the drives operate, though sometimes silently, in *language*, and their development is inextricably bound to the development of sexuality. Not only are the drives the basis of language, but their movement in psychic life depends on the deployment of language. The close relationship that Freud maintains between sexuality and the life drive is based on this notion of anaclisis, of propping on and away from the function of biological survival.

As the theory of the drives develops into Freud's last dualistic model, however, sexuality occupies an ambivalent position between the life drive and the death drive. One could say it has difficulties with commitment. In *Beyond*, the main opposition is between the death drive and the *sex* drive. Freud uses the latter signifier synonymously with the life drive. Laplanche and Pontalis point out a major shift in Freud's thought:

> We are justified in asking whether this conflation [between the life drive and sex drive] does not reflect a shift in sexuality's location in the framework of Freud's dualistic conception. Up until this point [in *Beyond*], sexuality had played the part of *an essentially subversive force*, represented by the first components of the major antithesis recognized by Freud: free energy as opposed to bound, primary as opposed to secondary processes . . . With the advent of the final instinctual dualism, the death [drive] takes over as the 'primal,' 'daemonic' force which is of the essence of instinct, while sexuality—paradoxically—goes over to the side of the binding process. (242 emphasis added)[10]

Because of the groundwork that Freud provides in the *Three Essays on the Theory of Sexuality* (1905), which emphasizes the primary *conflictual* role sexuality plays against repression in psychic life, the close tie between sexuality and the binding of the life drive does not really hold. Even in *Beyond the Pleasure Principle,* Freud's discussion of the conjunction between reproduction and individual death places sexuality in a precarious position relative to binding. Sexuality maintains its "essentially subversive force" even when the death drive in Freud's thought comes to occupy sexuality's former disruptive role. Due to their characterization by Freud as essentially subversive *at divergent points in his thinking*, sexuality and the death drive are connected through a slippage that becomes a conceptually fertile ground for queer theory.

Given the confusion regarding sexuality and binding, Freud's radical hypothesis about the primal necessity of the death drive becomes less difficult to accept. Even in economic terms, the destructive components of psychical life are logically consistent. To say that the aim of all life is death is easy compared to the introduction of and accounting for the life drive, which bears the speculative fruit for difficult thinking. The life drive, and sexuality for that matter, disturbs the tautological peace of Freud's theory about death, inciting many productive contradictions in the economic model of the psyche. Laplanche and Pontalis argue that "from the economic standpoint too the life [drives] fit badly into the energy-based model of the [drive] as a tendency towards the reduction of tensions. In certain passages [of *Civilization and Its Discontents*] Freud goes so far as to oppose Eros to the general conservative nature of the [drive]" (242). The question of how the life drive binds or unifies *through* "breaking the peace" runs throughout my book, and the conclusion will finally attempt one answer.

II. Economic Binding as the Death Drive: The Critique of Totalitarianism

Before discussing the *dynamic* conception of binding in relation to thought, it is necessary to consider how the *economic* link between binding and the death drive manifests in relation to totalitarianism. The economic conception of binding explains how the death drive fuels dominant totality, constitutes authoritarian subjectivity, and provides the groundwork for a definition of queer as a radical undoing of social and linguistic forms. Max Horkheimer and Theodor W. Adorno's influential book *Dialectic of Enlightenment* (1944) is established in critical theory as an incisive critique against reified subjectivity. For the Frankfurt School, fascism signified much more than a political dictatorship in which speech was censored and human rights were considered void. Fascism pervaded the cultural sphere and dictated the conditions of possibility and limits for meaning production on a large scale, invigorated of course by mass production and consumption. In this system of identitarian logic, voices of dissent threatened to become not simply prohibited but rather impossible. The power to signify, to make meaning with words and images, became contested on a cultural and political battlefield. From the threat of inexorable subjugation to a totalized language, the imperative toward queer representation emerges, particularly the paranoid imperative of queer antisocial critique. In acknowledging the conditions of semiotic totality, the paranoid imperative perpetuates the economic metaphor of binding that Horkheimer and Adorno lament, thus capturing only a fraction of the mobile drives.

In *Dialectic of Enlightenment*, Horkheimer and Adorno provide arguably the most convincing and horrific account of cultural totality, its link to Enlightenment, and the inextricability of what we call civilization in the twentieth century and a global death drive. Their first chapter, "The Concept of Enlightenment," illustrates Enlightenment as a totalitarian death drive: the apex of the economic binding process in thought, the reification of psychic structures, the homogenization of difference, and the phantasy of omniscience. Horkheimer and Adorno's personification of Enlightenment (they speak of it as a character, without the definite article, "the") renders human beings the parts of a single social body. Their opening sentences tell the whole story: "Enlightenment, understood in the widest sense as the advance of thought, has always aimed at liberating human beings from fear and installing them as masters. Yet the wholly enlightened earth is radiant with triumphant calamity" (Horkheimer and Adorno 1). Their opening links omniscience with catastrophe. Enlightenment has become the catastrophe it wants to avoid. The avoidance of fear corresponds to abolishing the anxiety arising from economic unbinding. The unconscious phantasy of Enlightenment, then, is the universally quiescent state of the earth. In phantasy, Enlightenment has developed that ideal, impossible external environment that Freud takes for granted in *Beyond* and which facilitates the human organism's project to die in its own way. Enlightenment aims to dominate nature, to dispel myth, and to "overthrow fantasy with knowledge" (Horkheimer and Adorno 1). Such aims are mere phantasies disavowed by reified knowledge. Throughout my book, I distinguish fantasy from phantasy in the Kleinian sense: the former is conscious, such as a daydream or in this case, narrative myth, while the latter is unconscious and can mediate psychic structures. In creative life, fantasy is something to celebrate while phantasy is something to mourn. This distinction is imperative to thinking about the ways in which Enlightenment purges itself of the fantasy in myth in order to perpetuate its own phantasy of epistemological omnipotence.

Enlightenment's abstraction of nature into a system of formulae enacts an emptying of content into form. The unit of thought itself empties out from concept to formula, making thought the very vehicle of homogenization against the multiplicity of nature: "Thought is reified as an autonomous, automatic process, aping the machine it has itself produced, so that it can finally be replaced by the machine" (Horkheimer and Adorno 19). On a metaphorical level, such abstracted lines of formula links with Freud's little monad, baked through from the cortical to the innermost layers by reified neuronic pathways that direct the content of energy.[11] Reduced to formula through deductive logic, the natural world acquires the quiescence of the inorganic state. The repetition compulsion serves only economic binding of the social body. A universal quiescent hardening is what constitutes totality, which Horkheimer and Adorno describe as an inexorable tendency toward unity, again invoking the function of binding.

Going back to the first sentences of the *Dialectic* quoted above, however, from whence does this disavowed "triumphant calamity" come? The difficulty in reading Horkheimer and Adorno stems from their dialectical methodology, which blurs the distinction between myth and reason. Binding and the death drive become mutually contingent in this conception of Enlightenment. Yet binding, in this case, serves the phantasy of omniscience, of absolute mastery. Enlightenment both epitomizes the bound psychic state and emits a "radiance" of triumphant calamity, of free-flowing, unbinding, destructive energy. Horkheimer and Adorno's dialectical approach suggests that Enlightenment is the negation of myth and magic, those resources of past civilizations that emerge through ritual and that prefigure art. As negations, myth and magic return as Enlightenment's omnipotence.

Wallowing in the infectious phantasy of global binding, Enlightenment disavows its utter dependence on the operation of dynamic *un*binding. This very disavowal constitutes the momentum of its power in triumphant calamity. The power of totality stems from an *imagined* capacity to bind and control human experience universally. Enlightenment would then resonate with Freud's description of the tendency toward a fully quiescent state as a mere unconscious *wish* that can never materialize. The path toward death, according to Freud, in which the pleasure principle operates on a radical register, uninterrupted, mediates the organism's defenses as a *projection into the future*. Enlightenment assumes an ever-anticipatory and paranoid stance to maintain its path toward a universally bound state through the distortion of thought processes. Horkheimer and Adorno's critique of Enlightenment crystallizes the economic link between binding and the death drive in Freud as operating only through the level of the subject's phantasy. Let us recall that the death drive operates quietly: so too does the dynamic unbinding of the subject and of society, such that Enlightenment is not conscious of the calamity of its mythical "new barbarism" (Horkheimer and Adorno 25).

Ostensibly impotent, this phantasy of universal economic binding nonetheless asserts a manic power. Thinking differently, specifically in critique, becomes void as it enters into the economy of Enlightenment's paranoia and negations. Within the culture industry, pain, unpleasure, uncertainty, and anything excessive to the phantasy of ultimate binding, transform into "jovial denial" (Horkheimer and Adorno 112). The replacement of art with faith in Enlightenment resonates with Kristeva's notion of the maladies of ideality, which replaces curiosity with belief. What was previously regarded as the transcendent work of art consists of "those traits in which the discrepancy emerges, in the necessary failure of the passionate striving for identity" (Horkheimer and Adorno 103). A dialectical oscillation between curiosity and failure is the ongoing project of art and of psychoanalysis. The culture industry transformed such dialectics of failure into a belief in the Absolute as sameness.[12] While these theorists lament art's former intimacy with failure, the project of queer analysis keeps art and failure alive, as a discussion of Bersani explores below.

Horkheimer and Adorno's treatment of the death drive unwittingly bridges the two separate types of economic and dynamic binding. The stealthy operation of the death drive in this case would require the two types of binding, which are now more than different stages of psychoanalytic thought. If the death drive applies to the cessation of individual and cultural development, then cultural totality depends upon a phantasy of economic binding that veils a dynamic unbinding, a triumphant calamity. In doing so, Enlightenment also disavows its death drive as an illusion of survival. The conditions of Enlightenment illuminate the fraught relation of epistemic certainty, the avant-garde, and politics. Queer aesthetics emerges from this historical relationship between art and totality.

The image of the death-driven totality attenuates the power of subversion and disorients the transgressive. Because of the death drive's role in totality, Horkheimer and Adorno see the drive in a politically negative light. On the other hand, Edelman's polemic in *No Future* romanticizes the death drive, articulating it as the only transgressive force within Symbolic totality. *No Future* holds a heavily cathected, affectively soaked place within the field of queer theory. Edelman's controversial popularity is most likely due to his non-negotiable stance. More specifically, however, I attribute this book's prominence to the desire and subsequent failure to think beyond the death drive in social and literary theory. Whether his book is dismissed or admired, *No Future* provides a reference point for queer theorists, from Snediker's *Queer Optimism* to Stockton's *The Queer Child*. The debate *No Future* has spurred indicates a turning point in the collective journey of thinking through queerness.

Edelman conceptualizes queer as *the* unbinding force that ruptures totality. Given that the signifier bestows only a promissory identity at which we, as signifiers, can never arrive, queerness negates such deferred promises within the fissures of signification, thus rupturing identity and meaning. A death-driven position places a unique responsibility on the queer subject. As Edelman urges: "the queer must insist on disturbing, on queering, social organization as such—on disturbing therefore, and on queering *ourselves* . . . For queerness can never define an identity; it can only ever disturb one" (*No Future* 17, emphasis in original). If, according to ideologies of reproductive futurism, no future exists for queerness, then queerness must in turn insist on the negativity that pierces the phantasy of futurity, which the Symbolic uses to defer its own nothingness.

In the phantasy of binding, Enlightenment has repressed its death drive in its assumption of complete knowledge. When the emergence of the AIDS crisis marked a crisis of scientific mastery, the Social projected its death drive onto queers in order to maintain its phantasy.[13] Edelman's focus is less about the AIDS crisis—though it surely haunts his prose—than about the rejection of imagined futurity through nonreproductive queer sex. Edelman's theory attacks Enlightenment, which he calls the Social, the Symbolic, Politics, the image of the future, but through a tactical reappropriation.

In doing so, however, Edelman reinforces Enlightenment's phantasy of omniscience and, along with it, the assumption that totality is the globally quiescent state materialized. Edelman romanticizes the power of unbinding the economically hardened social body: "by assuming the 'truth' of our queer capacity to figure the *undoing* of the Symbolic, and of the Symbolic subject as well, we might undertake the impossible project of imagining an oppositional political stance exempt from the imperative to reproduce the politics of signification" (*No Future* 27, emphasis added). Playing along with the logic of negation in the social body, Edelman's reinforcement of Enlightenment's phantasy constitutes his creative strength and theoretical limits all at once.[14]

Edelman's *No Future* struggles with three major contradictions. His resistance to viable politics is a call to queer modes of existence, which he defends as at least conceptually viable. Edelman reminds his readers repeatedly, perhaps himself as well, that no outside exists within totality, and that "liberation" from the system is an impossibility: "Neither, indeed, is there any ground we could stand on outside that logic [of the Symbolic]" (*No Future* 17). The imperative he brings to bear for queers depends on an investment in "rupture" as emancipatory, as a refusal of totality that accompanies the recognition that there is no outside of totality. In a second contradiction, Edelman paradoxically offers a representation of the unrepresentable, a queer *figure* that *unbinds* the congealments of identity, an *embodiment* of the disembodying death drive.[15] Edelman's proposed strategy, which again constitutes both a strength and limitation, is a negation of a negation. The queer performs a double negation that idealizes the transgressive forces of undoing.

The first two contradictions have been well established in the critical reception of *No Future*.[16] Yet a third contradiction is relatively unexplored and holds major implications for how the concept of the drive relates to queer aesthetics: the simultaneity of Edelman's insistence on the death drive and his repudiation of its temporal structure. Insofar as the death drive is particularly distinct from death in that it is a *drive*, a push toward dissolution, deferral constitutes the very temporal processes of the drive, such that it cannot logically be equated with the finality Edelman seems so readily to embrace. His excoriation of the endless entrance into intelligibility also contradicts the intimate engagement with discourse that defines the project of psychoanalysis. Edelman envisions a transformation within the Symbolic without repeating the law of the Symbolic. Although Edelman embraces the death drive, he cannot celebrate the repetition compulsion that characterizes it. His insistent distinction between transformation and repetition is logically precarious.

The insistence on immediacy, on the negation of deferral, for an "enjoyment that is always '*at hand*'" (*No Future* 91) that runs through Edelman's critique culminates in his call for no future—a call that he himself cannot quite answer. One could say that the future is repressed in this book. The book's title, *No Future*, at once appropriates the rhetoric of the conservative right and fails to purge this utterance of the unconscious effects of negation: that there ought to be, that there is, a future for queerness for which Edelman may be calling. If his readers are to remain faithful to the implications of his theory, his call to link queer with the death drive condemns queers to a silence not only unrepresentable in a way that signals the institutional death of queer theory, but which also completely contradicts Edelman's own polemic.

Edelman's thinking can be problematic, but his alignment of queerness and unbinding aptly characterizes art's subversion. The fantasy of shattering reified intelligibilities in a kind of cathartic trauma pervades many influential ideas of the twentieth century, such as Benjamin's concept of the dialectical image, the convulsive beauty of the surrealist image, Deleuze's call to deterritorialization, Butler's "troubling" endeavors in *Undoing Gender*. From the Surrealist movement, to late modernist texts such as Djuna Barnes's *Nightwood* (1937), to the Beat movement, particularly William Burrough's *Naked Lunch* (1959), both literary and visual art forms have encouraged an identification with an *unbinding* force, one that breaks through the placid oppression of rational, totalized life. Even Foucault's *History of Sexuality* (1978) theorizes a tautology of discourse as an ever-binding and regulating network that the subject cannot escape. The postmodern valences of Foucault's book emerge at the postulation of resistant discourse. Like Horkheimer and Adorno's, the paranoid imperative of queer antisocial polemic subscribes to the economic definition of binding only: the world is in a reified and ultimately bound state, and freedom can be found in shattering it through the inarticulable remainder, abjection, and *de*subjectivization. Lending itself as a metaphor for social totality, the economically bound organism disavows its death drive through its fixation on the pleasure principle. This fixation leads to a romanticization of negative aesthetics that, paradoxically, reinforces the disavowal of the death drive in the dominant order. So long as the concepts of binding and unbinding manifest in theory and art in their one-dimensional, economic fashion, the reparative project will struggle against the idealization of the negative. Laplanche and Pontalis's differentiation between two conceptual types of binding is imperative and has long been overlooked when interrogating the relationship between subject and the social body.

Queerness has long been associated with a kind of undoing, a psychical unbinding that has acquired a transgressive urgency against the stasis of normative life. This metaphorical unbinding of gender formations, normative sexuality, and the nuclear family makes sense in light of Horkheimer and Adorno's image of Enlightenment as a bound, hardened totality. Edelman crystallizes this association between queer and unbinding to a conceptual *breaking point*, such that he wakes us thinkers up in a way that his text does not set out to do because of his own denial of the life drive. Edelman's anticipatory anxiety stems from his opening up to intellectual revolt for the sake of thinking things through. Recall Freud's description of the life drive as "breakers of the peace" (*BPP SE* 77), much more perceptible than the quiet workings of the death drive. What Edelman seems to do in practice, unwittingly, is a life-driven breaking of the peace, and other scholars have followed suit in revolt against his brazen call. Queer theory in the twenty-first century, including Edelman's, paradoxically, has revived a fight for life, particularly for the life of thinking.

III. Dynamic Binding as the Life Drive: Reparative Formations

If the queer reparative moves away from the fantasy that envisions an instantaneous shattering of the articulable world, then the elasticity of time in relation to reading becomes redefined and foregrounded. The project of queer theory is thus not a perpetual insistence on the negative and the destructive as the sole means to fight against cultural totality. Rather, queer theory's project involves the constant effort toward the recognition of its own thought processes, its own negations and phantasies of omniscience—every process Enlightenment itself negates in its own machinery. The effort of queer thinking necessitates reparative practices. This queer fight for the life of thinking constitutes a rethinking, a close reading that, like art, refuses to shy away from failure.

At this point, my narrative of theory shifts from considering the concepts of binding and unbinding in an economic sense and in their social manifestation to a dynamic sense as they manifest in the relationship between text and reader. Social critique often neglects the condition that the drives relate specifically to the movement of thought. The oscillation of the paranoid imperative and queer reparative does not reject textual coherence, conventional forms of knowledge, and institutional thought from the outset. Rather, this method reads these structural phenomena queerly: that is, by tracing the development of intelligible thought up to its point of failure.[17]

I borrow Jacqueline Rose's use of the term, "vanishing-point" (*Why War?* 18), to describe this literary journey to failure. Rose often applies the term to mark an aporia or gap in thought, but she does not consider fully the implications of the metaphor. A term commonly applicable to visual art, a vanishing point describes a point on the horizon at which perspectival lines converge to produce a three-dimensional effect of distance on a two-dimensional plane. While vanishing points attest to the depth of an image, they also mark the limits of human eye, locating where visibility collapses. In material reality, these perspectival lines do not intersect, but human perception suggests that they will at a *projected* point in space, a point that the human subject can see but at which she can never arrive. A queer relation to failure that I propose does not involve a repudiation of intelligibility that valorizes the immediacy of traumatic undoing. Metaphorically speaking, queer failure submits to the allure of the vanishing point, allowing one to traverse with care and perversity the planar lines of thought that produce a pleasurable three-dimensionality. Far from repudiation, queer marks a devotion to an endpoint. In the following chapters, my readings identify the vanishing point of each novel that produces conceptual depth and marks conceptual failure. The metaphor of the vanishing point illuminates a paradox: the point in the narrative that attracts the desire for omniscience and anchors the promise of conceptual depth is the very point of epistemological crisis. The vanishing point reminds us that, in a queer reparative textual engagement, the reader still needs her phantasies of omniscience in order to sublimate the drives. While the paranoid imperative develops through phantasy, the queer reparative unfolds through literary acts of signification.

The life drive perpetuates the life of the signifier. Reparation and sublimation are linked through the dynamic binding of language. My elucidation of the life drive considers how a fight for thinking and a fight toward conceptual failure play out in Bersani's reading of Freud. Although Bersani wrote *The Freudian Body* almost two decades ago, its enduring resonance marks a belatedness that characterizes the practice of queer theory. In keeping with the queer agenda that strives toward the dissolution of being and meaning, Bersani's *Freudian Body* performs a theoretical analysis of what could be characterized as a queer death drive in Freud's speculative thinking. Bersani develops an "esthetics of masochism" (*Freudian Body* 107), articulating the necessary breaking points of conceptual categories that structure the capacity to think. As a self-effacing project, an "esthetics of masochism" locates vanishing points of psychoanalysis—conceptual blind spots that both structure and undermine psychoanalytic thought. I think through how the reading process itself becomes queer through the reparative function of literary sublimation.

By exploring the vanishing points of conceptual thought through close reading, Bersani posits a point at which categorical distinctions converge; subject to a vanishing point, conceptual depth eventually succumbs to its own limits. Bersani celebrates a kind of failure in Freud's writing, indicating the structural necessity of conceptual vanishing points: "the psychoanalytical authenticity of Freud's work *depends on* a process of theoretical collapse . . . The collapse of the argument is, as we shall see, a function of its own development" (*Freudian Body* 3, emphasis in original). The vanishing points that Bersani traces throughout Freud's oeuvre appear at moments of repetition, at reinstatements of conceptual definitions. Freud's definition of the sexual, in particular, comes into question. Bersani's insights allow him to articulate the ways in which art practices, both visual and literary, contain a subversion of conceptual categories.

The Freudian Body becomes central to thinking through queer theory's place in the field of epistemological inquiry and practices of aesthetic sublimation. Bersani's text provides a link between, on the one hand, the politics of sexualized queer practices that burgeoned in the wake of Foucault and, on the other hand, a difficult, slow, and often solitary relationship with words. Bersani describes theory and practice as symptomatic oppositions that "both reveal and disguise the antagonism internal to thought itself . . . [in which] a threatened rationality formulates the process of its own inevitable collapse" (*Freudian Body* 4). Practice and lived experience become a secondary concern when the integrity of the thought processes that render experience intelligible comes to be at stake. Simply put, "sex," whatever that might have meant to whomever, becomes a problem of thought.

What follows in Bersani's text challenges a reductive reading of Freud that understands sublimation as a mere mastery of the drives in the service of civilization. According to this conception of sublimation, desire becomes obscured or hidden. Instead, Bersani risks a kind of theoretical carelessness in his conclusions by equating sexuality, the sexual, civilization, death, pain, pleasure, and sadomasochism, albeit through meticulous close readings of Freud's texts. In doing so, Bersani traces "relational imprecisions" among psychoanalytic concepts. At the vanishing point of Freud's thought, these concepts do converge and only through their convergence and failure do we receive a sense of three-dimensionality to the body of Freudian thought. Through these inevitable slippages in thought, Bersani asserts, psychoanalysis moves back from the necessary "capacity to institute the categorical as a relevant mode of differentiating and structuring our experience of reality" (*Freudian Body* 5). He asserts the primacy of the sexual as a force that reduces the categorical in Freud's texts to what he calls an "oceanic textuality" (*Freudian Body* 21).

Bersani demonstrates the vagueness that plagues Freud's notion of sexuality, both across and within his major works. Symptomatic of this vagueness is a kind of obsessive repetition on Freud's part, where he explains, re-explains, and revises his concepts. Repetition is both a condition for the formulation of Freud's ideas and the agent of their disarticulation: "In Freud, an intense and explicit straining toward intelligibility frequently subverts the communication which appears to be its aim, as if the very effort of concentrated lucidity produced the secretive and pleasurable phenomenon of a self-destroying intelligence" (*Freudian Body* 12). The force that unbinds concepts for Bersani is the sexual, both the catalyst for sublimation and the vanishing point of sublimation.

Bersani questions the aim of the repetition compulsion, a question implicit in Freud's thinking in *Beyond the Pleasure Principle*. He states: "the mysterious repetition (and even intensification) of something unpleasurable is explicitly seen as inherent in sexuality. Freud seems almost on the point of suggesting that beyond the pleasure principle we find—sexuality. It is, in any case, repetition . . . which blocks Freud's attempts to define the sexual" (*Freudian Body* 34–35). Bersani clarifies what lies beyond the pleasure principle: not only a drive toward death, as Freud claims, but also its supposed opposite, the life drive. The drives come together in a contaminating friction to produce sexuality.

The Freudian body of work is literary insofar as its author is not afraid of conceptual failure. According to Laplanche's reading of Freud: "in sublimation 'a component instinct of sexual desire' escapes from the 'wave of energetic sexual repression' which terminates infantile sexual resources, and is transformed . . . into intellectual curiosity" (Laplanche quoted in *Freudian Body* 45). Another word for intellectual curiosity is epistemophilia. Libidinal energy is no longer attached, however, to original complexes of infantile sexuality. Intellect, Bersani argues, is not substitutive of infantile desires. The developing intellectual curiosity eventually leads to the acquisition of language, thus fostering the *anaclitic* (propping) character of the drive, but epistemophilia simultaneously maintains an *unbound*, sexual force. Bersani prioritizes the emancipated component of sexual desire that becomes the basis of intellectual curiosity: "In this form of sublimation, *sexuality would therefore provide the energy of thought without defining its terms*. Or to put this in another way, we would have *a nonreferential version of sexualized thought*" (*Freudian Body* 45, emphases in original). Although sexuality activates the formation of categorical thought, its energy remains independent from the relationship between sign and referent in the structure of signification. The fuel behind conceptual thought is a sexual excess that moves alongside but can never be subjected to repression.

Bersani's conclusion challenges Freud's notion of pleasure and threatens to rid Freud's *Beyond the Pleasure Principle* of its ambiguity about the relation of pleasure to sex and death. Bersani relates the sexual to sublimation, the argument, and an inevitable failure:

> Sexuality would, then, be inherently opposed to that psychic peace to which Freud seeks to reduce pleasure in *Beyond the Pleasure Principle*. The *work* of mental development involves a binding of the agitations I have just referred to, or a desexualization of the moves of consciousness. I want to suggest that this binding process re-stabilizes thought so that it may proceed, relatively untroubled, with, for example, precisely the kind of narrative argument . . . which as we have had occasion to see, Freud does *not* succeed in making. The narrative binding of thought is the repression of a desiring mode of operation, a repression on which philosophical discourse has perhaps traditionally depended. (*Freudian Body* 65–66, emphasis in original)

The process of binding involves a desexualization of thought that can never be completed. In this moment, Bersani attempts to foreclose a relationship between binding and the sexual. As Laplanche and Pontalis anticipate, Bersani in effect conflates sexuality and the death drive because he identifies both as subversive. Bersani points out how ineffectual the subject's disavowal is of the independent component instinct of the sexual that is the by-product of sublimation. The sexual is a constitutive outside. This very sexual desire constitutes the tear, the point of failure, in the structure of rational argument, a tear that grows upon every repetition of the argument's utterance and leads to unbinding.

That Bersani identifies an unbinding with a radical sexuality points to the slippage in queer theory between the death drive and the sexual. His theory resembles the paranoid imperative in the claim that a kind of conceptual unbinding constitutes the theory of sexuality. However, his framework also implicates the necessity of sublimation as the conditions of possibility for the unbinding force of sexuality. The processes of binding and unbinding, in other words, come together in a continuous dynamic. Bersani's unconscious insight in *The Freudian Body*, an insight crystallized in this passage and that differentiates him from the paranoid imperative, is that he employs both types of binding: the economic type that leads to an idealization of unbinding, and the dynamic type that occasions the movement of conscious thought, which makes ideas intelligible and susceptible to associative linking. The former is what provides the basis for Enlightenment and fosters metaphors of undoing in radical subversive practices, while the latter requires conceptual failure in order to prevent epistemological stasis.

At stake in light of Bersani's textual analysis are the modes of cultural discourse that make visible the libidinal forces in consciousness. He qualifies his emphasis on the nonreferential sexuality that underlies language, cautious of the postmodern, nihilistic celebration of the finality in the linguistic signifier: "[Literature] forces us to be aware of the density of words not as a function of their semantic richness, but rather as a sign of their inadequacy to the mobile sense which they cannot enclose" (*Freudian Body* 67). In this sense, art replicates and emphasizes the unconscious disruption in signification. Although this insight is certainly not a new one, Bersani's originality comes out of his close readings that expose the movement of the sexual inscribed in the interstices of conceptual thought. Because literature is structured by the repetition compulsion of mimesis, Bersani's prioritizes literature as a unique platform for sexual expression. He states: "The social function of literature—its critical power—consists in its demystifying the force of argument, argument's claim to truth. By initiating a designifying mobility within a text, the author's silent, insistent voice undoes that security of statement by which we can so easily be seduced, and possessed" (*Freudian Body* 67). If literature "mocks and defeats the communicative projects of language" (*Freudian Body* 67), then Bersani identifies a sense of (sexualized) irony inherent to the mimetic drive of literature. The association that Bersani draws between irony and sexuality evokes an expansive relationship to time, repetition, and sublimation. Irony becomes a kind of queering mechanism necessarily embedded in literature that hinges on this moment of failure.

A recasting of sublimation is in order, then. At the heart of language is the nonreferential manifestation of sexuality, coming out of but independent from infantile sexuality. This nonreferential, component instinct of sexuality is a necessary precondition and by-product of sublimation and contains the seeds of sublimation's failure. Bersani's agenda for a psychoanalytically oriented criticism becomes clear. Such criticism strives beyond naming hidden desires to "that moment of self-reflection which locates the *erasures of form* in art" (*Freudian Body* 111, emphasis in original). Bersani implies that the "gloss" of polished thought, where it is slickest, is exactly the point at which thought glosses over those shattering effects of desire. The question in reading is not the content of desire but its function: that is, not what art is but what it does in relation to the reader. The process of reading art, whether visual or literary, ought to be invested in locating precisely the moments where the effects of desire produce a pleasurable disarticulation.

Ending up with what becomes a rather broad definition of sexuality—or an anti-definition of sexuality, as it were—Bersani renders synonymous the sexual and the unconscious, either wittingly or unwittingly. According to Bersani's characterizations, both the sexual and the unconscious disrupt and constitute moments of conscious intelligibility. Like the unconscious, sexuality inhabits representations at the very place of symbolic failure. Perhaps missing from Bersani's text is the emphasis that the *de*-forming force of the sexual, its very existence, depends on the movement of signification and the repeated structures of conceptual categories. In other words, the *dynamic* processes of binding are necessary for a queer working through.

At times, Bersani takes repression for granted, as it enables the conditions for the unconscious. As Klein's patient, Dick, demonstrated, the unconscious does not exist *a priori* in relation to language.[18] The movements of sexuality and language are not only co-dependent. The emergence of the sexual in infant life is characterized by the supplementarity and displacement of nutrition, both of which parallel the function of signification itself. As Laplanche clarifies in his reading of Freud's *Three Essays*, "sexuality, in its entirety, in the human infant, lies in *a movement which deflects the instinct, metaphorizes its aim, displaces and internalizes its object, and concentrates its source on what is ultimately a minimal zone, the erotogenic zone*" (Laplanche 23, emphasis in original). The politicized sweep to discard Symbolic Law as a phallogocentric monolith or a system of phallocentric false consciousness comes into contradiction with itself, since the qualities of supplementarity and displacement that may render language unsatisfying, empty, untrue, or oppressive are the very qualities that bestow on sexuality its subversive force. Intelligibility as a result of repression, then, is still necessary.

The potential slippage in queer theory between an attitude of sexual freedom and the idealization of the unconscious as unequivocally emancipatory—while appropriate to narratives of, say, "coming out" to oneself and to others—can pose potential problems for psychoanalytic theorists. As Jacqueline Rose remarks in *Why War?,* "By seeing the unconscious as the site of sexual or verbal free fall, the humanities have aestheticized psychoanalysis" (*Why War?* 144). In *The Psychic Life of Power* (1997), Judith Butler also points out the tendency of critics in the humanities to forget that the unconscious catalyzes not only a site of liberation but also one that facilitates the desire for a complicit subjection to power (7). The point is that the unconscious does not have any political allegiances, and that it can be as much an agent of emancipatory representation as it can be a function of authoritarian power.

In a similar vein that cautions against idealizing the unconscious in her book *Melanie Klein* (2001), Kristeva laments that some of Klein's patients could be "precursors of today's gratuitous killers, of the mindless robots without a soul, and of *A Clockwork Orange* . . . Today, some of these fragmented personalities find refuge in art exhibits and other schizoid manifestations whose minimalist obscenities are welcomed by publishing houses claiming to be 'avant-garde'" (*Klein* 135). Did Kristeva just class gratuitous killers with contemporary avant-garde artists, both of whom can find their only postlapsarian savior in the psychoanalyst? She qualifies this strange condemnation by clarifying the philosophical agenda of Klein's work, which attempts to discover within those schizoid symptoms the preconditions for thought, "that is, within the very space that harbors the advent of psychic space and intelligence but that also accumulates the dangers of its suffocation" (*Klein* 135). In the failed symbolizations of these psychotics and artists, she suggests, the analyst has potential access, depending on her process of reading, to the repressed prerequisites for both thought and its subsequent failure. Kristeva identifies the importance of the anxieties at the root of signification, as these anxieties bring the analyst (and the critic) closer to the function of the drives in the acquisition of language.

Kristeva points to a crucial function of failure in symbolization that becomes the prerequisite to thought, something that Bersani gestures toward but, for all of his close reading, does not articulate. Bersani equips us, however, with the tools to think through the relationship between a queer death drive and the dynamic bindings of thought. As a cornerstone of queer theory, and coming out of a queer history fraught with love and death, Bersani brings me closer to articulating what I call a queer reparative. Bersani's "esthetics of masochism" encourages readers to see conceptual and visual forms through to their moment of undoing. Perhaps the reason Bersani prioritizes the concept of the sexual over the death drive is that he wants to make more room for the theoretical articulation of love while maintaining the agenda of radical disintegration. After all, according to Freud, the sexualization of the death drive stems from its ongoing tension with the life drive. A Kleinian perspective would clarify Bersani's insights in relation to when and how thought breaks down, as well as how breaches in thought can activate creativity.

Throughout her writings, Klein examines the relationship between the primacy of the death drive—its presence during early infancy and its dominance throughout life—and the development of thought. In her essay "The Importance of Symbol Formation in the Development of the Ego," Klein explains that an early, primordial Oedipus complex plays out during infancy when sadism predominates:

> Sadism reaches its zenith in this [early] phase, which is ushered in by the oral-sadistic desire to devour the mother's breast (or the mother herself) . . . The child expects to find within the mother (*a*) the father's penis, (*b*) excrement, and (*c*) children, and these things it equates with edible substances . . . Thus the child's sadistic attacks have for their object both father and mother, who are in phantasy bitten, torn, cut or stamped to bits (96).

The child's sadism triggers an overwhelming primal anxiety about potential punishment by the united parents, an anxiety brought about ultimately by an inner destructive force and internalized in relation to the early super ego. The destructive drive is present, then, at life's inception. As Kristeva notes, Klein revises Freud's theory of sexuality, asserting that the foundation of psychic life is not desire but anxiety.

The infant enters into a "paranoid-schizoid" position, defending against this anxiety (unpleasure) by projecting the destructive force onto bad objects that she cannot control, including the breast. A process of splitting binarizes the first love object into good and bad. As the infant experiences nourishment from the breast, it becomes idealized into a good breast, which the infant internalizes to negate the presence of destruction. The infant then experiences the unpleasurable deferral of nourishment, not as an absence of the breast but as the bad, persecutory breast. As Klein states in her essay "A Contribution to the Psycho-Genesis of Manic-Depressive States," because the baby projects its own aggression on to these objects, "it feels them to be 'bad' and not only in that they frustrate its desires: the child conceives of them as actually dangerous—persecutors who it fears will devour it, scoop out the inside of its body, cut it to pieces, poison it" ("Psycho-Genesis" 116). These part objects, or "imagos," as Klein calls them, are phantastically distorted pictures of material objects, existing for the subject in both the outside world and, through incorporation, within the ego.

The infant's world is thus built on a universe of part objects in which absence is disavowed. Although the paranoid-schizoid position is a first, unrefined attempt to stave off the destructive drives, such drives remain dominant as the infant's psyche tears objects apart, including the primordial ego, into good and bad. In the universe of part objects, the child feeds a phantasy of omniscience through both a disavowal of the mother's absence and a sense of mastery developed by the manipulation of object relations. For the subject, meaning depends on the degree of her anxiety. A surge of anxiety leads to a process of "projective identification," in which the subject equates primordial objects—penis, vagina, breasts—with many other things, such that she builds a series of equations that constitute her symbolic universe. In the paranoid-schizoid position the subject projects destructive part objects into the world and defends against them as external dangers. This universe of external and internal objects allows her to direct aggression to bad objects and idealize good objects. The dynamic unbinding force of the death drive characterizes this splitting process. Because the statuses of ego and object are so fluid and precarious, Kristeva claims that in this stage we can speak only of an *abject* rather than an object as such.

The infant enters the "depressive position" when she recognizes the mother as a whole autonomous other. The infant then realizes the mother's absence and mourns the inner world of part objects that previously defined reality. The depressive position is characterized by repairing the part objects into a whole, but, as Eve Sedgwick emphasizes and as I explain, one that is unlike any preexisting whole (*Touching Feeling* 128). The reparative moment constitutes a creative relation toward the other. According to Kristeva, the child "is capable of experiencing the loss of a *whole object* (the mother herself, and no longer simply the *part* object that was the breast) as a result of his diminished degree of splitting" (*Klein* 74, emphases in original). In other words, the work of mourning the lost object facilitates the transition from symbolization, based on the logic of sameness, to signification, based on the logic of difference. In the acquisition of language, the word is not a metaphoric substitute for the lost object, as is the case in phantasy, but a metonymic mark of difference and transition from that which the child must let go. For the rest of life, the speaking subject oscillates between silence and language, between phantasy and mourning, expanding in complexity, intricacy, and deferral.

The psychic defenses of phantasy give way to the acquisition of language. Fueled by the life drive, signification is characterized by the process of dynamic binding. This process narrates how the death drive gives way to reparation under the life drive: "objects become less malformed; projection diminishes; integration increases; and the separation from the ego and the Other becomes more tolerable" (*Klein* 75). The capacity to tolerate ambivalence, uncertainty, absence, pain, and above all failure, provides the foundation for creativity, sublimation, and love. Traumatic failure applies not only to one's own self-image, but also more generally to one's entire perceptual universe. The reparative project for which such Kleinians as Kristeva and Sedgwick call and to which I respond foregrounds the importance of binding part objects together in the depressive position as a process of working through loss. As Sedgwick clarifies posthumously, the depressive position is a difficult space in which to be still because it designates a psychical capacity for both destruction and creativity: "despite its name it comes to encompass, for example, both the preconditions of severe depression and also quite a varied range of resources for surviving, repairing, and moving beyond that depression. It is the site for Klein's explorations of intellectual creativity" (*Weather* 136). For the remainder of her life experience, the subject will deal with the oscillating transitions between structures of symbolization and those of signification. This oscillation takes the respective forms of, on the one hand, Enlightenment, reified language, dogma, or in a Bersanian sense, rational argument, and on the other hand, creative and difficult thinking.

The transition from symbolization to signification that marks the subject's introjection into language is, for Klein, an act of sublimation. She argues that "not only does symbolism come to be the foundation of all phantasy and sublimation but, more than that, upon it is built up the subject's relation to the outside world and to reality in general" ("Symbol Formation" 97). Although symbolism occurs through the manipulation of part objects in the paranoid-schizoid position, this death-driven stage is absolutely necessary for the development of sublimating practices. Because Enlightenment refuses to sublimate and resorts to suppression, as Horkheimer and Adorno argue, its phantasy of a world globally bound by formula remains at the level of symbolization and thus remains death driven.

Klein describes sublimation as the repairing of objects that have been torn apart by the destructive drive. More particularly, "symbolism is the foundation of all sublimation and of every talent, since it is by way of symbolic equation that things, activities and interests become the subject of libidinal phantasies" ("Symbol Formation" 97). As Kristeva states, "If it is true, as Freud believed, that sublimation results from a successful abandonment of both the aim of the drive and the residual effects of the death drive, Klein adds that such abandonment occurs through the work of mourning, with the residual effects of the life drive" (*Klein* 80). Mourning marks a turn from the dominance of the death drive to that of the life drive, and from symbolization to sublimation and signification. Bersani's intervention into the Freudian body of work notes, however, that inherent to the process of sublimation, haunting its structure, is the nonreferential, independent component of sexuality that has escaped desexualization and that always already promises to unbind what is made manifestly intelligible. The regression from a stage of binding to a stage of unbinding, an oscillation between the reparative and paranoid-schizoid position, is necessary to the movement of thought and representation itself. Queer thinking enables this capacity to think about economic and dynamic binding and unbinding together.

While this discussion divides the death drive and the life drive neatly into the paranoid-schizoid and reparative position, respectively, the drives really never become independent of one another. Rather, one drive is more dominant or manifest than the other at any given moment. Reading Bersani in dialogue with Klein illustrates how sublimation involves both death and life drives. As Kristeva reminds us, the anxiety that results from a reaction to the death drive, and which is very much bound to that drive, is constituted by an instinct for survival, a fear for life, a fear for loved ones, ultimately the contamination of the life drive. Conversely, the survival facilitated by the world of language marks, at least for Lacan, the death of the object, its absolute loss, as it comes to inhabit the cold, dead letter. The opposition between dynamic binding and unbinding characterizes the life drive and the death drive, respectively. Ambivalence emerges from the task of identifying what constitutes binding and unbinding in cultural production, especially when poststructuralism has called into question value judgments inherent to categories of socially acceptable products of sublimation. As we have seen in Kristeva's text, the cultural value of the avant-garde is precarious. This ambivalence arises also from the argument that the dialectical endpoint of sublimation in the project of Enlightenment facilitated, according to the Frankfurt School, the Nazi Regime.

As Britzman explains in her essay "Queer Pedagogy," reading involves risking the self, "confronting one's own theory of reading" and insisting on alterity inscribed within identity (94). For her, then, queer pedagogy is not about "getting identities right" or identities represented as ends in themselves: "the point is to read—in radical ways—the insufficiencies of identity as positivity and to examine and to refuse 'cases of exorbitant normality'" ("Queer Pedagogy" 94). She refuses an understanding of difference against the idea of normal. Rather, difference lies in the reader's relationship to her own negations, otherness, unconscious, and failure. The reading practice for which my analysis calls takes this queer detour into the death drive in order for reparation to occur: locating and pausing at the failure of thought; recognizing the part objects that constitute narrative structures; entering the work of mourning; and recognizing the dynamics of reading and thinking as a series of contingent and provisional identifications. This process is precisely how I define reading queerly, a practice that is distinctly reparative in that a difficult act of putting things together follows the impulse to take things apart. Queer theory, then, offers an alternative to the practice of critique as a dominant mode in twentieth-century thought. Consequently, for me, the aesthetics that become queer closely resemble systems of totality but incorporate a reparative turn.

My formulation of queer reading above risks, like so many queer theorists such as Sedgwick have done previously, the universalization of queer. A queer kernel resides in thought processes generally. The social specificity of "queer" that resists universalization in order to retain politicized clout for a certain group of people requires a shift in logic, from regarding "queer" in terms of object choice, source, impetus, or aim to defining it in terms of identity. In moving toward a practice of reading and thinking, this queer oscillation moves away from the explicit, particular agendas of identity affirmation for the LGBT(TIQQ2SA) community. Rather, my thinking incorporates the history of theorizing sexuality through a queer lens, which comes out of a particular history of activism and social change, but that simultaneously requires a kind of universalization insofar as the sexual is a universal condition of human relations. Consequently, the queer "referent" in this book is tenuous, provisional, and not always immediate due to the condition of failed knowledge I myself have set out. Despite, or because of, the theoretical discussion above that locates queer in intimate proximity to failed thought, I accept "queer" as a lost object, a slippery signifier.

I have arrived at the vanishing point of queer theory, and I have experienced a pleasurable kind of failure when the particularity of queer comes into question. What defines "queer" when, in Dean's words, "psychoanalysis *is* a queer theory" (*Beyond Sexuality* 215, emphasis in original)? As soon as queerness has experienced a flourishing of theoretical definition, it threatens to disappear. If, indeed, queerness locates the unintelligible within every moment of signification, if it celebrates the disintegration of meaning and coherence, then it risks becoming universalized into a transcendent space, a new sublime. Rather than the negation of meaning in signification, it becomes the metaphysical embodiment of the universal meaning it aimed to dismantle. Queer theory gets caught up in a performative contradiction, as its universality loses the historical specificity of queer politics out of which it emerges; as a ubiquitous force that is the constitutive "outside" of every system, queerness also reproduces the very identitarian logic it set out to critique, since it could potentially see traces of itself in everything. In its association with the death drive, queerness ironically becomes threatened by its own theoretical disintegration.

According to Klein, the paranoid-schizoid position limits the field of object relations. She states that although, "on account of his persecution anxiety and his suspicions, [the subject] develops *a very strong and acute power of observation of the external world and of real objects*, this observation and his sense of reality are nevertheless *distorted*, since his persecution anxiety makes him look at people mainly from the point of view of whether they are persecutors or not" ("Symbol Formation," 126, emphases added). A split occurs between persecutors and queers, between the social fabric and figures of total and radical negation. As the literary analyses in each of my chapters demonstrate, epistemological certainty houses the very seeds of its own undoing when the thinking subject follows her conceptual world faithfully to their vanishing points. Paranoia is but a resistance to and defense against that necessary undoing.

Contrary to Sedgwick's claims, the movement of the drives and the reparative turn are not mutually exclusive. A focus on the drives emphasizes how instrumental the negative is for a reparative turn. The queer reparative operates on a dynamic binding process that does not shy away from the failures of economic unbinding. If Enlightenment is caught in a phantasy of universal economic binding which enables and occludes a dynamic unbinding, then through the forces of the life drive, a queer reparative reading would tolerate an economic unbinding—loudly breaking the peace of conceptual homeostasis—in order to enable a dynamic binding.

A formulation of the "queer reparative" in a practice of reading necessitates a reexamination of queer love. The "whole" that Edelman repudiates as a love object is presumed in phantasy to be a knowable and thus narcissistically affirming whole. The whole object that Klein says we love, on the other hand, requires a letting go of narcissistic attachments, loving an unknowable whole that the subject nonetheless posits in reality as something that she can never possess with her faculties:

> Full identification with the object based on the libidinal attachment, first to the breast, then to the whole person, goes hand in hand with anxiety for it (of its disintegration), with guilt and remorse, with a sense of responsibility for preserving it intact against persecutors and the id, and *with sadness relating to expectations of the impending loss of it.* These emotions, whether conscious or unconscious, are in my view among the essential and fundamental elements of the feelings we call love ("Psycho-Genesis" 125, emphasis added).

Only then can the subject regard the other in an ethical way, recognizing the autonomy between subject and object and, in a way, letting the object go by *accepting the mediation of signification that nonetheless allows an elaborative, albeit abstract, relationship* between subject and object. My use of the term "autonomy" follows Winnicott. He postulates the stage in which a *potential space* develops between mother and child in the latter's move from dependence to autonomy through creative play: "Independence does not become absolute, and the individual seen as an autonomous unit is in fact never independent of environment, though there are ways by which in maturity the individual may *feel* free and independent" (Winnicott 188).[19] Klein's conception of love does not function at the level of the Imaginary, but it does involve compassion and guilt operating at the level of signification.

Klein's conception of love is intimately linked with a sense of failure and anxiety. Although this conception may encourage a kind of narcissistic self-loathing, it appropriately accounts for how subjects deal with the destructive drive: "The processes which subsequently become defined as the 'loss of the loved object' are determined by the subject's sense of failure . . . to secure his *good, internalized* objects, i.e., to possess himself of it. One reason for his failure is that he has been unable to overcome his paranoid dread of internalized persecutors" ("Psycho-Genesis" 121, emphasis in original). Failure has a direct relationship with letting go of the possibility of mastery, particularly over the drives, a mastery that is in itself a narcissistic endeavor. The reparative, then, is not a material effort to compensate for the subject's lack in a narrative of accountability toward the other; that is, it has little to do with a material relation of power, which unfolds *a posteriori* in relation to a psychical working through. Rather, the reparative process involves a process of sublimation and signification that affords a growth of psychical interiority: "there is anxiety how [*sic*] to put the bits together in the right way and at the right time; how to pick out the good bits and do away with the bad ones; how to bring the object to life when it has been put together; and there is the anxiety of being interfered with in this task by bad objects and by one's own hatred" ("Psycho-Genesis" 124). This conception of the reparative involves the process of dynamic binding: unifying and synthesizing part objects in a way that facilitates a letting go of melancholic attachments and takes the form of sublimation, particularly within a system of signification.

The reparative takes place in the wake of a traumatic internal violence. The death drive, then, is always already present. In the Kleinian model, the death drive is not disavowed but neither does it hold a place of finality; it rather spurs the subject toward creative life. While both Edelman and Klein define love as a letting go, the former urges his readers to let go of a narcissistic whole for the part object while the latter calls the subject to let go of the part object for an unknowable whole. As Sedgwick suggests, love is a creative process and deals with aesthetic engagements: "This is the position from which it is possible in turn to use one's own resources to assemble or 'repair' the murderous part-objects into something like a whole—though, I would emphasize, *not necessarily like any preexisting whole*" (*Touching Feeling* 128, emphasis in original). To say, out loud, that one loves unknowable wholes is indeed a queer freedom.

The tension between the two drives, between binding and unbinding, plays out through language, particularly through literary representation. A queer reparative reading practice, then, involves an intimate relationship to conceptual failure within the text. The text, in turn, becomes the space to elaborate love.

The theoretical narrative in this chapter makes contributions to three debates. The first engagement synthesizes the current split in queer theory between the anti-social approach, based on the death drive, and the reparative turn typically anchored in the language of affect. The second negotiation reintroduces *two* drives: thinking through the primacy of the death drive and the necessity of the life drive by sorting out the theoretical confusion about economic and dynamic binding. The third facet explores the status of the signifier in the new millennium, after the dominance of identity politics and critique.

Winnicott's differentiation between object-relating and object-usage helps to think through the implications of the three interventions that I propose for a specific approach to literature. In object-relating, the object has become meaningful through projective identifications: "the subject is depleted [. . . because] the subject is found in the object, though enriched by feeling" (Winnicott 118). In object-usage, the object must be "real" as "part of shared reality, not a bundle of projections . . . not as a projection, but as a thing in itself" (Winnicott 118). Object-usage involves an acceptance of the object's independent existence. The transition from "relating" to "usage" involves a recognition that the object is outside the subject's omnipotent control. A process of mourning occurs when the subject destroys the object in phantasy as it becomes external, and the "*object survives* the destruction by the subject," thus developing its own autonomy and life (Winnicott 120, emphasis in original). The act of reading, of playing and fighting with words, occasions the destruction and reparation of the object through the transition between object-relating and object-usage. As a love object and as a transitional object, the literary text survives reader identifications, and the reader is then free to indulge her own narratives of attachment and destruction through phantasies and their failures. As a device to mediate object-relations, the literary object serves as what Winnicott calls "transitional phenomena" in order to help readers through difficult thinking.[20] Like all transitional objects—our teddies, blankets, and bears that are part of both inner and outer worlds—literary fiction is both found and created. Our capacity to phantasize is what transforms the inert into the animated, the discarded into the treasured, the destroyed into the enjoyed.

Transitional objects, which are the basis of our capacities for representation, have neither beginning nor end, but rather exist in economies of attachment. Creative thinking with the other begins with objects that already exist in reality. Conceptual objects that are found, re-found, and charged with desire must pass through the other. Affinity, intimacy, love, is not about being too close, too immediate, but about the mobile elasticity between two people that transitional objects (narrative objects) make possible.

Creative sexuality unfolds out of a perverse relation to the text. By perverse, I refer to the undulating attachments, identifications, and certainties that build up and break down as reading happens. The historical specificity of such sexualized experience allows us to think about how perverse sexuality/textuality reinvigorate thinking and reading. The chapters that follow perform conceptual failure and reparative reading. Because the book theorizes and performs a queer reading practice, the literary analyses posit an imagined reader, and the close readings dramatize a process that is consistent with the methodology outlined in this first chapter.

In the subsequent chapters, the queer reparative emerges in a fashion that is particular to each novel, and so it is difficult to characterize in general here. The queer reparative varies from chapter to chapter depending on the kinds of phantasies that the paranoid imperative allows us to indulge. As I will show, the queer reparative is related to the transformation of melancholia into mourning. The process of mourning phantasy gives way to: an expansion of transitional phenomena; a diffusion of libidinal investments throughout a crystalline network of narrative pathways; an agility that negotiates the tension between the proliferation of signifiers and their limits; and a capacity to slow and stretch the experience of one's pleasure.

CHAPTER TWO

"A Tempest in a Test Tube"

The Paranoid Imperative of *Scientia Sexualis* and Psychoanalysis in Vladimir Nabokov's *Lolita*

> A lesson—any lesson—cannot simply be confused with the words, the terminology it uses to articulate itself. A reading lesson is, precisely, not a statement; it is a performance. It is not theory, it is practice . . . a practice, therefore, that can be exemplary only insofar as it is understood to be a model or a paradigm, not for imitation but for (self) transformation.
>
> —Shoshana Felman, *Jacques Lacan & the Adventures of Insight,* 20

I. Introduction

In the wake of emergent discourses on sex produced by Havelock Ellis, Alfred Kinsey, and the field of psychoanalysis, Nabokov published *Lolita* in 1955, a novel about confession and sexual deviance. As a middle-aged, erudite, narcissistic, self-reflexive "nympholept," Humbert details his journey toward pedophilic satisfaction through his twelve-year-old love object, Lolita, only to be circumvented by his rival and doppelgänger, the equally aged and erudite Quilty, whom Humbert eventually murders. This chapter investigates the relationship between Humbert's confession, the sexual sciences, and the problem of psychoanalysis in order to evaluate what, exactly, is queer about *Lolita*. "Queer" not only indicates sexual preference but also operates in the process of reading, the unfolding relationship between reader and text. *Lolita* is queer not necessarily because of its representation of transgressive sexual subjects but because of its relation to epistemological crises. Through a return to psychoanalysis, I argue that the transgenerational intimacy between Humbert and Lolita is a red herring that occludes the novel's central sexualized practice: Humbert's confession. Humbert's symptom resides not in his pedophilia, but rather in the excess that characterizes his phantasy of omniscience: his self-reflexivity, his encyclopedic deployment of *scientia sexualis,* his resistance to psychoanalysis. Indeed, the novel's sexual taboo takes a back seat to Humbert's seductive and imploring appeal to the reader.

As my introduction and first chapter establish, the term "queer" holds a fruitful albeit precarious and tentative position in the interstices of the literary text, because it no longer depends on explicit manifestations of sexuality as its sole anchor point for expression.[1] "Queer" refers to the crisis of knowledge. The reading below aims to resituate the queerness of *Lolita* from the problematics of sexually transgressive acts to conceptual vanishing points, thus highlighting moments that lure the reader to such points. The relationships among Humbert, Lolita, and the reader become refracted repetitions of one another, and they become queer when anxiety feeds on the over-enjoyment of mastery and certainty. *Lolita* is a story about Humbert's seduction of his reader and his simultaneous struggle with his epistemological drives. A paranoid imperative with *Lolita* will encourage various narratives of omniscience—Humbert's, the reader's, and those of the sexual sciences—in order to bring to crisis interpretive mastery over the text. The queer reparative will show that, if Humbert's self-construction as omniscient authority is sadistic, then his sadism is also a foolish one. The reader's moral outrage becomes attenuated by the uncomfortable identifications that I detail below. Through the queer reparative, we learn that despite its promises, epistemophilia sets us up not for omnipotence but for failure, which leave us raw, chafed, and vulnerable to the touch. That is, epistemophilia does not foster the body armour of reason but peels away narratives of certainty for new "skins" of thinking to grow.

While many of the issues this chapter addresses—parody, naturalism, and psychic life—run through Nabokov's oeuvre, especially in texts like *Strong Opinions* and *Pale Fire*, *Lolita*'s provocations are most pertinent to my argument. Famous for its controversial subject matter of pedophilia, *Lolita* is for Nabokov an allegory of his love affair with the English language (*Annotated Lolita* 316). The novel's focal displacement of transgressive sex practice for literary aesthetic is immediate because sanctioned by the author. But my chapter elucidates this aesthetic focal point from an uncomfortable angle that Nabokov would find distasteful, not only through a queer lens but also one that is psychoanalytic. Nabokov's well-documented, vehement aversion to psychoanalysis has invited criticism, such as Geoffrey Green's (1988), that links the author to Freud, but such attempts have neglected a thorough dialogue between Nabokov's novel and psychoanalytic texts. Because so glaring, such an aversion is a symptom that invites a reading.

Lolita at times distinguishes, other times homogenizes, psychoanalysis and sexology. The novel's representation of sexual subjectivity points to a difficult question about the role of what Klein calls the epistemophilic impulse ("Symbol-Formation" 98), particularly in sexual science and literature: in other words, the way in which the "drive to know" plays out in different discourses, in the different methods of possessing an object through the deployment of knowledge. Epistemophilia, the drive to know, is a temporally strange psychic position; as the basis for curiosity, it refers to conceptual mastery that is withheld or in deferral, an urge to contain the unknown with the intellectual capacities at hand. On the other hand, epistemophilia also leads to "the question," to a position that breaches moments of certainty. Paradoxically, the drive to know both seeks and sabotages conscious knowledge. The springboard to all intellectual activity, epistemophilia has sexual roots, as it is for Freud what fuels children's polymorphous perversity and sexual precocity when they encounter the primal scene (*Three Essays* 2). If, according to Sedgwick, queer resides in epistemological crisis, then queer reading has to do with the reader's relationship to the insatiable operation of epistemophilia.

Both Nabokovian criticism such as Charles S. Ross's and queer theory like Edelman's caution against the sanitization of sex or transgression.[2] Even Kathryn Bond Stockton's recent queer reading of *Lolita* in her book *The Queer Child* (2009) potentially sanitizes the novel as it allegorizes the queerness of Lolita through the symbol of the dog and the car.[3] Stockton's reading exemplifies how the queer child operates in a world that economically and socially disempowers her. Stockton's insight inverts the phallic authority of Humbert's narration, turns it on its head, as it were, by extracting the queer force of Lolita's sexuality from Humbert's incurious observations about her motivations. Contrary to the perceptions and expectations apparent in Humbert's dexterous self-representation, the mojo lies with Lo, and for all his narrating Humbert fails to get it back.

Like the more sanitized allegorical approaches to *Lolita*, Stockton's queer reading still depends on the ways in which Humbert's narrative lends itself to the displacements of metaphor, as she traces the queerness of the heroine through the metaphor of the dog and the car. My own reading appreciates the sovereign potential of Lo's mojo, but I do not posit Lolita as a material child. Indeed, Humbert is not the master of his own narrative, but my chapter does not locate the rupture in Lolita as an active human agent. He is, after all, telling his story in retrospect, painfully aware in several episodes of her budding sexual agency that gradually slips from his abusive control. In Humbert's narrative, Lolita does not exist as such, and so neither does Lolita as an intelligible queer figure. I do not directly contradict Stockton's reading, however, since the novel gives room for both interpretive approaches. Insofar as the queer child is extra-discursive according to Stockton, she remains aligned with the repressed unconscious that both structures and disrupts Humbert's conscious thought. Lolita is the point of epistemological failure, the vanishing point, the slippery object that Humbert cannot contain with language and around which he compulsively revolves. Lolita is not a child but one (disembodied) focal point of the queer aesthetic. Humbert and the reader can know Lolita (both character and novel) only as a part object whose absence Humbert disavows in a phantasy of omniscience and omnipotence. Humbert's narrative becomes the drive that infects and seduces the reader into its centripetal exertions. Because Humbert's confession is a return to the event and so an event in itself, the more immediate object of his seduction is his reader.

While recognizing *Lolita* as Nabokov's affair with the English language, my close reading is far from offering a "sanitized" allegory that imposes a phantasy of safety in talking about pedophilia. While appreciating the affective charge of the novel's taboo, I explicate the reading process as distinctly sexual. Parody imitates the conventions of genre for comic effect. As a repetition (in the case of *Lolita*, a repetition compulsion), parody disrupts the referents on which it depends. Through parody, *Lolita* exemplifies Bersani's claim that literature mocks and defeats the communicative aim of language (*Freudian Body* 67). As a result, the objects that *scientia sexualis* attempts to contain and regulate in relation to the novel become very slippery. This chapter draws out the sexualized irony that Bersani implies as the mimetic drive of literature.[4] As the previous chapter asserts, the queer literary form of irony disrupts the coherence of narrative. The various engagements with uncertainty catalyze a readerly desire. *Lolita* offers a unique stage for this reading process because it so potently blends affects of shame and pleasure that the resulting confusion becomes the glue that maintains our attachment to the text.

The ambiguity that stems from the novel's parodic representation of sexual science and psychoanalysis problematizes the author's position on the epistemology of sex. The gap between epistemophilia as *desire* and epistemic *certainty* misrecognized in consciousness marks the expansive space of the persistent question—the enigma of the text. In Shoshana Felman's words, "Where does a text (or a signifier in a patient's conduct) precisely make no sense, that is, resist interpretation?" (80). As a parody that resists the reader's search for ordered "levels of meaning" (*Annotated Lolita* xix), the novel brings into question sexual science, psychoanalysis, and literature as various reading practices upon the body. Indeed, in *Jacques Lacan and the Adventures of Insight* (1987), Felman celebrates that

> What *can* be read . . . is not just meaning but the lack of meaning; that significance lies not just in consciousness but, specifically, in its disruption; that the signifier can be analyzed in its effects without its signified being known; that the lack of meaning . . . can and should be interpreted as such, without necessarily being transformed into meaning. (45, emphasis original)

What can be read, in other words, is how literary *form* leads to a conceptual vanishing point: the compulsion to repeat, slips, negations, displacements, condensations. For Felman, "The analytic reading is thus essentially the reading of a difference that inhabits language, a kind of mapping in the subject's discourse of its point of disagreement with, or difference from, itself" (Felman 21). But this very difference, the unconscious, can never be resolved in a conscious translation. The non-sense embedded in language is the unconscious, from which no erudite, omniscient consciousness can ever escape—even Humbert's or Nabokov's or any astute reader. Unlike the popular conception of psychoanalysis in the 1950s, Felman points out that the outcome of psychoanalysis is not taxonomical or hermeneutical certainty, not even knowledge about the self, but rather the performative articulation of the failure in consciousness.

Because the central sexualized practice in *Lolita* is Humbert's confession, the sexual relation he attempts is a transferrential relationship with the reader. In *The Language of Psychoanalysis,* Laplanche and Pontalis define the theoretical development of "transference," which describes classically the fulfillment of unconscious wishes, predominantly Oedipal, through the relation between analyst and analysand (456). Freud regarded transference initially as a symptom, a resistance that perpetuates the patient's neuroses. As Laplanche and Pontalis point out, Freud revises the notion of transference later, however, as a displacement of affect from one idea to another, suggesting that the process of thinking carries an originary sexual charge. Freud concludes it necessary that transference emerge as memory, while cautioning against transference that arises as a repetition of a desire. Humbert offers his confession as a memory, but the more he hails and seduces the reader, especially through the intimacies of humor, the more he enters into a repetition of a desire to contain and construct his love object, as he did with Lolita. This time, the intimacy he attempts is not physical, as with the other object, but verbal, through the playful language of humor.

Like sex, humor, if it works, involves a similar reciprocity, awkwardness, surprise, vulnerability, and inconvenient but exciting encounter with the other. In *The Joke and its Relation to the Unconscious* (1905), Freud differentiates wit from the joke: whereas the former refers to a "play with ideas," something that "the witty man *possesses*," the latter describes a "*playful judgment*," something that he *makes*" (*Joke* 3, emphasis in original). The pleasurable effects of the joke stem from an economic short circuit that facilitates a discharge of a repressed desire (*Joke* 115). Freud claims that the pleasure derived from *delight* in *power* is secondary to a repetitive return to the familiar, typically found in the structures of rhyme, alliteration, and refrain (*Joke* 117). The play with words, a kind of sense making, alternates with unleashing nonsense. The pleasure of the joke, then, stems from this paradox of sense and non-sense, which Humbert's prose alternates. Given that, in the joke, power is secondary to repetition, Humbert's power is secondary to his more vulnerable invitation to the reader to engage with narrative desire and, in doing so, to engage in a repetition of conceptual failure.

This chapter addresses two literary approaches to *Lolita*. The first approach interrogates psychoanalysis in relation to sexual science; the second approach returns to psychoanalysis by exploring the psychic effects of the confessional mode as literary parody. The chapter bridges these two approaches by showing that *Lolita* provides an intersection for the workings of both Foucauldian critique and psychoanalysis, two discourses that have a tumultuous history within the field of queer theory because of their supposedly antithetical commitments, the former to the critique of discourse and the latter to the catharsis of confession.[5]

II. The Weaves of *Scientia Sexualis*

The critical task of relating psychoanalysis to Nabokov has entered and reentered the literary reception of his oeuvre on a regular basis, no doubt fueled by Nabokov's passionate, perhaps intimate, repudiation of psychoanalysis. In negated form, psychoanalysis is Nabokov's constant companion. In the novel's afterword, Nabokov asserts: "I detest symbols and allegories (which is due partly to my old feud with Freudian voodooism and partly to my loathing of generalizations devised by literary mythicists and sociologists)" (*Annotated Lolita* 314). Alfred Appel Jr.'s annotated edition of *Lolita* includes his personal consultations with the author and makes Nabokov's opinion of psychoanalysis clear outside of the literary text. As Nabokov notes about Freud, "Let the credulous and the vulgar continue to believe that all mental woes can be cured by a daily application of old Greek myths to their private parts" (*Annotated Lolita* 325). Appel provides an interesting background on Nabokov's ambivalence about sexual science and his vociferous denouncement of psychoanalysis, which by the 1950s had gained much of its reputation in America as a pseudo-science.

While provocative, Nabokov's rejection of American psychoanalysis was certainly not uncommon. Nabokov's resistance to psychoanalysis was at the time well founded. Led by Heinz Hartmann, the institutionalization of psychoanalysis in 1950s America manifested dominantly as ego psychology. The integrity of the ego took precedence over the subversions of the unconscious, and symptomatology depended heavily on the deductive application of Freud's theories.[6] In Britain, psychoanalysis was recovering from a major split between Anna Freud and Melanie Klein that prevented any methodological consensus and broke the institution up into several camps.[7] Like Nabokov, French psychoanalyst Jacques Lacan repudiated midcentury psychiatric practices in America that appropriated Freudian psychoanalysis, which led him to launch his own school. Given the ongoing crisis of the institution in the wake of Freud's death, Nabokov's resistance to psychoanalysis loses some of its polemical charge since his objections paralleled those unfolding from within the discourse.

Similar to the agendas of the revisionist psychoanalysts, Nabokov's fiction and interviews attacked the theoretical generalizations of Freud that circulated in the American popular imagination. Ego psychology translated symptoms into fixed meanings through hermeneutically reductive templates such as the Oedipus Complex. Psychoanalysts in Europe remained invested in Freud's emphasis on language, specifically that the unconscious is not some static, causal truth to be uncovered but rather an ever-displacing force, bound up with consciousness, that finds life in language and brings the subject both pleasure and pain in relation to the other. Like French psychoanalysts Lacan and Kristeva, then, Nabokov also refocused an investment in signification and desire. Nabokov identifies this reinvestment as a "game." In this game, Nabokov attacks the object in which American psychiatry was invested, namely, the ego. *Lolita* is a parody of the ego's self-expression and its comical, tiresome resistance to admitting failure.

While Nabokov attacks Freud, he is more open to scientists proper, particularly to Kinsey and Ellis, whose works abandon moral valuations for "scientific objectivity" to develop a taxonomy of sexual variation. Nabokov's divergent stances on psychoanalysis and sexology point to the problematics of the permeable boundaries that define science.[8] Nabokov's labor to redeem psychology as a testable, empirical science through his art required him to repudiate popular Freudianism. Nabokovian scholarship on the relation of *Lolita* to sexual science is contradictory, as are the relationships *Lolita* scholars draw between Freud and scientific discourse.[9] Unlike David Andrews, who associates Freud with science, Eric Goldman shares Stephen Blackwell's views of science as "pure" and myth, particularly psychoanalysis, as a misappropriation of scientific method. Both Goldman and Blackwell fix the binary between myth and science in a hierarchy organized according to presumed value judgments.[10]

The two central charges against Freud in Nabokovian criticism—that he is not scientific enough and that he operates with a moral agenda—are based on ideological presumptions about the discourse of science itself. The clinical milieu out of which *Lolita* emerged contributed to a vast production of sexual subjects based on taxonomical and statistical data. In the *Psychology of Sex* (1934), Ellis shares Kinsey's rejection of a moral norm in order to study sexual difference. Like Freud in *Three Essays,* Ellis challenges the societal dichotomy between normality and perversion. Ellis argues that because "morals are in perpetual transition," physicians have the responsibility to publish openly on matters of sex they previously could not address in private with their patients (5). A contradiction emerges in Ellis's statement: the claim that sexology distances itself from morals in its prioritization of objectivity and the recognition that it plays a performative role in moral systems. To a large extent, then, the responsibility (or power) to regulate the line between sanctioned and illicit subjects falls largely to the physician, due to his claim to greater scientific knowledge. Ellis works under an ideological framework of moral relativism, whereas Freud observes in *Civilization and Its Discontents*, perhaps more cynically, the poor ways in which civilization defers and displaces an implacable aggression. While Ellis undermines the fixity of morals through science, he nonetheless justifies his science as a moral referent, albeit one subject to historical change.

Goldman, like David Rampton, draws parallels between the representation of Lolita's character and Kinsey's *Sexual Behavior in the Human Female* (1953). The way in which Kinsey frames his study shares similarities with Ellis about the moral neutrality and rigorous method of science. In his report *Sexual Behavior in the Human Male* (1948), Kinsey describes modern taxonomy as a result of "increasing awareness among biologists of the uniqueness of individuals . . . The taxonomist is . . . primarily concerned with the measurement of variation in [a] series of individuals which stand as representatives of the species in which he is interested" (Kinsey 17). Kinsey's taxonomical approach to sexual variation in human males and females resists the construction of moral norms among difference. Kinsey and his team interviewed twelve thousand men to capture the wide range of variation in relation to "sexual outlets" by measuring the frequency of sexual acts, time of day, stage of life, type of objects—opposite sex, same sex, and animal—marital status, and other social factors that might affect sex acts, such as education and class. Kinsey's findings undermine the fantasy of sexual norms that plagued 1950s America.

At first glance, Kinsey's emphasis is concrete data, and this data comes from a wider range of subjects than Freud, who could speculate only from his clinical experience, an experience arguably recorded subjectively, through his own interpretations. But Kinsey and Freud share commonalities that critics have missed in reading Nabokov, which complicate the novel's relation to sexual science and psychoanalysis. Kinsey responds to his data in ways that resemble Freud's theorization of the sex drive in *Three Essays*. In Freudian terms, Kinsey traces various permutations and combinations of what Freud identifies as the sexual "impetus," the "aim," the "source," and the "object" among his sample of male subjects.[11] The wide range of behavior variation in the Kinsey reports serves a deductive logic that reduces subjectivity to a taxonomical structure. Kinsey claims that "the range of variation, the mode, the mean, the median, and the shape of the frequency distribution for the whole group" allows "the clinician . . . [to] comprehend the extent to which generalizations . . . may be applied to any particular case" (20). Here, despite the range of sexual variation he provides, Kinsey admits the convenience in the application of the general to the specific, a practice that amplified Nabokov's resistance to Freud. While Kinsey resists positing a moral norm, his methodology necessarily binarizes the difference between average male behaviors and deviant ones by graphing the degree of variation. While Kinsey's method is both abstract and taxonomical, Freud's method is both abstract and singular. It is singular because his method is based on the specific stories of each patient. Nabokovian critics often attribute moralism and deductive logic to Freud and thus reject psychoanalysis in favor of science. Such a distinction becomes tenuous in light of the ways in which Kinsey and Ellis, whose works figure heavily in *Lolita*, frame their studies.

But another similarity between psychoanalysis and these two giants of sexology is more troubling and neglected in the reception of *Lolita*. Despite Kinsey's and Ellis's noble intentions to proliferate sexual difference without a moralistic agenda, they contribute to the discursive "liberation of sex" that Foucault critiques in the first volume of *History of Sexuality*. Although, according to such scholars as Wardell Pomeroy, Kinsey attacks what he sees as the moralism and un-testability of Freud's theories, *both* Freud and Kinsey contribute to the discursive proliferation of sex as strategies that manage sexual subjects. For Foucault, *scientia sexualis* is a term that describes the scientific codification of the incitement to speak about sex, such that the confessing subject is exposed to clinical interpretation and pathologization. Foucault further postulates the mutual constitution of power and knowledge production: "The power which thus took charge of sexuality set about contacting bodies, caressing them with its eyes, intensifying areas, electrifying surfaces, dramatizing troubled moments" (Foucault 44). Kinsey's interviews engage the pleasure of power, which is intimately bound to knowledge production, and his sexual taxonomy contributes biopolitically to the management of populations. The will to power that reproduces the incitement to confess integrates the subject into the network of scientific discourse.[12] Kinsey's and Ellis's caution against moralism becomes void within the network of scientific discourse, in which power/knowledge gets deployed and is not "possessed" by any singular, disinterested scientist. Nineteenth-century Darwinian attitudes to species variation and phantasies of scientific disinterestedness have given way to cold-war panic. Despite Nabokov's agreement with Kinsey's and Ellis's view of science, his representation of all scientific discourse becomes a vehicle for critique.

The scandalous premise of *Lolita*, a transgenerational sexual affair, invites a deployment of sexual science in order to make sense of the deviance and to counter readerly anxiety in the face of sexual taboo. Within the narrative, sex and knowledge are inextricably bound. Kinsey's and Ellis's works do indeed assert a presence in the text, and the relationship between these sexologists and *Lolita* becomes a fraught one. On the one hand, Humbert presents himself as an object of inquiry for sexual science. He calls on the reader's psychiatric evaluations and differentiates himself from a "normal man" by self-identifying as an "artist and a madman, a creature of infinite melancholy" who is able to single out the "little deadly demon among the wholesome children" (*Annotated Lolita* 17). On the other hand, Humbert identifies with the sexologist. The taxonomic methodology in sexual science and psychoanalysis produces tension in the novel. Such methodology often arises in Humbert's descriptions of his pathology and scopophilic objectifications of Lolita. Humbert comes to terms with Lolita's rapidly growing body by describing her at length with anthropometric precision, thus indicating an expert knowledge about the science of measuring the body: "I could safely accept most of those January measurements: hip girth, twenty-nine inches; thigh girth (just below the gluteal sulcus), seventeen; calf girth and neck circumference, eleven; chest circumference, twenty-seven; upper arm girth, eight; waist, twenty-three; stature, fifty-seven inches; weight, seventy-eight pounds, figure, linear; intelligence quotient, 121; vermiform appendix present, thank God" (*Annotated Lolita* 107). Humbert's excessive evaluation makes him sound less like a father or lover than a medical researcher, especially when his evaluation extends to the interior of Lolita's body. Humbert's desire is scientific, methodical, and penetrative—a phantasy of omniscience. Humbert is both an object of inquiry through whom the reader enjoys a vicarious experience and a subject who takes sadistic pleasure in his deployment of knowledge. He illustrates the ambivalence of sexual science that simultaneously claims moral neutrality and disavows its pleasure of power.

Humbert's scientific knowledge allows him to acknowledge that his desire is totally impersonal. He reduces his young love objects to a statistical set. He recognizes that the qualities required to pique his desire are mere abstractions: "The bud-stage of breast development appears early (10.7 years) in the sequence of somatic changes accompanying pubescence. And the next maturational item available is the first appearance of pigmented pubic hair (11.2 years). My little cup brims with tiddles" (*Annotated Lolita* 20). His scopophilic dissection of the young female body at its "bud" stage suggests that his desire depends on the process of fragmentation: a kind of active splitting of an object. Humbert's scientific precision juxtaposes the whimsical tone of the alliterative rhythms in budding breasts, somatic sequences of pubescence, and pigmented pubic hair. His reflection on his brimming cup caps his evaluation of Lolita with an indication of pleasure. Humbert's alliteration and pleasure emphasize his tendency to *construct* his love object through discursive or rhetorical means.

The pleasure he experiences in his repeated discursive construction of Lolita exceeds the bodily pleasures of his sexual encounter with her. Humbert tells his readers repeatedly that he loves a Lolita that does not exist as such, but one he produces with his scopic drive and his use of language: "I knew I had fallen in love with Lolita forever; but I also knew she would not be forever Lolita . . . The word 'forever' referred only to my own passion, to the eternal Lolita as reflected in my blood" (*Annotated Lolita* 65). He even acknowledges that, by the time he experiences his first clandestine orgasm against Lolita's thigh, he has fallen in love with an object abstracted from the material person through a literary play, a fantasized object that is animated only by his will: "What I had madly possessed was not she, but my own creation, another, fanciful Lolita—perhaps more real than Lolita; overlapping, encasing her; floating between me and her, and having no will, no consciousness—indeed, no life of her own" (*Annotated Lolita* 62). Given his scientific approach to Lolita's body, Humbert's admission in this moment resonates with a later point when he expresses his frustration at not being able to kill Charlotte actively: "Perhaps if the year were 1447 instead of 1947 I might have hoodwinked my gentle nature by administering her some classical poison from a hollow agate, some tender philter of death . . . Nowadays you have to be a scientist if you want to be a killer" (*Annotated Lolita* 87). Even though, immediately afterward, Humbert claims to be neither scientist nor killer, he proves to be both in his linguistic deployments. He contradicts himself the moment he tries to rape Lolita in her sleep: "The science of nympholepsy is a precise science. Actual contact would do it in one second flat. An interspace of a millimeter would do it in ten" (*Annotated Lolita* 129). In his acknowledgment of Lolita's aesthetic abstraction lies both a recognition of the dehumanizing violence he perpetrates and an alibi to do what he pleases to the object that, to him, is not "Dolores" but "Lo," a product of his own will. Humbert's precise knowledge about the optimally developed love object exemplifies the problematics in the pleasure of power that accompanies a specifically scopic science.

The representation of psychoanalysis in *Lolita* is even more questionable. Nabokov's objection to psychoanalysis is concerned with the validity of its knowledge production, what counts as truth. Nabokov takes exception to psychoanalysis as, to his mind, a projection of scientific certainty that occludes its basis in myth and literature. The novel's narrator shares Nabokov's distaste for "neo-Freudian hash," fooling psychiatrists with invented dreams, staged symptoms, and "fake 'primal scenes'" (*Annotated Lolita* 34). Humbert represents psychoanalysis as an incomplete science: "Taboos strangulated me. Psychoanalysts wooed me with pseudoliberations of pseudolibidoes" (18). The alliterative repetition of three "s" sounds imposed upon invented compound words suggests another: pseudoanalysts.

Humbert's character echoes Nabokov's views when the former parodies the diagnostic power of something so dependent on literary "myth," such that psychoanalytic "insights" can be only half baked.

Humbert posits an originary trauma early in his confession that invites the reader to analyze his pedophilic tendencies. He explains that his preferred love object became fixed during his childhood when an affair with Annabel Leigh, a girl no more than thirteen, is cut short by her untimely death, thus stagnating Humbert's Oedipal processes in a melancholic attachment. He refers to himself in the third person in mock omniscience: "The able psychiatrist who studies my case—and whom by now Dr. Humbert has plunged, I trust, into a state of leporine fascination—is no doubt anxious to have me take my Lolita to the seaside and have me find there, at last, the 'gratification' of a lifetime urge, and release from the 'subconscious' obsession of an incomplete childhood romance with the initial Miss Lee" (*Annotated Lolita* 166–67). Humbert neither rejects theoretical models directly nor denies that he repeats his lost past as an act of melancholy. Rather, he confirms the repetition and justifies the diagnostic projections of the reader/psychiatrist. He does look for a beach to replicate the primal scene of his adolescence, but admits that by the time they reached that "Sublimated Riviera," his search, "far from being the impulse of the subconscious, had become the rational pursuit of a purely *theoretical* thrill" (167, emphasis added). In this moment, Humbert displays the power of his consciousness. His intellectual curiosity begs for a science experiment and disavows his unconscious repetition of his past. Humbert's scientific "rationality" reinforces his resistance to psychoanalysis, which arises at moments of uncertainty and becomes a vehicle for humor.

In the moment Humbert invokes "Annabel *Lee*," he subjects the reader to another layer of deferral. He refers not only to an Oedipal stagnation. The object on which he remains fixated is not the person, Annabel Leigh, but a textual figure, particularly the speaker's lover in Edgar Allan Poe's poem, *Annabel Lee*, a figure whose "sepulchre there by the sea" (Poe 40) renders her a lost object of melancholia. What Humbert desires to repeat by bringing Lolita to the beach for a "purely theoretical thrill" is the performance of a literary allusion, reducing Lolita's subjectivity to a mere relation to a textual figure. Humbert's reduction of Lolita to a repetition of his personal history, aestheticized through a double filter of both sexual science and poetry, suggests that his sexual excitement depends on discursive deferrals and not on any singular person.

Humbert mocks psychoanalysis as a hermeneutical project, because he maintains that the analyst deduces arbitrary meaning from arbitrarily chosen symptoms. He even reads Quilty's clues as symptomatic of pathology: "He did not use a fountain pen which fact [*sic*], as any psychoanalyst will tell you, meant that the patient was a repressed undinist" (*Annotated Lolita* 250). Ellis coined the term "undinist" to refer to a person, usually male, who derives erotic enjoyment from his object, usually female, urinating (*Annotated Lolita* 425). Humbert's detective work here homogenizes taxonomies of sexology and psychoanalysis; but humor stems from the logical gap between the symptom, in this case, the fountain pen, and the conclusion, undinism. Humbert attributes this logic to psychoanalysis and assumes that it appropriates and abuses science proper. When he writes a poem to express his distress over Lolita's abduction, he "psychoanalyzes" his poem and realizes: "it is really a maniac's masterpiece. The stark, stiff, lurid rhymes correspond very exactly to certain perspectiveless and terrible landscapes and figures, and magnified parts of landscapes and figures, as drawn by psychopaths in tests devised by their astute trainers" (*Annotated Lolita* 257). In the same spirit as Foucault, Humbert concludes that psychoanalysts are "trainers" by producing psychopathic subjectivities through the very methods of the profession. In Humbert's narrative, despite the claims of sexual science, his sexuality is less a fixed identity than a series of discursive displacements.

Humbert's discourse belongs to Enlightenment and its phantasy of universal economic binding, particularly a binding that reifies, contains, and consumes Lolita. Humbert exemplifies the "new barbarism" that attains a mythic status through a phantasy of omniscience that Horkheimer and Adorno critique. Humbert's universe is one of part objects. The attempts of Nabokovian scholars and even Nabokov himself to differentiate between the "myth" of psychoanalysis and the "science" of sexology or zoology resonate with the dialectical collapse of myth and reason in Enlightenment. Even though Humbert takes pleasure in written description, what becomes prioritized in the novel for him and for the reader is a paranoid imperative: the desire to know Humbert's, Lolita's, and the reader's sexual subjectivity; the impulse to secure the constellation of part objects in static coordinates, divided into good and bad; the drive to figure out the "truths" of this text and to read more comfortably because ego identifications become relatively safer. Far from the process of mourning in signification, Humbert's text attempts to symbolize a hermetically sealed totality of part objects, and its obsessive self-reflexivity implodes because Humbert's epistemophilia surrounding several enigmas of Lolita, Quilty, and the reader spurs him toward his conceptual vanishing points.

III. Parody and Psychoanalysis as a Practice of Reading

Foucault argues that a discursive totality produces rather than prohibits sexuality. Sexual transgression, therefore, would always already be subject to regulation and management. Such a totality, however, betrays a desire for omniscience and an anxiety that results from the necessary failure to acquire it. As Freud notes, something in sexuality is excessive to intelligibility. For example, Kinsey's compulsion to capture the greatest possible variation in sexual behaviors belies an anxiety of omniscience, or lack thereof. His premise articulates the limits of his study with a two-page chart of one hundred and twenty academic and nonacademic fields of human sexual behavior (Kinsey 22), including what Foucault calls *ars erotica* (Foucault 70). Although the listed limits of a study is standard in scientific procedure, the excess of Kinsey's list reads as symptomatic from a literary critical perspective. Kinsey's list claims to be conscious of where his study is lacking. His scientific method admits its limits only to disavow them by claiming knowledge of the unknown, a performative move that Foucault would critique in the discursive production of the truth about sex. The discourse of sexual science constantly confronts a crisis in omniscience when faced with the task to make sense of sex.

In contrast, psychoanalysis offers not a scientific but a literary endeavor to explore the silent effects that disrupt the phantasies of omniscience in both Humbert and the reader. The queer thing in *Lolita* is not Humbert's sexual transgression but the literary form of parody. As I will show, *Lolita* is a parody of the narcissistic sexual confession, one made obvious by the parodic metanarrative in which a Dr. John Ray Jr. offers Humbert's diary as a case study. For all of Foucault's tautological critique of sexuality's discursive power network, parody as a distinct and potentially erotic play of language is something he did not consider. Parody attenuates the will to power because, as *Lolita* exhibits, it mimics and thus undermines authoritative voice. In this case, parody depends on irony as a mode to produce humor. *Lolita* exemplifies the relationship of queer to irony and allegory. I agree with Edelman that irony is a "version of the death drive" in that it produces a "constant disruption of narrative signification" (*No Future* 24). Irony is an agent that disfigures articulable narrative. But, following de Man in "Rhetoric of Temporality," I depart from Edelman's contention that irony brings the reader to an unmediated relationship with the text. There is no such thing as an unmediated relationship to a text. That is a phantasy, and to literalize it does not make much sense because text *is* mediation, unless the reader was to eat the page or lick the black ink off the white fibers. I explore this phantasy of unmediated textuality more in my third chapter. In terms of de Man, irony in *Lolita*'s parodic form and the novel's allegorical attachments to the English language perpetuate queer temporalities of deferral and belatedness. Irony does draw attention to the signifier in Humbert's confession, but contrary to Edelman's link between irony and immediacy, irony defers certainty and begs rereading. The function of irony in *Lolita* illustrates its synchronic structure, which recaptures human existence as "a succession of isolated moments lived by a divided self" (de Man 226). Bersani in turn implies that irony operates through a queering mechanism because it sends the reader toward an epistemological vanishing point by tickling, provoking, alluding, and eluding the reader. Even though, in this case, parody and allegory have supposed referents (sexology, psychoanalysis, detective novel, the English language), the narrative form destabilizes such referents, using them only to seduce the reader and exacerbate her epistemophilia. The function of irony is in the service of the drive, in this case, the drive to read, through a repeated subjection to the mediation of the signifier that becomes eroticized in the moment of a chuckle.

Through parodic form, power becomes very slippery, dangerously so for the reader. Even Humbert associates queer with a certain kind of failed reading: "Queer! I who was jealous of every male we met—queer, how I misinterpreted the designations of doom" (*Annotated Lolita* 217). Parodic form both frames and disrupts the scientific themes of the novel. Nabokov's parody is queer particularly because it occasions an epistemological crisis that continues to provoke the reader's desire to know. Through Humbert's character, parody trips up the certainties with which the novel invites the reader to anchor interpretation. Around the novel's parodic form revolves all of the central problems that keep us reading *Lolita*: the hatred of psychoanalysis, the production of sexual subjectivity, the explicit abuse, and pedophilia. Parody brings these scenes to the reader, while foreclosing intellectual resolution. The process of reading becomes *drive* in the psychoanalytic sense: we read, we read on, and we read again, without abating our discomfort with the novel. This discomfort is distinctly epistemological. The process of reading as a compulsive drive points to renewable pleasures, not of sexual possession, but of conceptual failure. The reader's engagement with epistemological failure in *Lolita* constitutes what Bersani deems an "esthetics of masochism" (*Freudian Body* 107), which subjects the structures of the ego to a pleasurable compromise through aesthetic engagements.

In this view, psychoanalysis is not a taxonomical science of perversion, but a theory of reading. Many critics of *Lolita* who are interested in psychoanalysis reconcile Freud's or Lacan's writings to aspects of the novel or of Nabokov's persona. These readings pick up on various elements such as the doppelgänger, the uncanny, the death drive, or polymorphous perversity.[13] In general, however, critics employ psychoanalysis hermeneutically, as a mode of interpretation to see past the enigma of the text or charismatic author. Understandably, then, critics like Appel, Brian Boyd, Goldman, or Andrews are wary of Freud and his themes. The literary criticism of *Lolita*, however, neglects the condition that psychoanalysis takes the confession seriously. Thus, psychoanalysis allows the reader to think about where and how *Lolita* resists interpretation without diluting its aesthetic enigma.

A psychoanalytic queer reading aims to articulate both the desire that arises from the act of narrative confession and the desire it elicits from the reader. This intersection attempts to repair the split between Nabokov and psychoanalysis. At stake is not a thematic engagement of unconscious meaning, but rather a formal engagement between confessor and witness, particularly the unconscious dynamics between Humbert and his love object of the moment: the reader. He hails the reader into being and necessarily fails to contain her as he scrambles with various modes of address: "Ladies and gentlemen of the jury" (9); "my learned reader (whose eyebrows, I suspect, have by now traveled all the way to the back of his bald head)" (48); "gentlewomen of the jury" (123; 135); "Oh you, veteran crime reporter, you grave old usher, you once popular policeman, now in solitary confinement after gracing that school crossing for years, you wretched emeritus read to by a boy!" (134); "Oh Reader, My Reader!" (203); "the reader (ah, if I could visualize him as a blond-bearded scholar with rosy lips sucking *la pomme de sa canne* as he quaffs my manuscript!)" (226); "Winged gentlemen!" (230); "Reader! *Bruder*!" (262).[14] In these contradictory moments, Humbert betrays a frustrated phantasy, which mocks the possibility of identification between confessor and witness, thus accentuating the gap that alienates him from his addressee. The ironic effect of this situation is that for over half a century, readers of *Lolita* have been attempting to figure out the most comfortable way to situate themselves in relation to the text. Humbert's failed hails nonetheless keep working on us, and the reader becomes interpellated as such.[15] His hails frustrate us, entertain us, offend us, seduce us, engage us, and make us laugh. The point of identification between Humbert and the reader is not any kind of common moral position but the struggle of figuring out how to hold onto the other, how to conceive of one another in order to maintain a discursive engagement.

Whether the reader accepts his invitation and identifies with his love of language or retracts in horror at his obfuscation and silencing of his love object, the reader accepts a fraught and uncomfortable position through the process of readerly engagement. Specifically, the reader identifies with Humbert's desire for omniscience *as well as* with his anxiety, which proliferates in the wake of his repeated failure to possess his object. The frustrated desire to possess his object is less bodily than intellectual. His ample linguistic prowess compensates for a lack. Later in the novel, rival pedophile Quilty kidnaps Lolita and places Humbert in the role of detective by leaving erudite clues in their path. Humbert muses: "He challenged my scholarship. I am sufficiently proud of my knowing something to be modest about my not knowing all; and I daresay I missed some elements in that cryptogrammic paper chase" (*Annotated Lolita* 250). Humbert's wordiness in this admission to not knowing belies an anxiety that he tries to veil under a variety of contradictory virtues he pulls out of his head as tools of obfuscation: pride, knowledge, self-awareness, and modesty. In the end, his loss of Lolita coincides with his failure of knowledge, and Quilty's textual clues acquire meaning only belatedly. Because Humbert fails to grasp the truth of these clues, his love object slips through his fingers.

If *Lolita* is a parody of a case study, and the reader assumes the position of the analyst and Humbert the analysand, then conceptual failure becomes a point of identification between the two positions. Felman explains the dynamic process in the clinic: "The analyst, indeed, has first to learn . . . where his own textual knowledge is *resisted*. It is, however, out of this resistance . . . out of the patient's speech which says much more than it itself knows, that the analyst will come to *learn* the *patient's own* unconscious *knowledge*, that knowledge which is inaccessible to itself because it cannot tolerate knowing that it knows" (82, emphases in original). Felman's repetition of the root word "know" resonates with Humbert's symptomatic repetition of the same root word in his failure of Quilty's "cryptogrammic paper chase" (*Annotated Lolita* 250). The status of sexual knowledge in *Lolita* becomes precarious, because through it the reader encounters something at once intolerable and enjoyable. Felman's description of the knowledge that accumulates between reader and text (analyst and analysand) explains why the deployment of sexual knowledge in *Lolita* offers itself not as a stable ground for meaning but as a moment for laughter. The text hiccups, disrupts itself, in the very moments it forcibly attempts to assert certainty.

Through narrative, Humbert enjoys a certain mastery and a repeated objectification of Lolita. But he invites the reader to regard his confession as a cathartic sublimation of his sickness. The problematics of sublimation as the translation of an event into language figure heavily in Humbert's attempt to transform his frustrated desire for Lolita through narrative recollection. Humbert's contagious drive, which he passes onto the reader, resonates with my discussion of Bersani's *The Freudian Body* in Chapter 1. Bersani reads epistemological crises in Freud's repetition compulsion to develop his theory of sexuality. Through close reading, Bersani arrives at the point where conceptual thought unravels. The force that economically unbinds conceptual thought is the sexual. Recall Laplanche's clarification that in sublimation, a component drive of sexual desire escapes from repression and is transformed into intellectual curiosity, or epistemophilia. The silence embedded in signification is the persistent question of the sexual, which sublimation cannot enclose. In the symptom, both psychoanalysis and literature enjoy a knowledge that is not in possession of itself.[16]

Bersani's claim that the sexual fuels and limits sublimation resonates with Felman's conclusion that the unconscious embedded in mobile consciousness resides in literary form. Felman's emphasis on form parallels Nabokov's aestheticist celebration of art for art's sake. He reassures his readers in the afterword: "I am neither a reader nor a writer of didactic fiction, and, despite John Ray's assertion, *Lolita* has no moral in tow. For me a work of fiction exists only insofar as it affords me what I shall bluntly call aesthetic bliss, that is a sense of being somehow, somewhere, connected with other states of being where art . . . is the norm" (*Annotated Lolita* 314–15). Yet what Nabokov calls aesthetic bliss psychoanalysis celebrates as conceptual failure. The aesthetic bliss of creative language, the details in the particular moment, corresponds to Freud's focus on the narrative construction of the dream's scene, the atmosphere and environment rather than the act that the scene encloses. The interpretation focuses on the detailed dream images that emerge beside the dream's central events, the supposedly insignificant minutiae in the environment that disrupt the subjectivity of the dreamer.[17]

Felman's argument encourages a reading beyond a simple agreement with Appel that Nabokov's art is "artifice or nothing" (*Annotated Lolita* xviii), beyond the conclusion that the point of the novel is the mastery of form or the simple pleasures of description. The pleasure is distinctly a sexual experience, one that the narrator fuels by the awkward attenuations of the joke and the negative drives of epistemological failure. Contrary to the suggestion that *Lolita* exhibits a masterful command of language and the love for the particular, Humbert's narrative is a repetition compulsion toward the love objects that he cannot contain.

Appel's *Annotated Lolita* firmly establishes the text as a parody, and Nabokovians widely agree on the parodic tone as a given; yet critics including Appel depend on Nabokov's interviews in order to ground their arguments.[18] But this critical tendency responds to an anxiety in the wake of a failure to pin down meaning in *Lolita.* Nabokov's parodic mastery approaches the intensity of the mimesis, meta-citation, earnestness, irony, aesthetic distance, contradiction, and interpretive slipperiness that constitute camp, an aesthetic that takes pleasure in exacerbating hermeneutical anxiety in the reader or viewer.[19] Resisting a dependence on Nabokov's authoritative persona, the following analysis pauses in the discomfort of parody. And rather than uphold Nabokov as a postmodern master, my reading returns to a question of the reader's desire, which postmodernism attempts to foreclose in its repudiation of psychical depth.

The foreword introduces the parodic ambivalence of the novel. The foreword's fictitious author, John Ray Jr., PhD, sets up the narrative as a factual confession written by Humbert during his incarceration in the psychopathic ward prior to his death. Ray describes this madman's narrative as both a work of art and a case history that will become a classic in psychiatric circles. Ray's voice assumes a Kinseyan authority: "'*H.H.'s impassioned confession is a tempest in a test tube; that at least 12% of American adult males . . . enjoy yearly . . . the special experience 'H.H.' describes with such despair; that had our demented diarist gone, in the fatal summer of 1947, to a competent psychopathologist, there would have been no disaster; but then, neither would there have been this book*" (*Annotated Lolita* 5). Ray's assertion implies that the presence of proper science would foreclose the creation of literature; literature is a symptom of the lack of scientific truth and efficacy of method. As Appel notes, the foreword mocks "the conventional reader's desire for verisimilitude" (*Annotate Lolita* 322). That the diagnostic foreword is fictitious immediately problematizes the relationship both literature and sexual science have toward truth telling and the lessons that the reader can glean from the narrative.

The novel's parodic frame resonates with the clinical scene. Both relations—between text and reader, and between analyst and analysand—explicitly operate as a reconstruction and replication of intimate relationships. Given this parallel, psychoanalysis offers not necessarily a hermeneutical function, in which sexual meaning can be extracted from the text, but a way to consider how affective attachments form, evolve, and break down.

A parallel emerges between two slippery love objects: Lolita as a character and *Lolita* as the text. Some of the most rigorous Nabokovians such as George Ferger and Brian Boyd or critics from the 1979 *Modern Fiction Studies* special issue such as Christina Tekiner and Robert Merrill suffer quite productively from the epistemophilic contagion of the novel. These critics are determined to differentiate "real" events from fictive constructions in Humbert's confession in order to sort out the chronological inconsistency at the end of the novel, resulting in an ongoing debate in Nabokovian criticism. A temporal contradiction arises from the dates between the moments when Humbert receives Lolita's letter, sees her, kills Quilty, gets arrested, writes his memoir in the psychopathic ward, and dies from a heart attack. Dr. John Ray's dates are three days short of encompassing that entire chronology.[20]

Of course, this minor chronological inconsistency potentiates large ramifications for the reader's relation to the moral lesson and for the direction in which reader identification unfolds. While asserting different and opposing arguments, all of these readings depend on a common condition: the desire, much like Humbert's exhaustive detective work, to extract a line of logical consistency from a narrative of baroque contradiction in order to justify the contradiction. For any argument to work, each critic must assume the consistency of one figure at the expense of the others, thus attributing a single origin of contradiction to either the author's error, a character's phantasy, or a medicalized discursive containment. Ferger's reading—that John Ray, Jr., is the author of the last act—depends especially on the assumption that Humbert's character is not prone to contradiction, inconsistency, or ambivalence, the very qualities that seduce the reader. In a Nabokovian spirit, these critics enter into a linguistic game whose resulting close readings appreciate an artistic obfuscation "arrived at by diminishing large things and enlarging small ones" (Nabokov, *Speak, Memory* 167). But the terms of the game are self-defeating, since the ambivalence and contradiction that necessarily arise out of signification simultaneously produces and becomes threatened by readerly investments to pin down a unifying thread of meaning. The debate about the revisionist reading of *Lolita*'s conclusion engages a reading of irrevocable difference that materializes from within the text. In the process of close (detective) reading, the pleasurable frictions of the game—contradiction, ambivalence—occasion and are truncated by the object of the game—the desire for sense or meaning. Insofar as this object—meaning—is both an objective and a lost object, the reader encounters *Lolita* as an enigmatic signifier that initiates pleasure of the failed search for the lost object.

The novel's parodic form attenuates the reader's potential identification with scientific decoding and displaces Humbert's conscious deployment of sexual and psychoanalytic knowledge. Parody makes visible Humbert's paradoxical affinity for and resistance to such discourses. The form of Humbert's humor is Swiftian. Like Gulliver, for instance, Humbert casually juxtaposes the elevated and the base, often in the form of lists: he ruminates, "I doubt if much individual genius should be assigned to our interest in the plurality of inhabited worlds, competitive tennis, infinity, solipsism and so on" (*Annotated Lolita* 12). Both Gulliver and Humbert suffer from loquacity. Humbert holds an excessive attachment to long lists of examples, including the anthropometric and statistical dissection of Lolita's body. Humbert's lists produce the effect of narrative omniscience; however, the juxtaposition in the contents of those lists—between high and low, metaphysical and worldly, large and small, epic and mundane—reduces the omniscient narrator to flawed suspect, one who takes too much pleasure from synechdochic logic and free association to perform a posture of authority convincingly. A contemplative distance permeates Humbert's humor, as he often refers to himself in the third person when diagnosing his own pathology. Unlike Swift's, however, Humbert's narrative resists an unequivocal didactic stance. *Lolita* lacks the Swiftian break in parodic tone that expresses the moral or political lesson behind the comedic cautionary examples. As Nabokov claims in his interview with Appel, "Satire is a lesson, parody is a game" (*Annotated Lolita* 342). The text resists the dogmatic agendas of both sexual science *and* literature, thus attenuating its own repudiation of psychoanalysis as a mere posture of truth.

References to form devoid of content pepper the narrative. The text's emphasis on form draws attention self-reflexively not only to the text's parodic structure, but also to the possibility that the characters as parodic constructions cannot be imbued with any substantial meaning with or against which the reader can identify. Humbert's admiration of Lolita's tennis skills metaphorically reinforces the prioritization of the novel's mimetic form: "Her form was, indeed, an absolutely perfect imitation of absolutely top-notched tennis—without any utilitarian results" (*Annotated Lolita* 231). Lolita is a perfect formal replication of a sexually precocious, deviant child, and Humbert is one of a pathological pedophile, but these constructions serve no moral function. As with Lolita's form in tennis, the reader cannot find a utilitarian result from any character, as they are only formal constructs. The reader's sympathy for Lolita, compounded by the silencing of her suffering through Humbert's baroque linguistic solipsism, has value only between the lines of Humbert's narrative construction. Likewise, any identification with a sexual agency that Lolita might have outside of Humbert's control is contained within his narrative construction, through which the reader seeks clues of people's existence independent of Humbert's mind. In other words, a readerly connection to Lolita is foreclosed because Lolita exists not as a representation of a person but only as a replication of an already dehumanized love object, thus underscoring Lacan's controversial assertion that there is no sexual relation (*Seminar XX*). A parodic mode introduces the problematics of multiple narrative frames that destabilize the reader's identification, since the mode is established by a psychiatrist's voice that prefaces a confession, a confession in which the love object is abstracted to the extreme.

The reader's attachment can only be to the text's form rather than to its moral content, and to the way in which the content is presented as opposed to any substantial meaning one can glean from the content. Ray's lesson is thus undermined when he states: "*still more important . . . is the ethical impact the book should have on the serious reader; for in this poignant personal study there lurks a general lesson; the wayward child, the egotistic mother, the panting maniac . . . they warn us of dangerous trends; they point out potent evils*" (5–6). While Ray hails the reader to fit a significant model, the "serious" reader, apparently someone very concerned with the ethical lessons, Humbert interpellates the reader in the opposite way: "Mid-twentieth century ideas concerning child-parent relationship have been considerably tainted by the scholastic rigmarole and standardized symbols of the psychoanalytic racket, but I hope I am addressing myself to *unbiased* readers" (285, emphasis added). While "serious" and "unbiased" are not necessarily antithetical, Ray assumes that moral righteousness accompanies seriousness, a righteousness capable of identifying enemies to modern civilization. Ray depends on a deductive tendency in a potential reader that Humbert would likely see as biased. Such a clash of interpellations splits the reader and frustrates the ego identifications she may establish with the text.

The text repeats an ironic invitation for the reader to pathologize and diagnose Humbert as, for example, suffering from latent homosexuality. Humbert's numerous references to statistics, biological facts, and psychological theories about the development of female sexuality indicate an earnest interest in sexual sciences; but the parodic form of the text pulls the rationalized justifications of Humbert's pederosis into relief. Humbert's deployment of scientific knowledge about sex paradoxically facilitates and eschews the ethical violence of his behavior, thus problematizing the reader's own deployment of science as a tool to keep her vicarious experience of Humbert's perverse pleasure at a safe distance.

IV. The Loss of Lolita, the Unbinding of Enlightenment

The reader's experience with Lolita is a repetition of Humbert's experience with Lolita. The omniscience and sexual satisfaction Humbert seeks remain at the level of language. Humbert withholds a description of their first penetrative sex scene: "But really these are irrelevant matters; I am not concerned with so-called 'sex' at all. Anybody can imagine those elements of animality. A greater endeavour lures me on: to fix once and for all the perilous magic of nymphets" (*Annotated Lolita* 134). Humbert admits a drive to "fix" the magic of nymphets: that is, according to the *OED*, "to secure from change, vacillation or wandering"; "to give stability or constancy to (the mind, thoughts, affections, purposes); "To direct steadily and unwaveringly, fasten, set (one's eyes, attention, affections, etc.) *on, upon*"; "To make (the eyes, features, etc.) motionless or rigid (as in death)"; "To lose volatility or fluidity; to become firm, rigid, or solidified; to congeal, set"; "To preserve and harden biological material, esp. before microscopic examination." Humbert's desire to "fix" the nymphets evokes Freud's metaphor of the baked-through monad, implying a desire to reify his object, to petrify it with discourse. Humbert knows that his desire is for knowledge itself, and that in the end his language can penetrate only so deeply before it becomes frustrated by its own metastatic failure. As cancer distorts metabolic processes and grows through the overproduction of cells in an organic body, epistemological failure grows through readerly engagement with Humbert's language. Through parody, the repetition of reified knowledge leads to its inevitable unbinding.

When Humbert catches Lolita in a lie about attending piano lessons, she evades his accusation with an alibi that her friend Mona is able to confirm for Humbert on the phone. Like the reader's relation to the book, Humbert suffers from a drive to read Lolita. As Lolita slips from Humbert's conceptual mastery, she becomes an object of his rejection. After Humbert hits the wall of Lolita's transparent but substantiated alibi, his frustration transforms his perception:

> She sat right in the focus of my incandescent anger. The fog of all lust had been swept away leaving nothing but this dreadful lucidity. Oh, she had changed! Her complexion was now that of any vulgar untidy highschool girl who applies shared cosmetics with grubby fingers to an unwashed face and does not mind what soiled texture, what pustulate epidermis comes in contact with her skin. Its smooth tender bloom had been so lovely in former days, so bright with tears, when I used to roll, in play, her tousled head on my knee. A coarse flush had now replaced that innocent fluorescence. What was locally known as a 'rabbit cold' had painted with flaming pink the edges of her contemptuous nostrils. As in terror I lowered my gaze, it mechanically slid along the underside of her tensely stretched bare thigh—how polished and muscular her legs had grown! (*Annotated Lolita* 204)

Humbert's reading of Lolita's body resonates with the problem of the novel itself, that the novel lends itself more readily to rejection and repulsion the more it eludes the reader's grasp. The piano lessons episode causes Humbert's paranoia to disorient him and affect his own reading process of Lolita. Humbert's decline in omniscience exemplifies the notion that the reading process is indeed a paranoid one, in which the extraction of meaning requires a series of persecutory and identificatory projections.

Humbert's aim to "fix" nymphets collides with the undeniable corporeality of Lolita's body in the moment his phantasy of omniscience is taken away from him. The juxtaposition of different textures in the passage above speaks to the jarring disorientation Humbert begins to experience with his perception: fog, grubby, soiled, pustulate, smooth, tender, bloom, tousled, coarse, edges, tensely, bare, polished, muscular. With the perception of unpleasant textures, Humbert sees his reality in a stark visual display, as if multiple surfaces are emitting light. He ornaments his observations with words like incandescent, bright, fluorescence, flaming, flush. For Humbert, Lolita's interchangeability transitions from mythic nymphet to "any vulgar untidy highschool girl." Humbert's comic phobia of shared cosmetics indicates a phobia of bodily contagion, transmitted through the "soiled texture" of "pustulate epidermis." The contagion Humbert fears is less bacteria than subjectivity. The phantasy behind his disgust with skin assumes that Lolita will continue to grow away from "fixed" nymphhood the more she comes into contact with her growing peers.

After their fight, Humbert's relationship to signification shifts subtly and affects how he traverses the American highway. He begins to charge meaning into objects not in the pleasurable spirit of the pervert but in the paranoid discomfort of the neurotic: "We all have such fateful objects—it may be a recurrent landscape in one case, a number in another—carefully chosen by the gods to attract events of special significance for us: here shall John always stumble; there shall Jane's heart always break" (*Annotated Lolita* 211). As Humbert writes this reflection during his incarceration, signifiers of everyday life take on meaning belatedly. Humbert establishes the rhythms of suspense to activate the reader's anticipatory defenses, so that the reader inherits Humbert's paranoia and asks the question: when and how will he lose her? When Humbert builds suspense to prepare the reader for Lolita's loss, his self-reflexive use of language becomes exacerbated. During one of their tennis sessions, Humbert receives a sense of foreboding when the bellhop summons him away for a telephone call: "This, to use an American term, in which discovery, retribution, torture, death, eternity appear in the shape of a singularly repulsive nutshell, was *it*" (*Annotated Lolita* 235, emphasis original). Frustrated as Humbert is, the reduction of human experience to a signifier, "it," is his preferred mode of interaction and his only coping mechanism when physical and sexual abuses are no longer options. Language is the site through which Humbert confesses his sexuality, but it is also the site through which he processes loss.

The piano lessons episode functions as a turning point for Humbert on multiple levels. At this moment, Lolita's agency becomes undeniably manifest, a threatening agency that Humbert can no longer negate by infantilizing her mischievous behavior and relegating her inconsistencies to the whims of childhood. Right after the piano teacher notifies Humbert unwittingly of Lolita's absence, before the confrontation with Lolita, Humbert betrays his calm exterior by losing his queen to his friend Gaston in a game of chess: "I noticed through the film of my general distress that he could collect my queen" (*Annotated Lolita* 202–03). The immediate consequence to Humbert's failure of omniscience, signified by not knowing Lolita's whereabouts, occurs at the level of the game, again reminding the reader of the stakes in parody. The first serious breech of control over Lolita causes Humbert to lose his most precious object, the "power-femme" of all chess pieces, in a game of strategy, where omniscience is the key to victory.

Humbert's use of the word "film" in his reaction to the missed piano lessons marks a shift in the role of "film" for Humbert. At first, his prose exhibits a filmic quality. He describes his black diary in minute detail before reproducing its contents: "I speak of this neat product of the Blank Blank Co, Blankton Mass., as if it were really before me. Actually it was destroyed five years ago and what we examine now (by courtesy of a photographic memory) is but its brief materialization, a puny unfledged phoenix" (*Annotated Lolita* 40). Throughout Humbert's confession, the object itself does not matter. Humbert substantiates the photographic quality of his prose with filmic techniques of montage and close-ups. He likens his memory to the effects of film, differentiating between the scanning of a visual close-up and the traumatic flash of the glamorous face:

> There are two kinds of visual memory: one when you skillfully recreate an image in the laboratory of your mind, with your eyes open (and then I see Annabel in such general terms as: 'honey-colored skin,' 'thin arms,' 'brown bobbed hair,' 'long lashes,' 'big bright mouth'); and the other when you instantly evoke, with shut eyes, on the dark innerside of your eyelids, the objective, absolutely optical replica of a beloved face, a little ghost in natural colors (and this is how I see Lolita). (*Annotated Lolita* 11)

The image of Annabel assumes a series of deferrals similar to the function of writing. As the reader does not receive an understanding of the sentence until she reads all signifiers between periods, so too does the viewer not receive a sense of the whole picture until the close-up scans all elements of the image. The immediacy of Lolita's image in Humbert's imagination, on the other hand, recalls the aura of glamour, a film still that evokes a sense of royalty, even a perverse transcendent divinity.

Humbert is conscious of the difference between words and vision. Yet he expresses the desire to bridge the two, and he attempts to perform it when he discovers Charlotte's body and describes the scene of her death: "I have to put the impact of an instantaneous vision into a sequence of words; their physical accumulation in the page impairs the actual flash, the sharp unity of impression" (*Annotated Lolita* 97). He follows his admission with a long list of objects that, together, make up the scene that his visual faculties take in immediately. His prose, then, moves like a camera, or at least self-consciously attempts to and comically fails, zooming in and out, cutting to different scenes, seeing through various filters.

If film indicates the lucidity of Humbert's consciousness in the first half of the novel, then it becomes a screen that obscures perception and judgment through a series of dissociative episodes as Humbert gradually loses Lolita. Film transitions from a vehicle for sight, mythification, and projection, to a block, a fog that causes Humbert to lose his sense of time and space. Of course, as a technological phenomenon, the filmic medium facilitates both of these processes. The way in which film structures Humbert's perception and memory becomes a thread in his unconscious and, as his narrative progresses, parallels how he relates to Lolita, who herself is closely associated with American culture, including the seedy glamour of Hollywood.

The transition begins when film prevents Humbert from seeing his (chess) game clearly and culminates in the ultimate trauma of Lolita's escape with Quilty from the hospital. Humbert reproduces the effects of his trauma by narrating a dissociative episode that comes into focus very slowly:

> A bright voice informed me that yes, everything was fine, my daughter had checked out the day before, around two, her uncle, Mr. Gustave, had called for her with a cocker spaniel pup and a smile for everyone, and a black Caddy Lack, and had paid Dolly's bill in cash, and told them to tell me I should not worry, and keep warm, they were at Grandpa's ranch as agreed.
>
> Elphinstone was, and I hope still is, a very cute little town. It was spread like a maquette, you know, with its neat greenwool trees and red-roofed houses over the valley floor and I think I have alluded earlier to its model school and temple and spacious rectangular blocks, some of which were, curiously enough, just unconventional pastures with a mule or a unicorn grazing in the young July morning mist. Very amusing: at one gravel-groaning sharp turn I sideswiped a parked car but said to myself telestically—and telephathically [*sic*] (I hoped), to its gesticulating owner—that I would return later, address Bird School, Bird, New Bird, the gin kept my heart alive but bemazed my brain, and after some lapses and losses common to dream sequences, I found myself in the reception room, trying to beat up the doctor, and roaring at people under chairs, and clamoring for Mary who luckily for her was not there; rough hands plucked at my dressing gown, ripping off a pocket, and somehow I seem to have been sitting on a bald brown-headed patient, whom I had mistaken for Dr. Blue, and who eventually stood up, remarking with a preposterous accent: "Now, who is nevrotic [*sic*], I ask?" (*Annotated Lolita* 246).

The juxtaposition between the two paragraphs mimics the cut between scenes in film. He ventriloquizes the voice from the hospital, providing no quotation marks, as if he falls into the voice that breaks the news unwittingly about the lost love of his life. The moment Humbert discovers Lolita's abduction (or escape) on the telephone, he dissociates from his body, assuming an omniscient position in relation to the town. The idyllic image of the town gives way to Humbert's surreal phantasy of a unicorn in its pastures. From a peaceful panoramic sweep, Humbert brings the reader back to a fleeting action of a roaring car crash, and the narrative falls back into focus on a distracted drunk.

In this scene, Humbert watches himself in a violent rage at the hospital, as if he is both in front of and behind a camera. He is "very amus[ed]" at having side-swiped a car; he "[finds] himself" at the hospital, and "somehow" he "seem[s]" to be sitting on what turns out to be a patient. To convey his detached state, he relates the scene in one long, grammatically problematic sentence. Alliteration peppers his "dream sequence" with words like gravel-groaning, telestically and telepathically, lapses and losses, bemazed brain, bald brown-headed, reception room, roaring, ripping, rough, and remarking. The sentence ends with a reference to Freud, whom the patient/Dr. Blue ventriloquizes in Humbert's phantasy by remarking on Humbert's neurosis with a German accent. The loss of Humbert's love object brings him back, in his phantasy, into the discursive clutches of sexual science.

The sexual economy of *Lolita* is a discursive one, but, perhaps contrary to Humbert's desire, the body still plays a role in his narrative structure. From the moment of the piano lessons episode, Humbert's loss has to do with the body and its irreconcilability with language. His desire for omniscience becomes cannibalistic: "My only grudge against nature was that I could not turn my Lolita inside out and apply voracious lips to her young matrix, her unknown heart, her nacreous liver, the sea-grapes of her lungs, her comely twin kidneys" (*Annotated Lolita* 165). Such phantasies of penetrating her unseen depths recall his scientific abstraction of Lolita. Humbert phantasizes consuming Lolita's organs, but that phantasy is always already frustrated. Contrary to the scintillating, tabooed promises of the novel's premise, the materiality of the body often disrupts Humbert's pleasure. Chapter 26 in its entirety demonstrates an extensive narrative disruption, in which Humbert brings the reader back to his present moment:

> This daily headache in the opaque air of this tombal jail is disturbing, but I must persevere. Have written more than a

> hundred pages and not got anywhere yet. My calendar is getting confused. That must have been around August 15, 1947. Don't think I can go on. Heart, head—everything. Lolita, Lolita, Lolita, Lolita, Lolita, Lolita, Lolita, Lolita, Lolita. Repeat till the page is full, printer. (*Annotated Lolita* 109)

He refers to his present moment again after he completes his story, but his admission midway about the conditions of his body and mind jars the narrative flow, especially with the sentence fragments that contrast the rest of his story. Certainly, Chapter 26 implies his physical decline and foreshadows his death. Yet Humbert displaces his corporeal limitations with a repetition of his favorite slippery signifier, of the object which he cannot possess, "Lolita, Lolita, Lolita. . . ." The displacement of body with word in this moment becomes a synecdoche of his narrative process throughout the novel.

The body—its contagions, its functions, its instincts, its necessary existence—serves as a metaphor for Humbert's epistemological failure. Humbert finally loses Lolita when he contracts a fever from her. The double physical sickness of subject and object, the irrevocable fact of their biological existence, is what brings the death-driven narrative of highways and motels to an end and steers Humbert toward the conclusion of his story. His initial trauma—the prelude to the ultimate trauma of her escape—occurs in the supposedly momentary absence of Lolita: "I found myself unable to assimilate the simple fact that for the first time in two years I was separated from my Lolita. All at once it occurred to me that her illness was somehow the development of a theme—that it had the same taste and tone as the series of linked impressions which had puzzled and tormented me during our journey" (*Annotated Lolita* 241). The absence of the love object initiates the narrator's act of literary interpretation. To cope with his loss, Humbert creates a sense of aesthetic distance from his own life by extracting theme, taste, tone from a series of signifiers. As in his verbal mimicry of the filmic medium, Humbert attempts to mediate his experience by reproducing it in abstract form. Humbert presents the reader not with a sequence of events but with a reading of his experience. The reader has access not to an articulation of an event that she herself can decode but to a self-reflexive construction, preemptively decoded, that borrows from a number of discourses: science, psychoanalysis, film, and literary studies.

A heightened, visually rich atmosphere attends Humbert's loss. A repetitious pattern of color emerges through Humbert's desperation at

Lolita's initial absence. He muses: "I imagined that secret agent, or secret lover, or prankster, or hallucination, or whatever he was, prowling around the hospital—and Aurora had hardly 'warmed her hands,' as the pickers of lavender say in the country of my birth, when I found myself trying to get into that dungeon again, knocking upon its green doors, breakfastless, stool-less, in despair" (*Annotated Lolita* 241–22). Humbert phantasizes a ghostly agent that takes his love object away from him. He anchors his sense of foreboding by framing the unknown agent of his defeat with the red-oranges of aurora, lavender, the blackness of a dungeon, and green doors. The colors with which Humbert paints the hospital, the site of permanent loss, are the very same ones with which he concludes the last pages of the confession: "This then is my story. I have reread it. It has bits of marrow sticking to it, and blood, and beautiful bright-green flies. At this or that twist of it I feel my slippery self eluding me, gliding into deeper and darker waters than I care to probe" (*Annotated Lolita* 308). His description of viscera produces an echoing visual of red, purple, green, and the depths of black—colors that he presents almost in the same order as his description of the hospital, which becomes the stage of his loss.

The gruesome image of flies and flesh that Humbert draws in his mournful conclusion is inconsistent with the playful prose he enjoys throughout his confession. He commits crimes, indeed, but the saturated, putrescent, visceral abjection he attributes to his story characterizes it more as a gothic horror than a comedy, parody, detective story, or pornography. The question arises of whose body bits he imagines sticking to the story: Lolita's, Quilty's, his own, or all of them? Or, does the text itself acquire an ugly corporeality that Humbert knows is out of his control? If the material body is a metaphor for the aporia that ruptures Humbert's omniscience, then the body bits could signify all of the things I suggest, especially since they are associated with the loss of the self in the "deeper and darker waters" Humbert is too afraid to examine. He attaches both sets of color patterns with an extreme sense of loss, as if the elusive object that ruptures his omniscience and sense of self is clad with surfaces that are vibrant, beautiful, and horrific: a visually pleasurable metaphor for the novel as an object of inquiry and its relation to the reader.

V. Conclusion

Humbert is aware that he bestows upon his addressee the drive to read. Earlier, when he prepares for his first penetrative encounter with Lolita at the Enchanted Hunters hotel, he seduces the reader: "Imagine me; I shall not exist if you do not imagine me; try to discern the doe in me, trembling in the forest of my own iniquity; let's even smile a little. After all, there is no harm in smiling" (*Annotated Lolita* 129). What begins as a plea to the reader for his existence becomes a directive to smile in the first-person plural form. In this moment, Humbert displaces the reader, and for the rest of the novel the reader experiences a vicarious disorientation with Humbert in relation to a lost love object. Humbert's seduction attempts to engage the reader through humor, using the performative speech act of telling us to smile, as if to say that no one will get hurt if we just submit ourselves to the economy of the joke. The narrator's usurpation of the reader's safety is something that Mark Danielewski takes to a parodic extreme, which I will explore in my next chapter. In the case of *Lolita,* the gesture of including the reader in Humbert's joke renders her vulnerable to the same epistemological crisis the narrator attempts to work through.

Lolita is not so much a barometer for scientific validity as it is a flirtation with, co-optation, and subversion of epistemic certainty, of the will to power that accompanies supposedly unquestionable knowledge, whether that knowledge is related to scientific certainty, to the moralism with which the reader may distance herself from the text, or to the literary form of parody. Even if parody subtends scientific and literary dogmatism, it cannot save Nabokov, Humbert, or the reader from epistemophilic frustration. Humbert's parodic form of address attempts to master all excesses of uncertainty through the mimetic logic and self-reflexivity that perpetuate a paranoid desire for an impossible omniscience. If Humbert successfully orchestrates anything, it is a circle jerk. Kinsey, Freud, Ellis, Nabokov, and the reader rub up against problems of epistemic certainty, and those frictions proliferate in the novel.

The novel is less about pedophilia than it is about epistemophilia, the hunger for knowledge, in this case, about one's own sexual subjectivity. Humbert's epistemophilic instinct is never satisfied because he cannot transcend his status as a discursive construct, regardless of how much sexual science he can deploy to master himself and his reality. He admits this when he realizes his love for Lolita beyond his projection of nymphet: "I loved you. I was a pentapod monster, but I loved you" (*Annotated Lolita* 284). Humbert's claim to have replaced his perversion with ardent love is merely, as Appel argues, something that the reader wants to hear (*Annotated Lolita* 226). Humbert's realization is a simulacrum of an ethical regard for his love object, a potential departure point for reparative reading but an unsatisfying one. But something strange emerges when one considers the temporality of Humbert's confession. Its verisimilitude attempts loyalty to the affects immediate to the past events they describe. In some moments, the reader receives a strong sense of Humbert's perverse enjoyment when consuming Lolita; in other moments, Humbert conveys deep remorse. During the time of his writing, then, Humbert performs the split of subjectivity, more loyal to the process of writing and his destabilizing seduction of the reader than to a moral regard for his love object. As Couturier observes, Humbert claims "to have purged himself of his perverse desire, but he has not: the composition of his narrative is but a testimony of his durable lack of being, a pathetic attempt to possess, poetically and symbolically, an object that kept eluding him in real life" (Couturier 43). Couturier identifies Humbert's confession as a perverse repetition of his failure to possess his object. Through narrative, Humbert both disavows and draws attention to this frustrating failure. Humbert's love is not personal. Rather—and this is more queer a reparative than Humbert's performance of morally redemptive love—his love is a recognition of his relation to epistemophilia not as a drive toward possession but a playing out of desire in phantasy. This kind of impersonal love engages the reader because of its contagion. The premise of the novel forecloses the stakes of the romance. Really, no one cares whether the pentapod pedophile "really loved" the child or not. Rather, they care about why they are enthralled and how that implicates them. Epistemophilia is a phantasy of overcoming a lack, a phantasy that Humbert sees repeatedly to the point of failure.

Nabokov's novel elucidates the anxiety inherent in literature and sexual science in relation to the status of knowledge. As the novel questions science's proximity to the truth about sex, it self-consciously questions its own proximity to truth as a piece of literature. Insofar as knowledge is synonymous with taking possession of an object in response to anxiety, the novel frustrates the reader's epistemophilic instinct because one does not know how to relate to, to take a hold of, the text. Should one enjoy vicariously in the confessional mode or define oneself differentially from the confessor? Should one follow Humbert's example and rationalize the fact that readers are still, after over fifty years, "enjoying their symptom" by continuing to read this text? The difficulty of *Lolita* stems not from the moral problem of sexual obscenity and taboo, but from an epistemic breach, which keeps open the question of how the text hails us to engage in the reading process. Queer resides not in the truth about sex, but in the linguistic relationship that undulates between reader and text and that prevents either object from ever becoming fixed. *Lolita* transforms the relationship between scientific and literary signification from a battle over meaning to a dialogical relation of indeterminate play. In a dialogical state, neither sexual science nor literary representation can retain the ethical upper hand. The novel reminds the literarily inclined of the indeterminacy potentiated within scientific discourses, especially when both literary erudition and sexual science constitute the seductive intellect of such an absurd, offensive, oddly endearing pervert like Mr. Humbert Humbert.

CHAPTER THREE

"An Ethics of Failure"

Visual Literalization as a Queer Vanishing Point in Mark Danielewski's *House of Leaves*

> Klein sees the artistic creation as more than just a diagnostic tool. The work of art can also serve as an initial—and perhaps even an optimal—way of caring for other people. Is it more effective than interpretation?
>
> —Julia Kristeva, *Melanie Klein*, 187

I. Introduction

In the context of Klein's theoretical development, the epigraph's question above refers to interpretation in clinical psychoanalysis. But in light of Bersani's assertion that art undermines the force of argument by seeing the movement of thought to its own undoing, "interpretation" in Klein's words can also refer to literary criticism, that ever-frustrated process of extracting an argument from the artwork. To what extent is literary interpretation possible in the wake of the artistic text? Far from a mere symptom from which the analyst decodes a meaning of pathology, art becomes analogous to the "talking cure" and so can be the curative act in itself. To a large extent, the work of art stands apart, autonomously as it were, from the work of its interpretation. As a curative, the literary text comes into question as it emphasizes the breakdown of conscious meaning and relationships between text and reader. Cautious against a romanticized, sentimental ideal of art, I ask: how does a death-driven text come to be a way of, in Klein's words, "caring for other people"?

Klein's narrative of infant development, which, as Chapter 1 addresses, delineates the transition from the paranoid-schizoid position to the reparative position, can be representative of the movement of thought throughout life. Given the ongoing tension between the binding and unbinding of the drives, Kristeva reminds us that "The capacity for gratitude must be forever cared for and protected—and such assiduous attention . . . demands that we constantly heed the destructive anxiety that works tirelessly by forcing love and gratitude into envy, if not by annihilating them through the fragmentation of the psyche" (*Klein* 131). If the binding forces of sublimation were unclear in Freud's thought, as Chapter 1's close readings of *Beyond the Pleasure Principle* and *The Freudian Body* show, then a question arises as to how one distinguishes the *symbolization* of part objects from the *signification* of a whole autonomous other.

In order to develop a "queer reparative," this chapter explores Mark Danielewski's novel, *House of Leaves* (2000), which performs the failure of thought through a regression from signification to symbolization. Unlike other contemporary artists who almost evacuate content by prioritizing form in a conceptually difficult "verbal free fall" (*Why War* 144), Danielewski presents narrative and visual coherence, retaining an excessive intelligibility. Danielewski's *House of Leaves* may gesture toward reparation but prioritizes the performance of desire, anxiety, and failure that are prerequisites for the depressive position. Conceptual failure is paradoxically the outcome of omniscience, and it figures in the novel as a road to articulating an "ethics of failure" (*Why War* 36). My analysis explores how the breakdown of intelligible thought lays the groundwork for reparation through creative thinking, which queer theory has struggled to define since Sedgwick's late work. The queer reparative emerges in the capacity to create what these characters have lost and found. The various agents of danger in the novel—the figure of the Minotaur, the contagion of the text, the loss of domestic comfort—are ambivalent sites in which characters find either catastrophe or art. The horror that each character experiences is a defense against sorrow. *House of Leaves* shows the impotence of omnipotence, however urgent the desire for it becomes in the face of tragedy. In the conflict between life and death, each character finds survival not in omniscience over the labyrinth but, simply, in the production of an artwork.

In contemporary literature, a recent turn toward the visual is characterized by its promise of immediate scopophilic pleasure that written signifiers traditionally lack. In such avant-garde fiction as Thomas Pynchon and William S. Burroughs, the overdetermination of the signifier increasingly takes on a self-reflexive performance, the narrative constantly breaks down, and the thematic meaning of the text becomes markedly obscured through the prioritization of formal experiment. Danielewski follows this tradition, but digital technology allows him to approach the breakdown of meaning in a new way. *House of Leaves* presents a coherent story, thus differing from such canonical postmodern texts as Pynchon's *Crying of Lot 49* (1966), Ann Carson's *Autobiography of Red* (1998), and Burrough's *Naked Lunch* (1959). Such critics as Brian Chanen, Mark Hansen, and Katherine Hayles celebrate Danielewski's novel as a primary artifact of the digital age that revolutionizes our way of reading print media.[1]

The novel incorporates unprecedented publishing demands. As a result, almost every page presents its own unique visual composition. *House of Leaves* is a parody of genres, themes, and reading practices: gothic literature; academic criticism (specifically the genre of the dissertation); difficult postmodern texts; typographical innovation; and the process of signification in general. Like *Lolita*, *House of Leaves* exacerbates readerly anxiety and perpetuates a paranoid imperative in the act of reading. Unlike *Lolita*, whose economy works on the joke, *House of Leaves* operates primarily on the affective register of horror and, as the reader learns, "not horror but another kind of -orro-" (Danielewski 300): that is, sorrow. The latter novel does have humorous moments—the index, for example, teases the reader with the possibility of navigating through this monster of a text with a kind of legend, only to index words like "and," "burrito," "can," "dildo," "in," "joke," and "so" (665; 668; 668; 672; 680; 681; 697). The parodic effect of Danielewski's text emerges from its excessive self-reflexivity. The novel plays with the phantasy of omniscience that drives epistemological endeavors. Such play extends to the extreme anxiety that could manifest in the condition of "being in the dark," both literally and figuratively. In a uniquely visual manner, *House of Leaves* dramatizes the failure of thought that Rose and Bersani theorize, as darkness swallows fantasies of identity and meaning. What becomes queer in this text is the reading process itself. For all of its flirtations with the death drive—with murder, the uncanny, and over-the-top terror—a reparative kernel renders its detour into creative reading and thinking a queer movement.

In the core narrative, Pulitzer prize-winning photojournalist Will Navidson and his partner, Karen Green, attempt to save their waning relationship by settling in the house on Ash Tree Lane with their children, Chad and Daisy. Navidson soon discovers that the house's fixed exterior dimensions contradict its growing and shape-shifting interior. With a supply of Hi 8 cameras, he produces the documentary, *The Navidson Record*, filming several explorations of the mutating black passages that defy the spatial logic of his new house. His estranged brother, Tom, and his scholarly friend, Billy Reston, become involved in resolving the house's logical gap. The house becomes life threatening, as its effects deteriorate characters' psychical, interrelational, and physical well-being. Navidson hires an exploration team, comprised of Holloway Roberts, Jed Leeder, and Wax Hook, all of whom get lost in the house for days during the disastrous Exploration #4. After Navidson's attempted rescue mission of the team, the house engulfs his brother. After Karen leaves him for New York with their children, Navidson explores the house once more, only to be found over a month later—mutilated by hypothermia and starvation—by Karen herself.

The novel's multiple narrative frames produce a spiral structure. Four central "narrators" inherit the story about the house from one another. Each narrator builds on the sequence of events through four narrative frames. Surrounding Navidson's narrative is the story of old hermit Zampanò, who finds *The Navidson Record* and devotes the end of his life to translating the documentary into written text, complete with academic research and annotations. Upon the discovery of Zampanò's body, Johnny Truant, a cliché of an unambitious tattoo artist, inherits Zampanò's manuscript and vows to complete the project, but Truant struggles with the text, as uncanny resonances of Zampanò's words begins to haunt his waking life. His personal experience of the haunting is relegated to the footnotes, but often dominates Zampanò's writing. Finally, anonymous fictional "editors" piece together the previous narrative frames and are allegedly responsible for the novel's publication.

The novel insists emphatically, however, that the fifth diegetic world is the reader's, disrupting the promise of an overarching metanarrative as the limits of the fictional world become the reader's own perceptual horizon. The reader encounters nothing in the novel's book jacket or title page to relieve her of the fiction she is pulled into, as all paratextual material is intradiegetic. The book jacket blurb, written by the "editors," narrates the way in which this novel materialized in its present form: "Years ago, when *House of Leaves* was first being passed around, it was nothing more than a badly bundled heap of paper . . . Now, for the first time, this astonishing novel is made in book form." At the back of the novel, after the appendices and index, the credits acknowledge various publishers for granting permission to reprint various canonical poems throughout the text, but the two last acknowledgments give thanks to the provision of documentary fragments and photographic images of the house, neither of which actually exist. Hayles calls this type of storytelling not representation but remediation: "the re-presentation of material that has already been represented in another medium" (781). The reader's ability to distinguish between knowledge and reality becomes compromised. With digital technology Danielewski updates the trope in American fiction of challenging the reader's sense of reality in ways similar to the framing of the foreword in *Lolita* by Dr. John Ray Jr.

The house becomes a metaphor for the novel itself, since the novel is also a "house of leaves" whose interior grows and shrinks according to the reading process. The visual structure of the novel parodies mimetic desire in words. The words on the page visually imitate the architecture of the very house they describe, incorporating size, font, color, and location into their signifying function. Words fall down the page when characters encounter a drop into darkness. They spiral and squeeze through massive margins as characters traverse winding staircases and crawl through cave-like crevices. The word "snaps" becomes the very rope that fails Navidson as its letters scatter across three pages (Danielewski 294–96). This labyrinthine architecture of signifying chains becomes increasingly visual and convoluted. The visual elements become the only threat to narrative coherence. While, as the previous chapter explores, Humbert associates his omniscience with a scopophilia, and while film technology informs and enhances his mode of perception, *House of Leaves* explodes the association between scopophilia and omniscience. *House of Leaves* induces a drive to read that visually traverses perspectival lines of meaning to conceptual vanishing points. The more resentment grows against mediation, the more monstrous the novel becomes.

II. What Is Queer about Failure?

Danielewski's text resonates with the ways in which *Lolita* undermines the dichotomy between science and art, fact and myth. The death-driven subject trapped within a totalized system chooses from two conditions: language as abstract formula that serves as a circular guarantor of epistemological certainty, or language as melancholic resemblance of the unknown. Humbert stumbles over the former while Navidson stumbles over the latter.[2] Insofar as word becomes image in the attempt to master the ontology of darkness, *House of Leaves* performs a dynamic unbinding as signification regresses into symbolization.[3]

The characters caught in this house negotiate their alienation, their unconscious, and their capacity for love to save them. Hansen points out the historical correlation between the novel and the body: "Danielewski manages to submit the novel to a formal transformation, one that literally compels its adaptation to our allegedly 'post-hermeneutical' informational culture and that does so, precisely, by treating the novel as a body subject to development and deformation" (599). The novel itself resonates with the ever-mutable, unknowable queer body that resides at the heart of domesticity and thus disrupts the mundane comforts associated with the nuclear family and leisurely reading.

Queerness emerges when the reader's panic-induced loss of oneself feeds a perverse curiosity. The text performs the uncanny in a queer way, what Rose describes as "repetition as insistence . . . as the constant pressure of something hidden but not forgotten" (*Field of Vision* 228), which is the condition for sexuality. The compulsion to repeat the entrance into darkness illustrates a psychical attraction to conceptual vanishing points out of an urge to gain omniscience. The impossibility of totalized "economic binding" through the containment of knowledge perpetuates the paranoid-schizoid position as a dominant mode of object relations within the house. In "Saving the Subject," Hayles's diction is resonant with Freud when she explains that the inversion of inside and outside between Johnny's and Zampanò's narrative frame "make clear that the book refuses to lie quiescent in its 'binding tomb'" (800). The desire for and failure of economic binding leads to their demise.

The house magnifies the process of projective identification. Omniscience overcompensates for an implacable primordial anxiety, leading the subject to anticipate the object, to tear the object into bits and pieces in order to know it, to divide it into consumable morsels. The haunting of the house exacerbates such anxiety in order to compel the characters, ultimately, to tear themselves into bits and pieces, both psychically and physically. The death drive figures heavily in the narrative, not only from the fear of the house and the repeated desire to return to its vaginal, all-consuming depths. This drive emerges also out of the regression from signification to a paranoid-schizoid symbolization in the text, indicated by the transition of the signifier to visual image. The text, then, *abjects* itself into a universe of part objects in which anxiety dominates, and all who come into contact with the narrative struggle with this process of abjection.[4] The inversions from frustrated epistemophilia recall Freud's description of homosexuality as inversion (*Three Essays* 2). In *House of Leaves*, queer is very much bound up with the disruption of knowledge and the multiple layers of spatial and temporal inversions that result.

A question that arises is whether the visual image, unlike the written sign, necessarily presupposes an ontological referent. The scopophilic pleasures implicated in images invoke a sense of immediacy that counteracts the deferral of the referent in written signification. Hansen's thesis on digital topography in *House of Leaves* includes a challenge to Roland Barthes's concept of a photographic referent, a necessary reality without which the photograph would not exist: "Painting can feign reality without having seen it. Discourse combines signs that have referents, of course, but these referents can be and are most often 'chimeras.' Contrary to these imitations, in Photography I can never deny that *the thing has been there*" (*Camera Lucida* 76). Of course, the transition from analogue to digital technologies has attenuated Barthes's postulation of the photographic referent. But unlike any other medium, a self-conscious photographic form becomes ironic because of its historically presupposed intimacy with reality.

Scholars of the humanities have learned from Laura Mulvey's famous essay "Visual Pleasure and Narrative Cinema" (1975) about the conservative function of the unconscious in visual pleasure, cautioning against an idealization of pleasure as always already emancipatory. *House of Leaves* parodies and undermines the conservative function of visual pleasure. A literary detour into the visual invokes the failure of thought in tandem with the experience of pleasure—specifically, a visual pleasure that is inextricably bound up with sexuality. As Rose explains in *Sexuality in the Field of Vision* (1986) about Freud's reading of Leonardo da Vinci:

> Describing the child's difficult journey into adult sexual life, he would take as his model little scenarios, or the staging of events, which demonstrated the complexity of an essentially visual space, moments in which perception *founders* . . . Each time the stress falls on the *problem of seeing* . . . The relationship between viewer and scene is always one of fracture, partial identification, pleasure and distrust. (227, emphases added)

Sexuality, then, builds on the subject's troubled, erotic relationship to a visual scene. Sexuality develops from a scopophilic disjuncture, and identity materializes in a refracted way through a failure of vision. The simultaneity between conceptual failure and pleasure within the context of digital manipulation updates Bersani's notion of a "self-shattering" pleasure at the heart of literary texts. Through visual pleasure, failure becomes an opportunity for pause, play, ambivalence, and the active desire for hyperreal repetition—not a doomed finality, in other words, so much as a chance to be seduced by one's own fear.

The field of visual art problematizes the status of photographic image in relation to ego integrity. Danielewski's *House of Leaves* revels in an excess of (re)mediation, in which the referent becomes lost through multiple narrative frames within the visual mise-en-scène. Unlike the flat affect of postmodernism, desire and symptoms of reading figure heavily in the text. Pleasure is always already ambivalently positioned with anxiety. Conceptual failure marks the merging of categorical lines into their vanishing points, which remain on a two-dimensional surface. The reader/viewer's penetration into any conceptual depth remains a phantasy to which she becomes attached as her conceptual world of clearly defined self-and-other object relations gradually collapse. For Danielewski, conceptual failure involves neither verbal free-fall nor extreme visual abstraction. Nor does failure invoke an oppositional stance that negates oppressive structures of the system, as Halberstam argues in *The Queer Art of Failure*. On the contrary, failure in *House of Leaves* involves the excessive and malignant replication of a system's coherence; far from oppositional, the readers of the house become infected with a destructive devotion, a romance gone terribly wrong.

The text's self-construction as underground-turned-popular literature reinforces Mark Hennelly's claim that "the Gothic always returns with new *unconventions* which dissolve the boundaries between outside and inside, victims and victimizers, readers and texts" (84, emphasis in original). Because the house on Ash Tree Lane exists only through a multinarrative mediation, the novel underlines that the object of narrative discourse, in this case the house, is in perpetual deferral. Both the house itself and its "proof" of existence, *The Navidson Record*, are absent presences in the novel. That Zampanò is "blind as a bat" renders the viewing of the documentary impossible. Through the technological shift in book publishing, the unreliable narrator such as Humbert gives way to "the remediated narrator" (Hayles 785): a new split subject who enjoys a consciousness that is not in possession of itself because it is mediated by other narrative voices. The layers of inscription technologies that structure the novel revise Bakhtinian dialogism by lifting the silence that represses the multiplicity of narrative voices.

The novel presents a network of remediated narrators, each fragmented by an unconscious that emerges between each narrative voice. Truant acknowledges, "the irony is it makes no difference that the documentary at the heart of this book is fiction. Zampanò knew from the get go that what's real or isn't real doesn't matter here. The consequences are the same" (Danielewski xx). The text's self-reflexivity contradicts the Winnicottian claim that not knowing whether something is real is a form of creativity (*Why War* 30). Truant's observation, however, implies that the consequences of the narrative, whether real or not, lead to destruction. Insofar as queer theory questions ontological stability, the text enthralls the reader with the threat, or perhaps promise, of the destructive absence that compels her to read.

Like Freud's relationship to his theory of sexuality, like the infant to the elusive breast, the reader is confronted, again and again, with an absence around which words repeatedly revolve.[5] Although the novel's central object, the house, is an absence, it nonetheless haunts and structures the narrative. The house becomes the enigma to which the characters and the reader seek the answer. The reader and characters enter into a paranoid-schizoid position when the house's absence, like the breast, becomes disavowed through an overdetermined, excessive process of narrative symbolization.

The story about the house presents itself as a contagion, a curse, drawing a lineage of readers that bear the burden of the text. As infection, the novel falls into the reader's hands, and such bequeathal emphasizes the reader's responsibility for the narrative to take shape through her act of reading. As my second chapter discusses, Humbert displaces the reader's upper hand by appealing to a sense of responsibility, first presenting a plea, then a seduction, and finally a demand. *House of Leaves* hails the reader through negation. The dedication page reads: "This is not for you." This statement literalizes a common fact that dedication pages acknowledge a person who is typically not the reader. On the other hand, the dedication also reads as a warning against reading the novel. Of course, because it is a negation, the dedication presents an unconscious invitation: "This is for you." After Truant's Introduction, another page simply reads, "*Muss es sein?*" This question reinforces the dedication page. The German for "Must it be?" alludes to a reference (a double allusion) in Milan Kundera's novel, *The Unbearable Lightness of Being*, in which the protagonist, Tomas, considers the weight of his desire for his love object, Tereza, by repeating to himself a motif in the last movement of Beethoven's last quartet: "*Muss es sein? . . . Es muss sein! Es muss sein*!" (Kundera 32). Kundera provides a visual of the musical score to Beethoven's motif. As the weight and necessity of desire is what keeps Tomas bound to Tereza, so too does the reader's (nongendered) desire for the *House of Leaves* feel heavy and inevitable.

The reader confronts an ambivalence between safety and destruction that are both by-products of the desire for omniscience. A tendency toward self-destruction is most dramatically played out through Johnny Truant, who dictates the reader's identification with his experience of the horror that haunts him once he inherits Zampanò's text. He instructs the reader through direct address early in the novel:

> focus on these words, and whatever you do don't let your eyes wander past the perimeter of this page. Now imagine just beyond your peripheral vision, maybe behind you, maybe to the side of you, maybe even in front of you, but right where you can't see it, something is quietly closing in on you, so quiet in fact you can only hear it as silence. Find those pockets without sound. That's where it is. Right at this moment. But don't look. Keep your eyes here . . . you should be running, you should at the very least be flinging up your arms—you sure as hell should be getting rid of this book—you won't have time to even scream. (Danielewski 26–27)

This moment is a synechdoche of the entire experience the novel offers: paranoia, fixation, and a kind of narrative dictatorship. Truant draws attention to, on the one hand, the undeniable materiality of the book and, on the other hand, the unconscious that exceeds the margins of the text. The extent to which Truant dictates the process of reading borders on the absurd. The effect of Truant's sardonic humor distances the reader from the immediate threat of the text and exaggerates the reader's vicarious experience of fear. This moment is parodic of contemporary literature that emphasizes the reader's complicity in the unfolding of the text.[6] As Roland Barthes remarks in *S/Z*, the reader is an accomplice not of character but of the discursive code that governs the structure of the written text (145). The text exists only through the active engagement of the reader's desire. The unconscious resides in the movement of textual signifiers and disrupts the assurance of the immediately intelligible.

The moments in *House of Leaves* that draw attention to the necessity of the reader's engagement do not posit the reader as master and creator of the text in an earnest spirit celebrating the "birth of the reader." The death of the author rather inaugurates what Bersani refers to as an "esthetics of masochism," in which the integrity of the ego is perpetually threatened. Despite its parodic tone, the passage above effectively invokes fear in the reader. A slippage occurs between Truant's position and the reader's, as he warns the reader not to look but assumes she, like he, does. The text attempts to orchestrate not only the process of reading but also the physical movements of the reader's body. The process of identification integrates the reader within the narrative and forecloses any false sense of mastery over the text. Epistemophilic desire usurps the position of mastery. Truant realizes his relationship to Zampanò's text: "without me [the reader] it would perish . . . There's something else . . . without it *I* would perish . . . this thing has created me; not me unto it, but now it unto me, where I am nothing more than the matter of some other voice, intruding through the folds of what even now lies there agape, possessing me with histories I should never recognize as my own" (326, emphasis in original). Contrary to Hansen's claim, Danielewski does not prioritize the figure of interpretation, posing a challenge to the reader whose complicity initially empowers her.

Zampanò's and Truant's attempts to foreclose the ambiguity of the text through excessive interpretation undermines the reader's own interpretive agency, thus rendering the act of reading *unheimlich*—German for "uncanny," familiar and yet disturbing because repressed.[7] In Kleinian terms, the uncanny is an example of projective identification: that which threatens the ego and cannot be mastered by the epistemophilic instinct becomes repressed and projected into the external world. In an uncanny move, Zampanò does the interpretive work for his critical readers. The text's self-reflexivity undermines the reading agency of the aspiring literary theorist, thus upsetting the text's status as an object of inquiry by holding up a mirror, as it were: "Numerous professors have made *The Navidson Record* required viewing for their seminars, while many universities already claim that dozens of students from a variety of departments have completed doctoral dissertations on the film" (Danielewski 6). Zampanò and Truant's interpretive practices threaten to foreclose creative thinking and, consequently, the reader's capacity to maintain an aesthetic distance from the text.

Gothic, uncanny, queer. The relationship among the three concepts as manifestations of the "return of the repressed" has been the subject of much scholarship. Judith Halberstam's Foucauldian study of the technology of monsters in *Skin Shows* (1995), Max Fincher's *Queering the Gothic in the Romantic Age* (2007), William Hughs and Andrew Smith's *Queering the Gothic* (2009), and Paulina Palmer's *The Queer Uncanny: New Perspectives on the Gothic* (2012), to name a few, surround a figure of abject sexual, gendered, or racialized otherness, onto which the reading subject projects her anxieties about identity. All three concepts—gothic, uncanny, and queer—involve the allure of a dangerous agency that breaks through the safe and placid surfaces of domesticity. In the readings by these various authors, the threat congeals into a queer figure, most often a villain or monster.

Steven Bruhm's article "On Stephen King's Phallus: Or the Postmodern Gothic" relates horror directly to language, or an "evil" phallic deftness to the Symbolic Order. In his queer reading of Stephen King, Bruhm argues that the author focuses on "the function of articulateness and intelligence in making one vulnerable to horror" (Bruhm 56). While the "Enlightenment Gothic" works on the fear of self-splitting from repressed desires, King's postmodern Gothic presents the fear of self-splitting as the result of documentation, writing and representing the self (Bruhm 58). Bruhm defines fear of a violently castrating Father as homoerotic. The terror begins with the fear of castration, or, in the Lacanian sense, a fear of verbal prohibition. He explains further: "the terror is not only, as Freud would have it, the father's castration: nor is this fear of castration, as Lacan would argue, merely the fear of verbal prohibition. Rather, the fear is specifically *homoerotic* in its projection. Like the homosexual in these novels, the protagonist demonstrates a desire for verbal acuity that is coded queer" (Bruhm 65). Good and evil struggle on the battlefield of material signifiers, and "this bringing out of the male desire to indulge the phallus of and with an other man, this having the penis and wanting the phallus, is accompanied by no small pleasure" (Bruhm 66). The protagonists' desire for verbal acuity, for the phallus of the signifier, is queer.

Whereas Bruhm connects the gothic with a particularly queer relation to phallic signification, I link queer and gothic through the failure of thought. This chapter moves away from the bodily manifestation of abjection to what I call the queer abjection of thought itself.[8] Like King, the horror in *House of Leaves* stems from the material signifier; however, fear for Danielewski's characters does not culminate in a projected manifestation of horror, such as a queer monster or castrating father. Rather, epistemological failure culminates in the encounter with infinite nothingness. The only horror our hero faces is the anxiety that he fails, again and again, to project successfully onto the external world.

If, for Bruhm, King's gothic horror stems from a verbal acuity that characterizes evil and that the protagonist lacks, then the horror in Danielewski stems from a verbal acuity that is contagious and subject to degenerescence.[9] The reader's fear develops vicariously through the characters' struggle to survive and to inscribe their experience. More importantly, however, that fear is exacerbated as the effects of the house bleed into the reader's reality. The ubiquity of the novel within multiple narrative frames, compounded no doubt by its self-constructed growing popularity and commercial success, suggests the impossibility of the horror's repression. Truant encounters strangers at a bar who are discussing the very book he has been trying to finish editing, entitled *House of Leaves*, whose editor bears his name. The book that Navidson happens to bring with him on his last journey into the black passages is *House of Leaves*, even though his documentary has yet to be transcribed into text by Zampanò, let alone edited. This temporal contradiction attributes a timeless quality to the text, which can travel spatio-temporally into any realm or universe with which it comes into contact. Truant's warning that the reader should not repeat his mistake in reading this book, as well as the burning of the novel by both Navidson and Truant at the brink of their fates, implies an impossible desire to erase the text from memory and to undo the experience of the readerly encounter.

The textual attempts to tie up all narrative excesses exacerbate its death drive.[10] Epistemophilia turns on its head from a desire for mastery to one for destruction, and language regresses from signification to visual symbolization. The reader then becomes a character doomed to repeat the act of reading that leads to Zampanò's and Truant's demise. All illusions of mastery become integrated in this compulsion to repeat the overdetermined process of reading. Once the reader finds her way out of the labyrinth, once she finishes the novel, then the sense of mastery becomes akin to a sense of having survived. In Bersani's terms, the *House of Leaves* explicitly "demystifies the force of argument" by incorporating rational argument into the structure of narrative fiction: that is, by displacing interpretive argument through a mimesis of academic criticism. In doing so, Danielewski renders the language of philosophy as always already literary. This performative move exposes rational explication as an impotent defense against the enigma of the house. The reader follows the repeated, inexhaustible deployment of rationality throughout the text to its own vanishing point.

III. *Visual Literalization*

The difficulty of reading this novel lies not in its conceptual abstraction but in the practical demands that it makes on its reader. While in both King and Danielewski, the evil power that emerges at the level of material signifier retains the license to kill, *House of Leaves* poses an unprecedented threat in the tendency for its material signifiers to transform into visual image at moments of heightened suspense. As the narrative voices and footnotes layer upon one another, the reader encounters difficulty in keeping separate the different fonts and formats that draw ever-diverging narrative paths, academic tangents, and episodic interludes. The degree to which the characters become lost in the house corresponds to the text's visual convolution. The dangers of getting lost emerge both on a diegetic level, within the house on Ash Tree Lane, and on a literal level, within the leaves of the book, as the reader necessarily loses the omniscient position the various narrators attempt so excessively to provide. Getting lost becomes synonymous with a conceptual failure that threatens subjectivity. While, in *Lolita*, the nymphet is both the object of desire and the conceptual vanishing point, the house as an object is the vanishing point of Danielewski's text: all lines of thought point toward it in narratives of attachment and fixation, but in doing so, these attachments fail to render the house intelligible and conceptual categories thus collapse.[11] The point of convergence at the vanishing point is a projection that marks the limits of human perception. In this mode of queer reading, desire and the compulsive, convulsive impetus of sexuality lead to a rupture of subjectivity.

The formal components of the narrative are symptomatic of a melancholic attachment to the ever-absent referent in signification. Émile Benveniste challenges Ferdinand de Saussure's claim that the relation between signifier and signified is arbitrary. The relationship between signifier and signified is necessary; arbitrariness lies rather in the relationship between the sign and what Benveniste identifies as a third term: reality (44). Benveniste recognizes a slippage in de Saussure's thought between the signified and reality, from which the sign itself is hermetically sealed. As if sensing that the sign is lacking despite the necessary bind between signifier and signified, *House of Leaves* symptomatically recognizes the shifting gap between sign and reality by attempting to jump the gap, transforming signs into architectural elements on the page. The text responds to the anxiety caused by the arbitrary and contingent relationship between sign and referent, buttressing the bond between signifier and signified with the third component of visual composition. The tendency to invoke the physical world via signification, either through visual aspects or through Truant's over-identification with the reader's body, suggests melancholic remnants of the signifying act.

Scholars widely address the materiality of the text, but no one takes into account psychoanalytic implications of desire in signification.[12] Mimesis assumes an extreme form as the desire in textual signifiers undergoes a process of what I call *visual literalization*. Nicolas Abraham and Maria Torok's *The Shell and the Kernel* theorizes the process of literalization in melancholia as the subject refuses to replace the lost object with words.[13] When the lost object fails to be introjected into language in a process of mourning, the melancholic subject incorporates the object into her own ego. In a paranoid-schizoid position, the subject would rather disavow the object's absence by consuming it in order to preserve its idealized, static image in a psychic tomb. Without language, the object retains a literal, that is, unrepresentable and haunting, status. Visual literalization is a term that plays off of Abraham and Torok's conceptualization. An unspeakable symptom renders the visual aspects of *House of Leaves* melancholic. From a Kleinian perspective, the visual components of the text symbolize rather than signify. In an attempt to impose a logic of sameness on that of difference, the visual compounds the destructive threat that the novel bears for the reader. The words in *House of Leaves* mimic the hysterical body, acquiring a double function of signification and a highly symptomatic physicality that does not speak but acts.

The immediate scopophilic satisfaction in visual literalization reproduces a phantasy of recognition, particularly of a knowable referent. Visual literalization stems from the death drive, a performative compensation of language's necessary failure to make meaning, and thus an implicit refusal of signifying logic. Such contemporary novelists as W.G. Sebald (2001) and Jonathan Safran Foer (2005) incorporate photographic images into their texts, but Danielewski employs visual literalization a bit differently. By turning word into visual image, narrative events into visual compositions, the *House of Leaves* performs the breakdown of the distinction between mourning and melancholia that have so concerned literary scholars. The performative self-reflexivity of the text becomes a queer moment that recognizes the failure of linguistic intelligibility. Through this visual symptom, the text becomes caught in a repetition compulsion of failure that seduces the reader into a queer attachment to the death drive. The failure of linguistic representation in the wake of the house occasions a scopophilic regression that enjoys the house's destructive agency. Visual literalization structures the conceptual vanishing point of the novel: in the characters' attempt to know the ontology of the house, the text collapses into illustration, gesturing toward an aporia that the characters can neither reach nor master.[14]

Visual literalization in *House of Leaves* exemplifies Rose's notion of the "*failures of vision*" (227) that become the basis for sexuality. Since literalization reacts to insurmountable failure, the drive to literalize darkness transforms into a perverse kind of reading. Truant remarks about Zampanò's writing: "he returns to the subject of light, space, shape, line, color, focus, tone, contrast, movement, rhythm, perspective and composition" (Danielewski xxi). Zampanò's close reading of the film mirrors his visual literalization of it. According to Truant, Zampanò and Navidson approach a paradoxical task of representing the ontological substance of the house, to "somehow capture the most difficult subject of all: the sight of darkness itself" (Danielewski xxi). Since vision depends on the play of refractions, reflections, and absorptions of light on material surfaces, the visual representation of the absolute absence of light is a doomed endeavor.

The writing of such visual representation translates this paradox into the challenge for words to represent absolute nothingness. As Truant discovers, Zampanò's representation of the house, the manifestation of emptiness, erupts into its opposite, a vast array of words that seem to indicate an infinite fullness: "Endless snarls of words, sometimes twisting into meaning, sometimes into nothing at all, frequently breaking apart, always branching off into other pieces I'd come across later—on old napkins, the tattered edges of an envelope, once even on the back of a postage stamp; *everything and anything but empty*" (Danielewski xvii, emphasis added). The system of words encroaches on multiple surfaces until it produces a totality into which the reader is pulled and which ultimately collapses into the nothingness that Zampanò seeks. The structural totality of the *House of Leaves* collapses into itself, as if drawing then subsequently submitting to its own vanishing point through a series of narrative, visual, and epistemophilic repetition. The text invokes the unbound, nonreferential version of the sex drive that feeds and frustrates structural intelligibility. Within the constructed totality of the text, the lost object—the house on Ash Tree Lane—becomes literalized into the novel, *The House of Leaves*. Melancholically, the reader consumes the lost object in the process of reading. Although the house becomes introjected into language through the medium of the novel, the visual literalization of the house's architecture disrupts the process of mourning that language affords. The reader's role necessarily echoes the other narrators of the novel as they obsess over knowing their lost object and perpetuate the movement of the story.

Certain moments of visual literalization exemplify the repetitive structures that fixate on the absent object of desire. For King's heroes, asserts Bruhm, the discourse of the Other represents both terror and possibility for triumph over evil; the protagonists face the law of the castrating Father by bringing their silence into speech, thus disempowering the evil

Other by overcoming the fear of language. In *House of Leaves*, the characters' phallic powers are the very things that entangle them in the depths of the labyrinth. The novel presents a number of masculine characters who equip themselves with various tools, be they linguistic, academic, filmic, or militaristic, to reduce the house to approximate intelligibility. During Exploration #4, hunter Holloway Roberts slowly descends into madness as he searches, rifle in hand, for the creature whose growls reverberate in the walls and whose claw marks appear in the black material of the house. His name plays on "hollow" and "hallway," both of which he unremittingly encounters as he traverses the darkness. Eventually, Holloway becomes the beast that he searches for; his fleeing teammates, Leeder and Hook, become his prey.

Zampanò gets caught on a tangent while detailing the exploration team's crisis, unceremoniously diluting the rhythm of narrative suspense. His tangent differentiates Hollywood and documentary films, claiming that the former relies on "sets, actors, expensive film stock, and lush effects to recreate a story," while the latter relies "on interviews, inferior equipment, and virtually no effects to document real events" (Danielewski 139). Ironically, the novel comments on the truth value of the documentary genre, while *The Navidson Record* does not exist. Zampanò provides supporting research in a footnote about Stephen Mamber's reflections on *cinema vérité*, which eliminates the technical, procedural, and structural "barriers between subject and audience" in order to convey "unmanipulated reality" (Danielewski 139). Navidson's explorations of the house follow the *cinema vérité* aesthetic, while Zampanò's visual literalization parallels the filmic attempt to minimize formal mediation in order to produce immediacy. The academic discussion ironically undermines the *cinema vérité* and literary realism of the suspense. At other times, the temporality of the reading process is mimetic of *cinema vérité*.[15] This strategy paradoxically represents unmediated experience of fear through multiple layers of semiotic mediation.

Mirroring *cinema vérité* on a visual level, Zampanò compensates for the absent referent of the documentary by incorporating visual elements into the formal structure of the written text itself. In the content of the narrative, the psychic tension and sense of panic increases as the exploration team gets lost in the labyrinth. When Holloway punches the wall out of frustration, a footnote appears off-center on the page with a blue border about two inches squared in dimension. This footnote lists in excess all of the architectural elements that this portion of the house is missing: "bathtubs, urinals, sinks, drinking fountains, water heaters . . . Bonus A-line,

75,000 watt, Wartzline, special service, e-bulb mercury" (Danielewski 119–41). The blue window continues for twenty-four pages, suggesting an "infinite" totality by listing "all" building elements needed for a house as well as architectural elements developed throughout history. In attempt to convey precisely the house's emptiness, the blue lined window delineates "everything and anything but empty," as Truant states earlier about Zampanò's writing (Danielewski xvii).[16]

Like the room that Holloway breaks into, this blue-lined footnote gives the reader a mere promise of exteriority. The window on the verso page parodies transparency in its reversal of the words in the previous recto page. As Zampanò reflects, "This desire for exteriority is no doubt further amplified by the utter blankness found within" (Danielewski 119). Additional footnotes on the margins of the verso and recto pages resonate with the discussion in my second chapter about Kinsey's list of limits to his study about sexuality in *Human Sexuality in the Human Male*. In both cases, an acknowledgment of conceptual failure is bound to an anxious desire for omniscience. In *House of Leaves*, the narrator's excessive knowledge in these lists is symptomatic of the anxiety stemming from the impossibility of narrative omniscience, an anxiety that infects the reader's own position. As the central object, the narrative itself gets lost in a sea of tangents. In an exaggerated and inverted spirit of nineteenth-century realism—in which the totality of household details contributes metonymically to the meaning of the unfolding drama among characters—the text attempts to convey the emptiness of the house through the negation of emptiness. The disjuncture between the emptiness of this house and a room full of household details in, for example, *Anna Karenina*, renders this narrative moment both a citation and displacement of literary realism.[17] In its mimetic efforts, the text widens rather than closes the gap between the immediacy of experience and the mediation of representation.

As the footnotes form textual blocks perpendicular to one another, the reader turns the book in a spiral motion for a number of pages, echoing the movement of the exploration team's descent down the stairway. The exaggerated degree of verisimilitude proves that, despite the textual efforts toward *cinema vérité*, unmediated representation of reality is not possible, and that form is constitutive of reality's conditions and limits. The melancholic, queer attachment between reader and novel develops from a paradox of a materially intimate yet highly mediated wish fulfillment of immediacy, which evokes an uncanny identification with the exploration team. The collapse of Zampanò's rational argument on truth depends on a relationship of anxiety and attachment with the text.

The "work" of traversing the house's shape-shifting labyrinth becomes equated with the "working through" required for reading the novel.[18] Right before Exploration #4 begins, Zampanò warns the reader about the vicarious adventure she is about to take into the house by theorizing how one escapes the labyrinth: "If the work demanded by any labyrinth means penetrating or escaping it, the question of process becomes extremely relevant" (Danielewski 115). As the reader continues deeper into the narrative, the prospect of "escape" threatens to disappear as the text becomes increasingly visual and melancholic. Zampanò observes:

> In order to escape then, we have to remember we cannot ponder all paths but must decode only those necessary to get out. We must be quick and anything but exhaustive. Yet, as Seneca warned in his *Epistulae morales* 44, going too fast also incurs certain risks:
>
> *Quod evenit in labyrintho properantibus:*
> *ipsa illos velocitas inplicat.*
>
> Unfortunately, the anfractuosity of some labyrinths may actually prohibit a permanent solution. More confounding still, its complexity may exceed the imagination of even the designer. Therefore anyone lost within must recognize that no one, not even a god or an Other, comprehends the entire maze and so therefore can never offer a definitive answer. (Danielewski 115)

In a footnote on the bottom of the page, the Editors translate the Latin quotation: "This is what happens when you hurry through a maze: the faster you go, the worse you are entangled." In the same footnote, Zampanò adds a remark from de Man's *Allegories of Reading*, also translated by the Editors: "If one reads too quickly or too slowly, one understands nothing" (Danielewski 115). The text's multi-level citations, which defer the reading process, contradict its warning to the reader about the pace of reading. Already these textual margins—the translations, the exhaustive academic tangents, the narrative layering—very quickly become constitutive of the story's content and formally reflect the process of losing oneself within the house. Reading becomes equated with the search for an escape out of a labyrinth. The novel hails the reader to heed the warnings of de Man, Seneca, and Zampanò as she begins to negotiate its textual maze.

More generally, however, the passage above suggests the trouble with the desire for omniscience embedded in knowledge production. Just as the traversal of all the paths in a shifting labyrinth is impossible, so too is the promise of omniscience behind any epistemic endeavor. The phantasy of omniscience emerges from a paranoid-schizoid universe of part objects.[19] In the passage above, Zampanò's reference to the incapacity for omniscience in god or Other is reminiscent of a Kafkaesque trial. Kafka's protagonist attempts to prove his innocence before the all-knowing power of the Law. The subject's fragmentation within a system of signs becomes deferred by a projection of omniscience onto an Other, who claims a capacity to affirm one's identity, but whose omniscience is mythical, constituted by the subject's own desire. Circular logic and frustrated desire are what ensure the Other's projected omniscience and power.[20]

The impossibility of exteriority renders the house a totality in itself.[21] As a narrator, Zampanò attempts omniscience like an all-powerful Other and cautions the reader about getting lost in the text, discouraging the reader from following him. As an inheritor of the story, Zampanò is trapped, like the reader, in an obsession with the object of inquiry that haunts him and exceeds his intellectual capacity. Zampanò's warning against getting lost recognizes the seductive dangers of one's own unconscious in the pursuit of knowledge: "Due to the wall-shifts and extraordinary size, any way out remains singular and applicable only to those on that path at that particular time. All solutions then are necessarily personal" (Danielewski 115). In phantasy, the subject becomes caught in a paranoid-schizoid disavowal of the house's absence. Zampanò instructs his reader that to escape, she must renounce her desire for omniscience, a move that Zampanò himself failed to accomplish.

Zampanò's inexhaustible desire for knowledge is the structuring force of the text. The contradiction between his academic *jouissance* and his warning to the reader points to a queer paradox: celebrating the death drive of desire and intuiting a reparative potential, however remote. Quoting a fictional Dr. Haugeland, Zampanò differentiates knowledge from boredom: "'knowledge is hot water on wool. It shrinks time and space. (Admittedly, there is the matter where boredom, due to repetition, *stretches* time and space . . .)" (Danielewski 167, emphasis in original). The narrator acknowledges the function of a parenthetical statement as an implicit emphasis rather than an aside by adding an extensive footnote. According to a Dr. Helen Hodge, "In those endlessly repetitive hallways and stairs, there is nothing for us to connect with. That permanently foreign place does not excite us. It bores us . . . Boredom is really a psychic defense protecting us from ourselves, from complete paralysis, by repressing, among other things, the meaning of that place, which in this case is and always has been horror" (Danielewski 167). Boredom, then, presents itself in the text as a defense against the unconscious and provides a link between knowledge and ignorance. Boredom counters conceptual failure with an active but futile and frustrated rejection.

In the house, certainty returns to ignorance. Such blending marks the slippage between epistemophilia (the desire to know) and what Lacan calls a "passion for ignorance," that, according to Britzman, the "more uncertain we are, the more we create harsh avenues of certainty" ("Pedagogy of Sexuality" n.p.). The house literalizes its epistemology. Zampanò's scholarship links an excessive and repetitious production of knowledge with its supposed opposite, complete ignorance. An attempt to "ponder all paths" becomes negated into knowing none. The accumulation of academic knowledge leads to its collapse, allowing the reader to become disoriented as she approaches a vanishing point of conceptual failure. Although the footnotes constitute the bulk of the novel and promise a more insightful reading of the house, they lead the reader astray. Avenues of certainty are bound to fail, even when boredom defends against ignorance with presumptions of certainty. Ignorance becomes constitutive of knowledge structures.[22] Like every character, the reader becomes seduced by the empty promise of omniscience and risks being swallowed up by the exponential anxiety in the face of darkness. Although Navidson is adept with navigational skills in dangerous circumstances, even his mastery diminishes as his repetition compulsion to explore the black passages nearly kills him.

IV. Failure and the Reparative

Like the physical explorations themselves, all academic exposition about the house exacerbate rather than satiate the reader's desire to know. The novel's object of desire that rational argument defers through its very efforts to contain it is a queer but disembodied "figure": the Minotaur. Halberstam's *Skin Shows* theorizes the gothic monster as the queer abjection that both haunts and structures normative identity. Subjects in gothic narratives experience terror through their struggle between fear of and desire for the monster.

Unlike the subject of Halberstam's queer gothic, Danielewski's monster never shows its skin. The Minotaur functions as a point of arrival, a completion of the labyrinth, which is coextensive with the explorer's death. The Minotaur haunts every corner of the labyrinth as an amorphous force of impending destruction, one that can never be "known" but that affectively structures the labyrinth. The Minotaur resides in a queer space just beyond the fields of vision, provoking the subject's scopophilic and epistemophilic drives. Danielewski illustrates the monster as a visual negation. In the main text, the Minotaur appears in traces, but its effects fragment the material signifiers on the page: "[ ]t d[ ]d have claws, they were made of shadow and if it did have te[ ]th, they were made of darkness. Yet even as such the [ ] still stalked Holl[ ]way at every corner until at last it did strike, devouring him, even roaring, the last thing heard, the sound [ ]f Holloway ripped out of existence" (Danielewski 338). The reader witnesses similar traces of an invisible beast: the deep claw marks beside Zampanò's body; the flashing claws as Truant falls down the attic stairs at the tattoo parlor; and the horrid stench.

The Minotaur intermittently peeks out in the text. The red text struck-through in black ink signifies the theme of the Minotaur. The blue-lined window footnote that Holloway punches through ends queerly. Its last line stands alone in red text: ~~"Picture that. In your dreams"~~ (Danielewski 141). The next recto page shows a blank, white window, its verso page reveals a black window, and the following recto page presents a visibly larger white window, without the confines of a blue border. This visual moment parallels Truant's panic attack in the parlor attic, when the beast's presence causes him to spill tattoo ink all over himself as he falls down the stairs. Hayles notes, "the 'foreseen' dissolution of [Johnny's] identity connects with the beast as a signifier of absence, a negation that spreads like an inkblot to encompass his subjectivity" (789). She remarks that after his panic subsides, he finds "himself" again, doused in ink, marking a return of the subject after a moment of re-inscription. The oscillations between negation and presence are very much closely aligned with the invocation of the Minotaur. The black/white/bleeding window repeats this pattern as the central footnote that becomes the vanishing point of Chapter 9. It calls the beast into being through the reader's dreams—the reader must "picture" the beast—and emphasizes that the base material of writing, ink, leads to a proliferation of absence. The growing window, which ends without the blue border, demonstrates the verbal acuity that afflicts the house's subjects, bleeds into anyone who touches it, and brings the subject into nothingness.

A visual contradiction arises between the invocation of the Minotaur and its analytical discussion in the footnotes. Traces of an invisible beast haunt the narrative. Conversely, any footnote discussing the Minotaur stands out visibly with red text, highlighted further by the black strike-through. Zampanò's extended footnotes of the Minotaur juxtapose the absent presence that kills Holloway in the main text. The explicatory footnotes about the Minotaur dilute the suspense in the central narrative:

> ~~*Creature* is admittedly a[ ] pretty clumsy description. Offspring of the Greek *Koros* meaning 'surfeit,' the implication of fullness provides a misleading impression of the mino[ ]r. In fact all references to the Minotaur[ ]self must be viewed as purely representative. Obviously, what Holloway encounters here is pointed[ ]y not half man/half bull. [ ]something other, forever inhabiting[ ], unreadable [ ]granting undeserved ontological benefits.~~ (Danielewski 338)

Zampanò's self-reflexive evaluation of the gaps, that the unreadable is granted "undeserved ontological benefits," mocks the terror the reader projects into the text's aporia. Located at the deepest recesses of the labyrinth, the Minotaur manifests visibly only through its negation.

Extended analyses of the Minotaur in Greek myth supplement discussions of labyrinthian architecture. These passages revise the myth of Daedalus and the labyrinth he constructs for King Minos to hide the monster (Danielewski 109–10). Zampanò bases his revision of the myth on science, claiming that human and bull cannot conceive offspring. He speculates that ~~"King Minos did not build the labyrinth to imprison a monster but to conceal a deformed child—his child . . . I am convinced Minos' maze really serves as a trope for repression"~~ (Danielewski 110). As the return of the repressed, the Minotaur emerges as a part of the self that each character must face: the more they want to know, the more dangerous the passages become. From Zampanò's explanation, the reader can predict what will happen to the characters in the *Navidson Record*: ~~"most of the Athenian youth 'fed' to the Minotaur actually starved to death in the labyrinth, thus indicating their deaths had more to do with the complexity of the maze and less to do with the presumed ferocity of the Minotaur"~~ (Danielewski 110). Zampanò draws from his published reception of Taggert Chiclitz's play, *The Minotaur*, which depicts the Minotaur as a gentle and misunderstood creature who slowly earns his father's love, only to be slaughtered by the ~~"drunken, virtually retarded, frat boy,"~~ Theseus (Danielewski 111). Zampanò's revision is consistent with the notion of the queer gothic villain, a figure who is ultimately sympathetic but serves as a receptacle for aggression projected from society proper.

While the Minotaur is an object of fear, the labyrinth's actual murderous agency is the infinity of walls that block, direct, mislead lost subjects. The only perception the walls give its victims to fuel their continual meandering is a vague sense of a rhythmic proximity to repressed desires: a way out, a death, a buried shame—in other words, the misunderstood Minotaur that will not kill but will unravel the phantasies of identity. The baroque labyrinth of text functions similarly for the reader. Zampanò later remarks:

> ~~Chiclitz treated the maze as trope for psychic concealment, its excavation resulting in (tragic[ ] reconciliation. But if in Chiclitz's eye the Minotaur was a son imprisoned by a father's shame, is there then to Navidson's eye an equivalent misprision of the [ ] in the depths of that place? And for that matter does there exist a chance to reconcile the not-known with the desire for its antithesis?~~ (Danielewski 335–36)

The question Zampanò poses at the end of this passage applies to Navidson, the reader, and anyone who enters the labyrinth. The potential to reconcile the desire to know with the unknowable is the paradox of reading and working through *House of Leaves*. At the heart of the labyrinth, a kernel resides onto which characters and reader project their fear and aggression, but instead of horror we find sorrow. According to Zampanò's revision of the myth, the struck-through passages about the Minotaur point to the shame of something one ought not to love. While the subject dreads and flees this unspeakable shame, she perishes in the repressive structures that conceal and imprison it. In the wake of that shame, a deep sense of loss that the labyrinthian structures disavow inverts into a force of otherness that turns the subject's insides out. The Minotaur, the unseen heart of the novel that nonetheless bleeds, is the central figure of loss. Found and (re)created in the text as that which one ought not to love, it transforms from the source of horror to the reparative kernel.

The drama of Navidson's last exploration acknowledges that reading is an act of working through, a process that is personal, singular, and solitary. Zampanò quotes Daniel Hortz: "By granting all involved the right to wander (e.g. daydream, free associate, phantasize [sic] etc., etc.; see Gaston Bachelard) that which is discursive will inevitably re-appropriate the heterogeneity of the disparate and thus with such an unanticipated and unreconciled gesture bring about a re-assessment of self" (114). Zampanò's application of "[sic]" is erroneous. While fantasizing is a possibility, the reader phantasizes in an unconscious sense. Each character in the novel engages in the labor of actualizing his or her own Minotaur, not as an inner monster that figures the death drive, but as a love that each cannot bear to acknowledge as lost. The most painful and profoundly repressed losses that the reader comes to know is Johnny's loss of his mother at a young age, as well as Navidson's loss of Delial and, along with it, a bit of his humanity, in exchange for international acclaim from his drive to "shoot" photographs. Each character either survives or does not survive a "re-assessment of the self," depending on how each negotiates the paranoid-schizoid and depressive positions.

The passage above on Chiclitz and Navidson is a footnote to a critical interpretation of The Holloway Tape. In particular, the passage footnotes Zampanò's personification of Myth: "the Vandal known as Myth *always* slaughters Reason if she falters. [ ] Myth is the tiger stalking the herd. Myth is Tom's [ ]r. Monster. Myth is Hol[ ]y's beast. ~~Myth is the Minotaur~~" (Danielewski 335). Zampanò's dichotomization of Myth and Reason parallels Horkheimer and Adorno's explication of their dialectical relationship. Myth threatens the bindings of Reason with the unbound excess, opening up to a world of the not-known.

Just as the Minotaur offers itself as an alternative queer figure with whom the reader can identify, Truant takes that possibility away. In a footnote of a footnote of the footnote above, he explains the struck-through passages: "Whether you've noticed or not . . . Zampanò has attempted to systematically eradicate the 'Minotaur' theme throughout *The Navidson Record*. Big deal, except while personally preventing said eradication, I discovered a particularly disturbing coincidence . . . I mean, that's what you get for wanting to turn **The Minotaur** into a homie . . . no homie at all" (Danielewski 336–37). As soon as Zampanò appeals to a more sympathetic regard for the Minotaur, noting that the latter is a trope for repression and a kernel of working through loss, he attempts to repress it. The Minotaur cannot be domesticated into a safe reconciliation with structures of conscious knowledge. While these passages hint at the theme of reparation, a possibility to work through shame and repression, Zampanò's attempt to undo his work indicates that reparative regard for the other is not easy and very much bound up with the uncontrollable drives. Both Zampanò and Truant—and, by implication, the reader—engage in queer reading, not by appealing to a liberal sympathy through an identification with the queer figure in the literary text, as so many texts of twentieth-century queer theory have encouraged, but by engaging in and confounding the process of identification itself. The development of an intimacy with the Minotaur renders identification ever unstable. The reader's identification follows a circular path that promises and precludes a "way out," presenting the Minotaur first as an unspeakable horror, then as a sympathetic figure of loss, and finally as a return of its radical alterity.

A contrast develops between an absent presence that forces characters to face their inner monster and its rational containment through academic discussion. The visual appearance of these discussions as struck-through red text is symptomatic of excess, something that is negated but, in being so, stands out. The red color of the words reflects the blood-filled eyes of Truant's beast. The visibility of the discussions' censorship signifies, in light of the house, the return of the repressed, which dominates the psychic landscape.[23] As Hamilton notes, the beast is not corporeal but appears as nothingness (12). If the minotaur appears as nothingness, and if the text structurally repeats a collapse into its own vanishing point of nothingness, then a queer force that sends the project of omniscient knowledge to its point of failure is ever-present in the novel. The Minotaur is not a figure *per se* but rather a vanishing point of thinking, representing the unspeakable horror and sorrow that is embedded in and disrupts structures of knowledge while simultaneously feeding the desire for knowledge. The Minotaur conveys visually the power of the repressed to exert psychic pressure, as if making the book bleed.

The queer gothic in *House of Leaves* is the repeated encounter with intellectual failure. The system of material signifiers that attempts to render the house intelligible, including its final manifestation in book form, becomes a labyrinth of the red herrings that elicit the subject's epistemophilic drive and that entangle her in winding paths of signification. Initially a defense against the unknown, the subject's epistemophilia is what dooms her to the labyrinthian architecture of the house. The threat to the characters' lives manifest in their incapacity to know, let alone represent, the ontology of its darkness.

Formally and thematically, *The House of Leaves* performs the failure of thought. The excessively visual components of the novel fail to capture the darkness: "Funny how incompetent images can sometimes be" (Danielewski 344). Again and again, however equipped with tools of knowledge (filmic, military, theoretical apparatuses), the characters/narrators/readers constantly confront the vanishing points of conceptual thought. Like Freud's repeated ventures into the concepts of "the sexual" and the death drive, the characters face a house that exceeds their epistemophilic mastery, with which they are nonetheless driven to engage. The process of reading *House of Leaves* is akin to the process of reading *Lolita* as *drive*. A perverse obsession with the enigma disrupts myths of domestic safety and the assurance of cultural sublimation. A point of identification for the reader is not a queer(ed) figure but an internal otherness that turns against each subject, carving out a space inside the subject as a locus of pain that the house then echoes infinitely.

While not exempt from the house's power, Karen is the foil to the phallic characters, with their cameras, guns, and theoretical penetrations. At first, Karen "refuses the knowledge. A reluctant Eve who prefers tangerines to apples. 'I don't care,' she tells Navidson. 'Stop drilling holes in my walls'" (Danielewski 30). Rather, she attempts domestic normality by buying bookshelves and practicing feng shui: "This demeanor is typified as denying as well as showing maturity, in which case maturity has everything to do with the acceptance of 'not knowing'" (Bemong n.p. 2003). Indeed, her feng shui defense disappears as she becomes ready to know the house, yet her motivations are different from all others entering. As Karen realizes that she must save her partner from the house, she, too, begins to explore what it is, overcoming her severe agoraphobia.

Her explorations differ from Navidson's, occurring predominantly outside the house, thus acknowledging that the house, if it exists at all, must exist in relation to exterior reality. Paradoxically, this reference to exteriority emerges through a double mediation, from within the labyrinthian leaves of the novel that mediates the *Navidson Record*. This blurred distinction between inside and outside tempers the reader's identification with Karen. For her, however, a grounding in external reality indicates a recognition of a world external to the ego, however mediated the perception of that exteriority may be, and prepares the subject for working through loss. In her recognition of exteriority, she posits a space that exists independently of the self, a space into which the self can release love objects as autonomous and independent wholes. Karen's first film short includes interviews with such famous thinkers as Kiki Smith, Stephen King, Camille Paglia, Jacques Derrida, Stanley Kubrick, Hunter S. Thompson, and Harold Bloom. Unlike Zampanò, however, Karen approaches these scholars not through their writing but through their personal reaction to the footage on the house.

The parodic ventriloquism of these scholars and writers with which Danielewski takes liberty provides some comic relief. That each intellectual speaks to Karen according to the idiosyncrasies of their writing reduces them to caricatures: "Derrida: Well that which is inside, which is to say, if I may say, that which infinitely patterns itself without the outside, without the other, though where then is the other? Finished? Good. [Pause] Hold my hand. We stroll" (Danielewski 361). Nearing the end of the interviews, Derrida speaks again conclusively: "The other. [Pause] Or what other, which is to say then, the same thing. The other, no other, You see?" (Danielewski 365). Derrida's fragmented, playfully obfuscating speech, though mimetic of his theoretical savvy, fails to be of any use to Karen. Conversely, Camille Paglia's character affirms Karen's position as she argues, "[women] know there's nothing there and can live with that knowledge, but men must find out for sure. They're haunted by that infinite hollow and its sense-making allure, and so they crave it, desire it, desire its end, its knowledge, its . . . essence . . . It really comes down to what men lack . . . The whole thing's about womb envy or vagina envy" (Danielewski 357–58). Although Paglia's reading holds some insight, the narrative frame that presents her undermines her interpretive power. Each scholar's reaction to the footage of the house as an unknowable object is characteristic of his or her authorial voice. The house is intelligible to them only insofar as it mirrors back what they already know. These character sketches are appropriately anticipatory. For readers of Paglia and Derrida, their reactions within the narrative make a disappointing amount of sense because they sound familiar. These interviews dramatize the circular logic inherent in theoretical knowledge.

Karen responds to her psychiatrist's question of what the house means to her personally. Her answer to this question results in a short film, "A Brief History of Who I Love," which focuses not on the dark corridors of the house but on what the house had cost her. A nonacademic endeavor, the second film is an exploration of Will Navidson through photographs of himself and ones he had taken: "The diligence, discipline, and time-consuming research required to fashion this short—there are easily over a hundred edits—allowed Karen for the first time to see Navidson as something other than her own personal fears and projections" (Danielewski 368). Karen's character previously suffered from psychosomatic symptoms due to her projective anxiety, and her condition becomes common among all characters who enter the dark hallways. As an unknowable object, the house immobilizes its victims in a paranoid-schizoid position, exacerbating the desire for omniscience, for freedom from the suffocating-yet-sublime interior of psychic reality. Karen is able to enter into the reparative position after the paranoid struggle of failing to make sense of the house and of one's own unconscious. In doing so, she recognizes Navidson as an autonomous other, rather than an assortment of part objects that she internalizes and projects onto the external world. Will's last venture into the depths of the house allows Karen to acknowledge his absence, and she is thus able to mourn the internal objects that she projected onto him. Only once she accomplishes this working through could she return to the house, live there, and find Will without getting lost.

Another reparative kernel resides also in what Hayles observes as the characters' condition for survival. She notes: "When relationships are not mediated by inscription technologies they decay toward alienation, and when they are mediated, they progress toward intimacy" (783). In this sense, the condition of possibility for the return of the subject is precisely signification. Reparation stems from the ongoing process of remediation, or re-telling the story. The economy of inscription technologies not only affords the characters an existence through the very condition of their representation, but they also use such technologies to work through "past trauma, reenvision damaged relationships, and understand the relation of themselves and others to the inscriptions that bring them into being" (Hayles 785). At this point, an opportunity arises to accept the economic unbinding of the text for a dynamic binding through a proliferation of signifiers, a proliferation that allows a growing intimacy with absence.

What Hayles identifies as the return of the subject through inscription is not, however, a Messianic recuperation of lost presence. In coming into being through the act of narration, the characters recognize loss as such. Although Danielewski postulates the possibility of reparation through identification with Karen's character, the text does not allow the reader a final resolution through analepsis.[24] The reader's identification with working through is momentary as the alterity of the text persists, not only in its haunting affect but also in the exhibits, appendices, and index located after the central narrative's denouement. Appendices include ten years worth of letters written by Truant's mother to him from an asylum. This appendix inflects Truant's editing practice as a personal working through of his own traumas, rendering his act of reading more parallel to Karen's, only after the fact of his physical and mental degradation within the narrative.[25] Like queer sexuality, the text resists the resolution of the primordial Oedipus complex, in which desire and identification are designated to the appropriate objects. True to the movement of the death drive, the resolution of the narrative fails to deliver along with the Navidsons' closure an unequivocal certainty or feeling of cathartic release. To its very last page, the novel emphasizes a deferral whose operation is extra-diegetic, at the level of the reading process, thus disrupting the finality of narrative conclusion.

Even though Karen and Will survive and get married, Zampanò questions the "happy ending": "The Navidsons may have left the house, they may have even left Virginia, but they will never be able to leave the memory of that place" (Danielewski 526). The *House of Leaves* comprises a burnt memory trace whose path characters repeat compulsively throughout the narrative frames; but the repetition compulsion of the house potentiates a discovery of one's own creative resources. While the house ultimately serves its intended purpose to repair a floundering relationship, Will's reconciliation with his "passion" has to do less with Karen than his drive to produce art: "Passion has little to do with euphoria and everything to do with patience . . . It does not mean to flow with exuberance. It means to suffer" (527). The resolution for Will and Karen is not the sudden disappearance of the horrific black aporia that inevitably defines their lives. Rather, a greater resolution lies in their arrival at their laborious, singular, continuous engagement with the unknown.

Navidson knows that the image provides not a final solution but a resource in the struggle to signify. In the last scene of the documentary, Navidson "suffers the responsibilities of his art and consequently must turn from the blind comfort found in those neatly framed photographs filling his home to follow his costume clad children out into the New England streets, their hearts set on sacks of candy, their paths hidden beneath cold coloured leaves" (Danielewski 527). The alliterative emphasis of the "costume clad children" whose hearts seek "candy" yet whose paths hide under "cold coloured" leaves implies an awareness of what Navidson is about to bequeath through his art: an identification with the other, an insatiable, even infantile desire, and an occlusion of safe paths by the leaves of the novel. The final shot of *The Navidson Record* suggests the refusal to bind the horror of the house within the casings of a book. Navidson's shot leaves Halloween's domestication of horror to pause on the documentary's final vanishing point: "he focuses on the empty road beyond, a pale curve vanishing into the woods where nothing moves and a street lamp flickers on and off until at last it flickers out and darkness sweeps in like a hand" (Danielewski 528). Here, the vanishing point is coextensive with depth, its simultaneous negation, and the completion of an artwork.

The novel's resistance to closure relates to what Kristeva critiques Klein for neglecting in the latter's own literary criticism. Indeed, Klein's articulation of the reparative in her literary analyses remains at the level of plot, as characters suffer through psychic struggles to arrive at recognition and love. Of Klein's readings, Kristeva remarks, "the mechanism of reparation certainly does not exhaust the creative process, no more than do the themes of falsity and of perversion, sadomasochism, or profanation . . . which are not addressed by our psychoanlayst-turned-literary-critic" (*Klein* 190). Klein's "naïve" approach, as Kristeva describes it, nonetheless belies the perseverance of the former's theory: "projective identification and its replacement by a reparation process that is wholly dependent on the experience of loss" (*Klein* 190). In light of Kristeva's insights, the *House of Leaves* is less a horror story than a drama about love and loss. The horror serves as a defensive screen that represses the unbearable pain of a traumatic past in which each character suffers the shame in longing for broken attachments.

V. Conclusion

The ultimate experience of loss is the reader's, since identification fails to guarantee any final sense of catharsis. Nor does the work to let go of omniscience, particularly of knowledge about the house, guarantee a completion of the self. The text exemplifies the reader's loss as both Navidson and Truant, at the end of their respective narratives, burn the book they have on hand, entitled *House of Leaves,* as a last resort to their survival. The enigma of the house as an unknowable lost object is negated momentarily in Karen's creative elaboration of her love for Navidson. Like Karen, Will continues a passion in producing art; for both characters, their relationship is secondary to their own creative solitude. Like object-relational conditions of the unconscious, the enigma of the house remains perpetual, transforming through a series of displacements until it lands on the reader's lap, prompting the reader to consume it as a lost object, whose visual literalization renders it an artifact of melancholia. As Kristeva notes, "Because the death drive is forever, reparation and gratitude are but temporary crystallizations of negativity as well as its dialectical resting points" (*Klein* 131). Danielewski emphasizes repeatedly that the text must necessarily remain open.

Reparation, then, occurs both diegetically and at the level of the reading process once the reader recognizes the experience of loss. Knowledge's failure marks the failure of the circular logic that bases itself on a familiar return to the same. In the wake of such failure, lost among the signifiers in the house of leaves, the reader realizes that the enigma of the lost object necessarily persists. She arrives at a queer moment in which she realizes the contingent and provisional identifications that perpetuate a fixation on textual enigma. Although the reader occupies the same structural position as Zampanò and Truant, the compulsion to repeat the engagement with the enigma of the text results in a "proliferation of identifications and critiques" ("Queer Pedagogy" 81) as the fates of these readers diverge into a network that informs the movement of the text. Through these provisional identifications, the text feeds the desire to know but forecloses the possibility of knowledge and undermines what Bersani calls the "force of argument."

If, according to Rose, sexuality emerges from failures of vision, then *House of Leaves* is a strange kind of pornography. The novel presents a multitude of visual fields, all of which mark fragmented and partial scenes to which the reading subject attaches. Danielewski's text allows for the working through of mourning only after a detour into a performative melancholia: a death drive whose symptom emerges from the text's visual literalization, which the reader must consume in order to continue the process of reading. The reparative potentials in this reading process require attuning to a queer temporality, a lag of recognition that requires multi-level mediation. The novel's characters both constitute and are subject to this temporal lag.[26]

One answer to the question posed at the beginning of this chapter—how a death-driven text comes to be a way of "caring for other people"—lies in the process of signification and remediation. The fragmented subject in *House of Leaves* returns through the signifiers that both mark absence and offer intelligibility. As sexuality unfolds out of the text's conceptual vanishing points, the reader slowly comes to terms with the uncertainties that abound in the text about where to read, in what order, how to navigate, what to skip or skim, and what to attach to. The phantasy of omniscience diminishes, and the reader is left with the desire to retell the story. In the wake of anxiety, the subject develops a desire to signify as a way to mourn narratives of certainty. Only then can she exit the labyrinth, or, more importantly, find the love object in the labyrinth without getting lost. With the provisional identifications that develop and break down, the act of reading *The House of Leaves* allows the reader to pause with the insight that otherness is more than a mere projection of the fragmented ego. The encounter with both internal and external otherness occasions a capacity to tolerate ambivalence, uncertainty, and the potentiality of object relations. *House of Leaves* shows that a death-driven text is first and foremost a text indeed. The contagion it passes on from one reader to the next is less an inescapable horror than a passion to signify sorrow: one that morphs from reader to reader into singular and particular enunciations of attachment and grief. For each character in *House of Leaves*, the act of reading becomes a difficult care of the self, a task that some do not survive.

CHAPTER FOUR

"Kill Your Children"

Queer Temporalities and Failed Identification in Timothy Findley's *The Wars*

The first intimacy is an intimacy with a process of becoming, not with a person.

—Leo Bersani and Adam Phillips, *Intimacies*, 114

I. Introduction

Consider a relationship to reading that embraces the irresolvable dialectics of the drives, as economic and dynamic binding and unbinding weave the subject in and out of phantasies of certainty and of identity. In a painful project of making experience intelligible, the subject nurtures a capacity to tolerate epistemological failure. The paranoid imperative and queer reparative is a process that maintains an erotic attachment to the text, an attachment that pulses with the oscillation of knowledge and its necessary failure as the subject initiates difficult thinking. Narratives of certainty that defend against such conceptual failure risk a stasis that forecloses the erotic elasticity of reading. This chapter explores how reading persists as an oscillation in narratives of certainty that operate at the level of nation. The literary representation of war illustrates the extremes of psychic splitting. In war, the phantasy of omniscience operates with broader stakes than those that motivate the domestic object relations in *Lolita* and *House of Leaves*. War envisions a cohesive social body that requires management and deployment against an alien other. The political totality of the social body is key to military victory, and the degree to which the death drive dominates in the subject becomes a matter of material survival. War results from a struggle to universalize epistemological certainty, and survival becomes tangled up with the effort to deaden the body against both the shocks of battle and the concurrent pace of technological progress. In a world of paranoid imperatives, intimacy emerges in the failure of phantasies that must be carried out and acted out for the discursive maintenance of the nation.

In *Why War?* (1993), Jacqueline Rose asserts that internal to the movement of thinking is an impenetrable alterity that forecloses the possibility of absolute knowledge. Like Bersani, Rose is interested in the failure of thought but through a particularly Kleinian lens. For Bersani, as the first chapter illustrates, sexuality is the vanishing point of psychoanalytic discourse, while for Rose, the death drive is that nonrepresentable point. She articulates the death drive as the ultimate disruption to the coherence of the psychic topography. Rose reiterates Derrida's claim in *Post Cards*, that the impasse of the death drive to Freud's thinking is the impasse to theorization itself, to knowledge, to mastery, to a metalanguage.

That the Freudian corpus is subject to constant debate led to the famous Controversial Discussions, a conceptual crisis that Rose identifies as the "war" between Klein and Anna Freud over the inheritance of the psychoanalytic institution from its deceased father. Rose describes war as the crisis of absolute knowledge that resists its own failure when consciousness becomes estranged from itself. War indicates a psychic splitting that occurs when the phantasy of omniscience is threatened by the otherness of the unconscious. The subject projects the threatening foreign body onto the external world and directs aggression outward with an aim to obliterate its difference. Rose names the symptom as "'alien,' the 'foreign body' of the repressed" (*Why War?* 19). Such a breach bears the seeds for an ethical life and thus articulates an "ethics of failure": "war breaks out, uncontrollably, because . . . we are not willing to fail *enough* . . . Knowledge will be possible only if we are willing to suspend the final purpose and ends of knowledge in advance" (*Why War?* 36–37, emphasis in original). War occurs in recourse to splitting and projective identification, in a disavowal of failure and an insistence on omniscience that denies the absence of the unknowable object.

The question of whether knowledge corresponds with exterior reality necessarily remains open. Rose notes that Winnicott locates creativity in the suspense of not knowing what is and is not real (*Why War?* 30).

The process of mourning allows the subject to let go of omniscience, to tolerate the painful position of not knowing and to pause with a form of thinking unable to possess itself. Paradoxically, thinking and certainty thus become incompatible: "if mourning initiates thinking, it also severs us once and for all from any certainty of thought" (*Why War?* 20). Splitting and projective identification saves the subject from the work of mourning, from letting go of the object of radical alterity. Conviction is a posture of omniscience that disavows the absence of the unknowable object. As the primary operation in war, splitting sets the subject on a path toward mastering part objects by consuming them possessively. Omniscience is thus inherently melancholic, and the creative potentials stemming from not knowing are foreclosed.

Psychic splitting manifests in a variety of scenes: on the micro level, within oneself or among individuals, as the first chapters elucidate, and on the macro level, among nations but also between schools of thought and critical trends. Rose reminds her reader of Freud's claim, that unification as an objective of war becomes a necessary violence. Subjects submit to the unifying force of cultural law from the exterior world because they fear a loss of love, but "like sexuality, Freud hints, the law of culture is arbitrary, uncertain, incapable of completing itself" (*Why War?* 36). The law of culture, culture's systems of intelligibility, provides only a promissory form of unification that depends on the process of splitting and a defense against the de-forming force of the sexual. Like queer sexuality, the law of queer culture is by no means exempt from uncertainty and thus from defensive impulses of splitting, either in its subgroups or in relation to the larger socio-political sphere. The split in queer theory between the paranoid imperative and the reparative turn to affect is predicated on a process of psychic splitting, projective identification, the wish for certainty, as well as a resistance to failure and ambivalence. The Kleinian framework is the key that differentiates the death drive operating in systems of totality from the death drive operating in queer theory, a difference around which such scholars as Michael Cobb and Lee Edelman have previously revolved but never explicated. The shattering force of sexuality is less a romanticized metaphor for the death drive than, as Derrida remarks, an expression of a "leap into the ethical," a "radical discontinuity" and a "heterogeneity" that results from the persistence of Eros *against* the death drive (*Without Alibi* 272), a persistence that endures against the stronger drive despite the odds.

Queer sexuality becomes an antidote to authoritarian and tautological systems not because it offers a manifestly subversive life, but because it keeps thinking alive through eroticized creativity within such systems. Previous critiques of totalitarianism would not agree; in *Dialectic of Enlightenment*, Horkheimer and Adorno argue that totalitarianism re-appropriates the sexual excess that constitutes the failure of meaning into the culture industry. This incorporation ensures the efficient operation of the system and complete subjugation of all individuals within its structures, which in turn retains the power to demand either complicity or death. Desire becomes implicated in the operation of this system and not a force that questions it. In this social body, the death drive persists, and reparation is foreclosed. In this situation, Enlightenment's Reason is in the service of the "new barbarism" of industrial warfare due to its production of docile subjectivity. The scientific categorization of the material world into a knowable system is based on formulae of deductive logic that imposed a taxonomical structure to external reality. The culture industry is so baked through with the logic of Enlightenment that the question of the difference between knowledge and reality ceases to hold creative potential. As a reified system of intelligibility, aesthetics has lost its reparative capacities in the wake of Enlightenment. Our post-Enlightenment system of categories denies the absence of the object, particularly the object of knowledge. The disavowal of absence, the phantasy of omniscience, and the splitting of objects have fixed systems of intelligibility in perpetual melancholia. This formulation of modern culture has led to a debate that challenges the distinction between mourning and melancholia.[1] In lieu of mourning, the culture industry produces the myth of dominant history as a narrative of capitalist and military progress.

For queer thinking, the death drive is a necessity but not a finality. This assertion is becoming increasingly apparent in studies that consider the futurity of queer, such as Sedgwick's later work and Bersani's 2011 article, "Shame on You." Queer thinking takes risks in order to enjoy the dangerous and wrenching intimacy that the drives facilitate in object relations. The queer recognition of the self-shattering that undoes the intelligible world initiates mourning. Even when Edelman in his article "Ever After" calls for an "impossible" counterproject "that's willing to forgo the privilege of social recognition" (114) through his queer figure that is opposed "to life and futurity" (113), his call challenges queer theory's institutional intelligibility in a way that sustains creative thinking through a capacity to tolerate ambivalence and paradox. Queer thinking attempts a reparative working through in its emergence within closed systems, and such difficult thinking involves an intimate relationship to the oscillation between epistemological attachment and loss. The ethical work of mourning that takes place in the wake of thought's failure is the precondition for reparative practices.

II. The Life Drive in War

Although their writings do not speak directly to one another, Bersani's and Rose's insights draw attention to the epistemological proximity between sexuality and war in the delicate and potentially violent project of bringing thought to life. Indeed, what kind of thinking is possible when the questions of war and sexuality are brought together? Timothy Findley's *The Wars* (1977) tells a story about an ethics of failure in the midst of war. In 1915, devastated by the death of his hydrocephalic sister, Rowena, Robert Ross enlists in the army at the age of nineteen and is sent to the front. He stumbles through his tour while his body and mind degenerate in his struggles with sexuality, masculinity, and loss. Ross's identification with animals is a strong motif and culminates in his own demise, when he betrays the Canadian army, "*King and Country*" (Findley 49, emphasis in original), by recovering one-hundred-thirty horses from a train wreckage in an attempt to save them from definite slaughter in battle. When he finds refuge in a barn, Canadian officers who are assigned to hunt him down light the thatched roof on fire, killing the horses and leaving Ross severely crippled and disfigured until his death about six years later. The reader receives the story of Robert Ross in fragments, pieced together by a researcher whose work is overseen by an archivist in an unnamed space.

The reception of *The Wars* peaked during the 1980s and 1990s, focusing on a few themes that preoccupied hermeneutical trends of those decades. The novel thus begs for a rereading in the current context, especially since *The Wars* persists as a prominent artifact in the cultural imaginary and as one of the most well-known novels of Findley's oeuvre. Two major themes of the novel mark a paradigm shift in representation at the end of the twentieth century: postmodernism and the explosion of dominant history. Linda Hutcheon's concept of the Canadian postmodern figures heavily in Findley criticism. Ronald Hatch, Evelyn Cobley, Herb Wyile, and Eva-Marie Kröller build on Hutcheon's intervention to reflect on the self-reflexive resistances and complicities that Findley's postmodernism offers in relation to dominant history. In his critique of historical fact over the potentiality of fiction, David Ingham explores the association between fascism and perfection in the novel, concluding that fascism and imagination are antithetical. The narrator's work of imagining Ross's life serves as an antidote to the proto-fascist context of World War I.

The literary establishment of *The Wars* as an example of postmodern fiction that ruptures official history has paradoxically fixed a closure of interpretation on the text. In a certain sense, the novel itself became subject to epistemological certainty. Few scholars tease out queer valences, such as Shane Rhodes in his 1998 article "Buggering with History," which investigates the implications of the link between sex and violence for the current of history. Ross's inarticulable homosexuality draws attention to history's closet, in which those excesses of singular personhood become subject to repression. The narrator's work of piecing together Ross's "sexual warfare" is an act of "historical reconstruction." This suggestion about sex and destruction is consistent with the radical manifestation of "queer" at which scholars arrived around the time of Rhodes's article: "*The Wars* literalizes the violence inherent in the tense interlining of homosocial and homosexual and the queer disruption of binaries in which homosexuality seems to exult" (Rhodes 45). Rhodes's link between sex and violence culminates in his reading of Nicholas Fagan's lines at the end of the novel, that a shout of recognition can come in a form of a shot. In other words, the most intimate recognition of the other is coextensive with the destruction of the other. While critical preoccupations in the twentieth century focus on hermeneutics of historical narrative, those few articles in the twenty-first century draw attention to representations of vulnerability. Some criticism, such as Diana Brydon's "A Devotion to Fragility," focus on the displaced value of fragile things in the novel but reduces the homoerotics that bombard Ross to "male friendship" (82). Most queer readings link sex not with vulnerability but with violence.

The conceptual relationship between the two positions in Findley criticism—the novel's shattering postmodernism and the attachment to vulnerability—offers unexplored implications about the unconscious and the economy of longing in the novel. The novel offers something beyond the irreducibility of such interpretive formulations as a "queer breakdown of meaning" (Rhodes 43), the explosion of metadiscourse, the subversion of authoritarian Other, the redemption of the closeted homosexual, the valuation of fiction over fact—the redistribution of value, in other words, between margin and center. The role of the archival fragments in the metanarrative carries implications about projection, mourning, desire, alienation, and the unconscious, all of which form an economy that organizes the drive to read. In this way, intimacies unfold out of *narrative* relationships.

Death abounds in the novel. Trenches become tombs that bind soldiers in an undifferentiated mass: the men "had all been gassed or had frozen to death. Those who lay in water were profiled in ice. Everything was green: their faces—and their fingers—and their buttons. And the snow" (Findley 146). The objects successfully bound in the trenches and fields are dead or deadened. Ross fails to take military action against any life[2] until the climax of the novel, when he shoots Captain Leather "between the eyes" (Findley 203) for closing the gate on the horses and mules, preventing their escape before enemy shells kill them all. The other soldiers whose stories contribute to the narrative exhibit the great failure to automatize in the national effort toward victory. Their failure indicates a refusal of "the forces of history" and the blind instrumentality of "history's 'orders'" (Hatch 93). Captain Leather is among the very few featured in the novel who are complicit with dominant history, and Ross's betrayal of his fellow officer solidifies his stance against the nation's narrative of certainty. The political enemy hardly manifests as material antagonists in the novel; for the most part, German soldiers are absent presences. The narrative of certainty with which the nation coerces its subjects is less against the Germans than, more abstractly, against the resistance to interpellation, against the otherness within individual subjects that threaten the unity of national identity. A contrast develops between the trenches that bind the soldiers to their graves and the researcher's narrative project that attempts to bind Ross's story together: "The mud. There are no good similes" (Findley 76). Such resistance to poetry resonates with the twentieth-century difficulty to aestheticize events of modern barbarity; and yet "you," the reader whom the novel addresses in second voice, are called on not only to envision the scene but to walk on the wet clay.

The tension between industrial modernity and precarious bodies runs throughout the novel. Structured by the plurality and repetition of conflict in both inner and external worlds, *The Wars* captures the death drive of war, colonial and imperial modernity, ecological devastation, and the imperative of heterosexual masculinity. As Donna Pennee observes, Findley's novel "figures an individual's resistance to modernity as an event only (re)producible through the point of intersection of the everyday and the epochal" (Pennee 94). In one of the first scenes, barely grown out of childhood, Robert Ross stands in a new trench coat clutching a new briefcase, waiting on the train platform to report for duty. His fascination with the steam engine foreshadows his demise: "Great clouds of steam billowed out around its wheels. The '*fire horse*': that's what the Indians called it. Robert looked to one side from under the peak of his cap, hoping that no one had seen him flinch from the steam or stepping back from the fire" (Findley 11–12). In a proleptic fragment pages before the scene at the train station, the reader receives an image of his fate: "*He leans along the horse's neck. His eyes are blank. There is mud on his cheeks and forehead and his uniform is burning—long, bright tails of flame are streaming out behind him*" (Findley 5, emphasis in original). Two images of the *fire horse* appear within the novel's first pages and haunt the narrative. Ross maintains his allegiance to the horses and, ultimately, to the vulnerability of organic life. In doing so, he rejects the violence of industrial technology. When Ross suffers his demise, he melds with his horse into a single fiery figure only to literalize the myth of industry and to repeat his premonitory rejection of its violence.

Throughout the novel, loss accumulates among singular relationships against the impersonalizing backdrop of an industrialized war. Near the end of the novel, the narrator notes, "So far, you have read of the deaths of 557,017 people—one of whom was killed by a streetcar, one of whom died of bronchitis and one of whom died in a barn with her rabbits" (180). The juxtaposition between the numerical abstraction of bodies and the very private deaths of loved ones outside of war draws attention to what the novel prioritizes: the refusal of reified subjectivity. The novel offers an ethics of failure through Ross's failure to reproduce heroic masculinity, to achieve normative heterosexuality or even to realize a queer one actively, to steel himself against vulnerability and death. In an interview, commenting on the effect of "our leaders" on soldiers, Ross's nurse, Marian Turner, aptly observes Ross's failure in "binding": "That's what binds us together. They appeal to our basest instincts. The lowest common denominator. And then we turn around and call them *extraordinary* . . . Robert Ross was no Hitler. That was his problem" (Findley 11). What economically "binds" subjects together in complicity with the state parallels Freud's deadened monad, in its invulnerability to stimuli and incapacity to undergo change. In his major struggle, Ross ultimately refuses the mandates of the Great War. As Phillips states in *Intimacies*, "The ego's essential perplexity was Freud's way of saying that the modern individual could have more existence only by having less life . . . Modern love was a self-consuming passion" (*Intimacies* 103). Repeatedly, Ross insists on more life, thus compromising mere survival. The novel offers a universal epistemological failure of Clausewitzian abstraction: ultimately, a failure of economic binding, of mastery in light of modern warfare.

In Findley's landscape, anything that is neither dead nor mechanized by military orders comprises a surreal tableau of stubborn attachments to delicate objects. In that "inordinately civilized place" (Findley 94), the dugout that is about to be bombed, Devlin treasures a panel of stained glass protectively. Rodwell nurses injured birds, rabbits, hedgehogs, and toads in a makeshift hospital. Poole plays music on his bugle after dinner and conversation. Levitt brings the book *Clausewitz on War*, the only unwelcome object in the makeshift home, yet he is the only one immobilized by shock from the bomb. In this notable scene, amidst the knotted rug, candles, homemade table, coffee pot, stove, and empty bookshelves, Rodwell tells the story of finding his disparate menagerie of little animals crouched under a single hedge. The men share their aesthetic preferences, their wishes, and their love of absurdities. As Devlin admits: "I'm devoted to fragility. Glass has a certain fineness and brittleness that a man with my bones appreciates" (Findley 94). The dugout scene stands out in the narrative as an insistence on domestic comfort and, paradoxically, an utter rejection of normality. Levitt's attempt at the ordinary in the context of war alienates him from his dugout companions as he lectures from his book: "Clausewitz says an excess of artillery leads to a passive character in war" (Findley 100). His reading captures a contradictory condition of trench warfare, not because technology prevents men from expressing an active heroism, but because, as the dugout scene demonstrates, military technology fosters the passivity connected to the empathic care for precarious life that war violently attempts to foreclose. Yet even Levitt's efforts to instrumentalize thought into a battle strategy strikes Ross as strange because in war, "*Ordinary* is a myth" (Findley 100, emphasis in original), marking the dialectical collapse of Myth and Reason. All of the pleasures in which the men indulge become perverse, even Levitt's obsession with Clausewitz. The dugout becomes a transitional space in which the men can insist on life pleasures. In this transitional space, the men reject the reality of war and simultaneously feed the will to remain still, in position, as ordered. The dugout is a luxurious place that allows the fantasy of an enriched life to proliferate in the face of impending destruction.

III. Narrative Remediation

As a space of repose, the dugout allows Ross a few moments of sleep. While he falls asleep to the sound of Poole's "harsh and liquid" breathing, the narrative jumps analeptically, as if the narrator mimics Ross's drifting back through the memory traces of waking life. This mimesis repeats events that are necessarily imaginative, events that no historical document could capture: "nobody dreams on a battlefield. There isn't any sleep that long. Dreams and distance are the same. If he could run away . . . But he kept running into Taffler. Throwing stones. And Harris" (102). Despite the battlefield, Ross dreams, and the reader gains access to his inner life. At the moment when dreams begin, Ross's repression relaxes on his desire for male objects like Taffler and Harris. For Ross and the reader, Poole's breathing draws an associative thread to the story of Harris, with whom Ross falls in love and who suffocates from his own congested lungs before he even reaches the battlefield. The reader learns how devoted Ross is to Harris's bedside: "no one since Rowena had made Robert feel he wanted to be with them all the time. *If* what he felt could be reduced to an understanding—that was it" (104, emphasis added). Harris's fragile body becomes the substitute for Rowena, and his impending loss pulls on Ross's desire to maintain a presence for the other that is bound to fail. Yet, implied by the qualifying "if," this feeling is analogous only as an approximation to Ross's relationship with Rowena. Ross struggles because what he feels cannot be reduced to conscious understanding.

Language mediates Ross's relationship to a dying Harris, and yet Ross's attachment to Harris painfully exceeds such mediation: "Robert didn't know, sometimes, what to do with Harris's sentences; where to fit them in his mind, or how to use them. He only knew they went somewhere inside him and they didn't come back out" (Findley 104). Words offer a profoundly mediated penetration. As unconscious otherness paradoxically enters into and envelops the self, Ross submits to a psychical shift. Harris's words not only feed Ross's attachment but also serve a transformative function, opening Ross to a kind of thinking unable to possess itself. Even though Ross's desire for Harris cannot be reduced to a mere conscious understanding, the words exchanged at Harris's deathbed mark the most intimate relationship in the novel. Each time Harris finishes a story about his young life, "he'd look at Robert—once he'd spoken. Never while he spoke. He was really only talking to himself, Robert guessed, before he slept" (Findley 105). In Ross's "guess," he disavows the weight of his role for Harris's last moments, suggesting that their relation is completely impersonal as Harris comes to terms with dying. This turning away acts as a mirroring between the men. Ross cannot quite articulate what Harris cannot bear to witness as he tells his story: a mutual recognition of a love that thrives because it lasts only as long as Harris does. This moment parallels Bersani's proposal of new relational modes in a world of intractable nonrelations:

> In the generous narcissism of the exchange between Socratic lovers, each partner demands of the other . . . that he reflect

> the lover's type of being, his universal singularity . . . by recognizing and cultivating that singularity as his own most pervasive, most pressing potentiality. . . . Socratic ideality . . . is more cultivated than it is contemplated. Cultivated through dialogue—intrinsically unending dialogue, for we are always either moving toward or falling away from the being it is our greatest happiness to 're-find' in others. (*Intimacies* 86–87)

The Socratic notion of the being that the self "re-finds" in the other is not synonymous with an inner identitarian "sameness." Rather, Bersani and Phillips describe this process of re-finding as the potentiality of both self and other that unfolds from contact, from their pressing on one another, from their supple resistance against and for one another in the very moment of encounter. Robert and Harris turn away as their devotion to words intensifies.

The reader learns about Harris and Ross's intimacy through the researcher's mimetic efforts to follow Ross's dream in the dugout. Such dream-like recollection is supplemented by the narrator's interview with Lady Juliet d'Orsey, who was at the time a twelve-year-old witness to the love affairs between her sister and her suitors, soldiers who turn out to be a little queer. This section of the novel, then, is remediated through both the researcher's and d'Orsey's voices. A disjuncture arises between d'Orsey's subjective testimony and Ross's private longing for Harris and blushing at Taffler's naked hands (106). Such disjuncture between the visible and the invisible emphasizes the condition that wish fulfillment necessarily saturates and disrupts the act of piecing together this past. The narrative mimesis of the dream's drift sutures this disjuncture into a seamless stream of story, whose unsettling rhythm is muffled by the momentum of free association. That the researcher fills in the gaps of history with omniscient re-imaginings of Ross's desire belies a wish that lost objects can be recuperated in their entirety. The narrative draws attention to its remediated condition in order to acknowledge the limits of representation: "There is an aspect of this interview which, alas, cannot survive transition onto paper—and that is the sound of Lady Juliet's voice" (Findley 157). Along with the disjuncture between the visible and invisible, such acknowledgment primes the reader to develop a relationship to loss.

The life drive emerges not only from the diegetic conflicts: resilient attachments to vulnerability, small creatures, majestic horses, dying sisters, or broken mothers. The life drive overshadows the psychic splitting in war through the archivist's reparative act of piecing together lost stories of intimacy from the fragments of history: photos, letters, newspaper clippings. Hayles argues that, in the posthuman era, when textual dialogism comprises the entirety of contemporary reality, the subject returns through acts of remediation.[3] In *House of Leaves,* characters who are remediated in a series of narrative fragments survive the murderous drive of the house. Unlike the conditions of the house on Ash Tree Lane, the remediation in Findley's novel does not ensure the characters' material survival retroactively. Rather, the subject returns in remediated form in order to prepare the reader for the work of letting go.

As a repeated remediated fragment, the letter functions in the novel as an object that maintains both distance and closeness. Like the ambivalent efforts of an adolescent striving for independence, the stories that Ross sends home are hedged with restraint. Ross's correspondence involves the contradictory desire to feel strong and to receive belief in that strength from his parents: "he didn't feel like sending love to anyone. It seemed unmanly. What he did do was enclose a photograph (official) and say to his father: 'This will show you that my draft makes a brawling, husky lot of men'" (Findley 51). Ross's whimsy disavows his need to project his masculinity for his parents, a need that the photograph conveys that words cannot. His letters become increasingly mediated throughout the novel, as his traumas build. His formal tone reflects the way in which his family archives him: "Week after week, Robert wrote with unnerving formality . . . All these letters, neatly folded and tied, were laid in an oblong lacquered box beside the silent, booted icon of ROBERT ROSS, SECOND LIEUTENANT, C.F.A. in the silver frame on the black walnut table in the parlour" (Findley 73). Ross's letters are bound in what seems like a little coffin, "laid" down to rest with as much formality as its contents.

For the majority of the novel, the reader does not receive a sense of how Ross's family reciprocates his letters. Mrs. Ross stores his letters in an archival tomb, and she fails to reflect back to him the pretense of familial strength for which he asks: "Robert's letters were read and re-read—numbered and catalogued and memorized. Mrs Ross would write him every day—long, meandering epistles angled down the pages of her blue notepaper—often (more often than not) completely indecipherable" (153). The persistence of these letters overturns the economy of failed intimacy between child and parent. Mrs. Ross's indecipherable meanderings parallel Ross's restraint; in both cases, the content ceases to matter. Behind each letter is a repressed knowledge that it may be the last one sent, so that the letter itself, regardless of its content, becomes a simultaneous declaration of love, persistence, and farewell. Other soldiers write letters to announce their farewell to their loved ones. At one point, Ross reads a letter that his friend Rodwell wrote to his daughter before committing suicide in no man's land. The letter states: "I am alive in everything I touch. Touch these pages and you have me in your fingertips. We survive in one another. Everything lives forever. Believe it. Nothing dies" (Findley 151). Because Rodwell's letter belies a keen awareness of his impending death, his insistence on life enduring is not a melancholic denial of loss, but rather a recognition that life resides in the letter, that is, in the signifier and its transferrential potentials.

The photograph is more ubiquitous than the letter, and it becomes the repository of even greater relational failure between self and other. Both Kröller and Brydon explore the role of the photograph in the novel. Kröller notes that postmodernist fiction often "exploits the ambiguous function of photography" (Kröller 69), since the photograph produces an illusion but, in the postmodern context, one that is a fragment of a montage, necessarily reducing an uncontainable scene onto a two-dimensional plane. Her discussion of the *camera obscura* in Findley's novel identifies in the visual text a desire to recuperate life through the fragment. Lorraine York also claims that the inclusion of the photograph points toward "its own constitutive processes" ("Violent Stillness" 193). Both *The Wars* and *The House of Leaves* link the camera with the gun. Besides the obvious parallels between camera and gun, that one aims and shoots both, with breath relaxed, eyes focused, and trigger finger slow, these authors explore the invasive violence of a camera ripping a scene out of reality in an instant. Unlike *House of Leaves*, no literal images litter the pages of *The Wars*, as the photograph emerges only through textual description. As Kröller points out, the photograph serves as a metaphor for a postmodern disruption of discourse's claim to truth rendering. As a textual metaphor, the photograph becomes deferred as its shapes are transformed into letters. In its remediated state, the photograph sheds its promise of immediacy for the rhythms of belatedness, becoming subject to the timing of its description, its contextualization, and the gap of lost history that it attempts to redeem.

In *The Wars*, belatedness is a motif that structures not only visual images and narratives but also the emergence of beauty. Lens-facilitated vision shifts from its association with the gun to the more tentative unfolding between self and other, a relation that is built on failed identification. Over and over, the novel presents such polarity between the immediacy of a gun and the belatedness of failed identification. In a scene that compromises the sympathy of his character, Ross and his company crawl out of a mud crater under the watch of a merciful German. When it is Ross's turn to climb out of the crater, in a symbolically telling moment, Harris's scarf gets tangled around the Lewis gun and Ross abandons the former to free the latter. When the German moves, Ross panics, trips, falls, then shoots his watcher blindly. When he recovers, he looks upon the scene with his "field glasses"—a lens—to discover why the German moved so quickly:

> Binoculars. He had only been reaching for his binoculars.
>
> Robert sagged against the ground. It was even worse than that. Lying beside the German was a modified Mauser rifle of the kind used by snipers. He could have killed them all. Surely that had been his intention. But he'd relented. Why?
>
> The bird sang.
>
> One long note descending: three that wavered on the brink of sadness.
>
> That was why.
>
> It sang and sang and sang, till Robert rose and walked away. The sound of it would haunt him to the day he died. (Findley 146)

Initially, the songbird "made him extremely nervous" since "anyone in hiding was an imitation animal" (142). The sound that at first provokes Ross's paranoia becomes the trigger for remorse, as he attributes the motivation for the German soldier's empathy to the bird's song.

The transition of the songbird's role from a vehicle of paranoia to that of mourning emphasizes the precariousness with which the subject relates to the external world. Although Ross cannot be certain in his causal logic about this sequence of events between the bird's song and the German's empathy, he identifies with his victim from this imagined yet unquestioned uncertainty. The gunshot is an immediate certainty that links Ross to his victim, and its sound rings sharply "around and around the crater like a marble in a bowl" (145). In contrast to the gunshot, the bird's song also links Ross to the victim, but through a phantasy that imagines that beauty can inspire recognition between enemies, a recognition that Ross fails to share with his victim in his moment of panic. Unlike the shot, the bird's sound is not trapped in an insistent, repetitive echo. Rather, its resonance blossoms: one long note, three wavering, and then the bird "sang and sang and sang" until the day Ross dies. Through this phantasy about slow and sad beauty, Ross sees his victim clearly. The German soldier's binoculars, Ross's blind shooting, his subsequent lens-facilitated remorse, and the bird's song reframe the function of looking in the novel. The act of looking at a fragmented scene through holes, scopes, and lenses is associated less with the immediacy of the gun than a tentative and vulnerable desire between self and other that unfolds, wavers, and rebuilds in time. Like Ross's phantasy about the songbird, this desire invites imagination, failure, slowness, uncertainty, and loss.

IV. Queer Temporalities and Failed Identification

For the researcher in the novel, the remediated fragments operate like the songbird from the crater. Narrative remediation inaugurates mourning in a depressive position through two strategies: its queer temporality and its treatment of identification. The remediated fragments exacerbate the novel's aleatory structure. Several anachronies, or temporal discontinuities, highlight the state of perpetual loss with which Ross struggles as he is moved inexorably by the current of war. Pennee observes that "The railways and Raymond/Ross Industries represent progress, confederation, and consolidation, but at a cost both in the past and in the future-to-come within the novel" (Pennee 104). She notes that the contradictions in the novel between technological progress and the pastoral, between infantile repetition compulsions and a coming of age, "figure clearly the contradictions that inhere in the *bildung* of colony to nation" (Pennee 103). The linear time on which the myth of progress insists gets crumpled up, as it were, as both Ross's coming of age and the narrative's development break into pieces.

I argue that belatedness structures the narrative through analepsis, or an invocation of events that have already occurred. Only after Ross is sent to a dugout at the front do we learn at length about the death of Harris, as if a memory disrupts the immediacy of trench warfare. We learn of how Ross's sister Rowena dies from a fall in the barn, beside her pet rabbits; but again, this memory emerges through narrative analepsis after we see Ross standing immobilized on the train station platform, already on his way to war to flee Rowena's permanent absence. We learn about the moment Ross sees his father for the last time before his tour, but only mediated through a letter written from son to father, asking why his mother was absent for that goodbye. We return to this moment from the parents' perspective, learning belatedly that Mrs. Ross's rapidly deteriorating psychic health prevents her from saying goodbye to her son. The timing of the circular analepses suggests the archivist's mimetic efforts to reproduce the characters' psychic life submerged in the relentless of war, an archival project doomed to failure. The project to retell the story occasions a dynamic binding that attempts to fill the silences of "the wars" taking place in the unseen insides of the characters. This narrative structure marks the return of the subject through a remediation that acknowledges loss and insists on the subject's return to disrupt the myth of progress that obfuscates the violence of war.

The novel presents loss also through two types of failed identification. The first type provokes the paranoid imperative, since it involves ideological interpellation with national identity. Similarly to what Slavoj Žižek points out about Kafka's characters,[4] Findley's characters experience interpellation while failing to identify with the ideology. Mrs. Ross protests the church mass that sends the soldiers off to war: "What does it mean—*to kill your children*? Kill them and then . . . go in there and sing about it!" (Findley 54, emphasis in original). Even then, she still finds it difficult to keep herself from singing the hymns. Such material interpellation forces an alienated commitment to war, one that many men do not succeed in making, either by dying from bronchitis, committing suicide, or turning on one another.

The second type of failed identification potentiates a reparative function. Aptly, Terry Goldie's reading of *The Wars* links passive queerness with the enigma of the researcher/narrator/reader. Goldie describes Ross as the "homosexual bottom . . . [who] submits while destroying masculinity" (*Pink Snow* 164). Goldie then notes that the reader is called into being as a bottom through the second-person narration: "the 'you' becomes like the soldier who is told by his commander to volunteer. The second-person is the subjectivity who is not the subjectivity" (*Pink Snow* 164–65). While the second-person narration forces an identification with Ross as bottom, this narrative mode holds other implications for identification between the archivist, narrator, and reader.

The researcher's presence in the metanarrative becomes apparent only gradually because her character is conflated with the reader, who is called into being by the repeated signifier, "you": "You begin at the archives with photographs . . . Boxes and boxes of snapshots and portraits; maps and letters; cablegrams and clippings from the papers. All you have to do is sign them out and carry them across the room. Spread over table tops, a whole age lies in fragments underneath the lamps" (Findley 3). The signifier, "you" attempts to close the gap between the reader and the researcher/archivist/narrator. Initially, the archivist and the reader are distinguishable by the pronouns "she" and "you." Through the reading process, however, a question soon arises about how, to whom, and to what extent the narrative is being transmitted: "The archivist is gazing from her desk. She coughs. The boxes smell of yellow dust. You hold your breath. As the past moves under your fingertips, part of it crumbles. Other parts, you know you'll never find. This is what you have" (Findley 3–4). As "you" sort through, receive, remediate, *breathe in* crumbling fragments of Ross's story, despite the resistances of time, of lost histories, of the body, "you" look up and see the archivist cough, as if she absorbs the fragments simultaneously while she gazes (at "you") from her desk. Such seamless transference of archival materiality from one body to another occurs simultaneously with the recognition of lost "parts" that are never found.

Similar juxtapositions between metanarrative figures both interrupt and structure the telling of the story. The reader both receives the narrative and, paradoxically, collects its raw data, since "you" accumulate the fragments at the archive and interview Ross's last nurse, Marian Turner, and Juliet d'Orsey. Yet once Ross's story is complete, the last page of the novel finds that the archivist, like the reader, "closes her book" when it is "time to tell us all to go" (Findley 218). At the novel's beginning, when the details of Ross's death are still murky, a haunting image of the fire horse sets the tone. Let us return to this scene. An image sees Ross in the moment of his demise, and its description brings the reader's senses back into the archival space of the present:

> *Robert Ross comes riding straight towards the camera. His hat has fallen off. His hands are knotted to the reins. They bleed. The horse is black and wet and falling. Robert's lips are parted. He leans along the horse's neck. His eyes are blank. There is mud on his cheeks and forehead and his uniform is burning—long, bright tails of flame are streaming out behind him. He leaps through memory without a sound. The archivist sighs. Her eyes are lowered above some book. There is a strand of hair in her mouth. She brushes it aside and turns the page. You lay the fiery image back in your mind and let it rest. You know it will obtrude again and again until you find its meaning—here.* (5–6)

The text draws attention to its remediative form, as Ross comes straight toward the camera that apparently captures him. As those "*bright tails of flame*" hits "your" eyes, Ross "*leaps through memory without a sound*" and "*the archivist sighs.*" Ross's leap toward the camera, "through memory" resonates with Derrida's description of Eros as a "leap into the ethical" (*Without Alibi* 272) against the death drive, and the Eros of Ross's leap that is transferred onto the reader produces a "radical discontinuity" through the repetitions and displacements of narrative remediation. The archivist's bodily reactions become seamless with the researcher's reading process. In this moment, the story transmits metonymically to the archivist through the wandering perception of the character, "you," as the textual fragments come together in the archival space. The gloss of the text is located in the slippery identifications of the reader with the various metanarrative figures. Such misrecognition accentuates the absence in the wake of the lost and dead objects, objects that the narrative signifiers replace. What we are left with in a remediation of Ross's story is a series of signifiers that emphasize the gap between self and other.

A tension arises in the passage above between the haunting image and the text itself: the image will obtrude repeatedly until "you" "*find its meaning—here.*" The motif of the tension between picture and text repeats throughout the novel. Elsewhere, the narrator qualifies the scene of Ross's convoy, "There is no good picture of this except the one you can make in your mind" (Findley 75). The last lines of the novel show a photograph that "you" spot before leaving the archive: "*Robert and Rowena with Meg*: Rowena seated astride the pony—Robert holding her in place. On the back is written: 'Look! You can see our breath!' And you can" (Findley 218, emphasis in original). While Kröller marks the breath in the last photograph as the happiest period in life, Brydon reads it as a giveaway in the trenches. The variety in the potential projection of meaning onto the image of Robert's and Rowena's breath contradicts the wish fulfillment that insists that "you can" see. In this last line, two voices address the reader from two different moments in history through two different mediums. On the one hand, Ross draws attention to the visibility of their breath on the archival object itself: "Look! You can see our breath!" The narrator confirms our capacity to see: "And you can." The object that becomes prioritized is not the photograph itself but, through repetition, the "you" to whom lost voices reach out in affirmation, the "you" who can see the lost and fleeting objects through the resistances of time, space, and narrative frames. Unlike the *House of Leaves*, the perception of the image is narrated but never delivered, as no image interrupts the written text, only the reassurance that we can see.

Like the bird's song above the crater, the remediated photograph's impact follows a similar slow rhythm of unfolding that crescendos upon every archival intervention and transmission. The book closes with a quotation from 1943 by the Irish essayist and critic Nicholas Fagan. Let us return to this moment as well: "*the spaces between the perceiver and the thing perceived can . . . be closed with a shout of recognition. One form of a shout is a shot. Nothing so completely verifies our perception of a thing as our killing of it*" (Findley 218). An alternative form of a shout to the shot is the text. While the shot destroys the object by piercing through the material body and obliterating its sensory system, the text destroys the object by mourning its materiality and giving it new life through the signifier, one that can pierce through time and space.

V. Conclusion

Ross is a queer figure, but not necessarily because of his unconscious desire for homosexual submission. Ross's sexuality expresses itself in a conceptual failure that bonds him to his love objects, built on identifications that are subject to vanishing points. In others—the researcher, Taffler, Harris, his family members, his political enemies—he shares an unspeakable recognition that leads to absence and loss. The mediated relationships that confuse and enthrall him culminate in remorse about lost if imagined intimacies. Ross's character bequeaths this attachment of conceptual failure to the researcher and then the reader. The reader's failure involves the inability to invoke a referential presence in the face of so much loss, typified by slippages into narrative omniscience. Through analepses and failed identification, the narrative both sutures and widens the gap between Ross, the archivist, and the reader. Failed identification perpetuates attachments to objects, teaching us that phantasies are vital components of psychic life that we must continually mourn and build.

If creativity emerges out of the suspension of certainty about what is and is not real, then the narrative about Ross brings creative thinking to the critique of dominant discourse. The knowledge about what happens to Ross is necessarily constructed. Unlike the postmodernist readings that merely undermine the validity of official history, a psychoanalytic reading invests in phantasy in order to suggest that phantasies, while subject to failure and mourning, are necessary for the subject to remain engaged with potentiality inside totalized systems. Such engagement is the condition of possibility for new relational modes between self and other. *The Wars* differentiates the repetition of ideological practices that serve national and gendered identity from the repetition compulsion of literary narrative.

Both types of repetition operate through the drives, but the latter accepts failure and mourning as structuring components to object relations. The "wars" inside each character unbind not just each individual ego but also the cohesive identity of nation. Yet in the wake of this unbinding, the repetition compulsion to tell Ross's lost story revitalizes the reader's relationship to history.

CHAPTER FIVE

Reading the Queer Reparative in Kazuo Ishiguro's *Never Let Me Go*

> Doors are let into the walls at frequent intervals to suggest deceptively the way ahead and to force the visitor to go back upon the very same tracks that he has already followed in his wanderings.
>
> —Mark Danielewski, *House of Leaves*, 114

I. Introduction

The process of reading the novels of Chapters 2, 3, and 4 adopts a kind of circularity. Each text compels its reader toward what seems like the same conceptual paths, much like Freud's compulsion to rehash and revise the theory of sexuality. Reading as a compulsion to repeat is a drive, a process accompanied by frustration and the experience of getting conceptually entangled. As a particular expression of sexuality, the oscillation between the paranoid imperative and queer reparative facilitates a relationship to the vanishing points of thought to which the reader becomes attracted and into which all lines of intelligibility collapse. In the first stage, the death drive dominates: with omniscience and exposure as objects of readerly desire, paranoia is the mode of engagement, and frustration blends with enjoyment. The life drive pushes back in the second stage: reparation is the mode of engagement, constituting a recognition of the love object as whole, a recognition that necessitates letting go of phantasy and omniscience. The way this process unfolds in literary reading is not as simple as it sounds, especially given Freud's reminder that neither drive can really be absent at any stage of psychic life.

As the previous chapters explore, economic binding tends toward static calm and rational containment, while dynamic binding involves the difficult and ongoing work of an introjection into language. Both types are necessary for creative thinking. The death-driven phantasy of economic binding, of containment through reason, compels the reader to invest in certainties that render the text intelligible or consumable so as to maintain cathectic (homeo)stasis. At the same time, the death drive lures the reader toward dynamic unbinding, toward the silences that preclude satiation, perpetuate desire, and exacerbate the paranoid-schizoid position. The detour of the death drive is inextricably bound up with the life drive in the constant process of signification through the depressive position. Reading as drive, in other words, develops intimate and sexualized relationships with epistemological failure, and the rhythm of moving in and out of such failure renders the reader's relation to the text as organic, provisional, and vulnerable.

Given that "queer" signifies an aesthetic as opposed to an identity, I offer a queer reparative reading of Ishiguro's novel by acknowledging the necessity of social critique while emphasizing the fissures from which vulnerability, love, and a passion for signification and singularity thrive. "Queer" comes to signify the necessarily interdependent play between the drives, between a paranoid and reparative reading, between having *no* future and deferring such negation in the face of ineluctable dissolution. Unlike a blind optimism, which turns away from the fruitful potentials and necessary primacy of the negative, this practice of deferral develops an intimacy with the death drive that appreciates the sexualized experience of epistemological failure. Queer does not bring the deferral of a promising future to a close through a Symbolic death. Rather, like Ishiguro's characters, queerness proliferates in the deferral of the future in order to displace prescribed futures from discourses that claim the right to determine the status of marginalized subjects. If, according to Freud, the aim of life is death, then perhaps the aim of love is not only to die but also to live in one's own fashion.

In her early work on the death drive, Kristeva posits the abject as an unspeakable remainder excessive to the subject, a domain of *unintelligibility*. Yet she implicitly invokes the sublime in conceptualizing a domain where things as they are in themselves are distorted by the phenomenal world of things as they appear. Hal Foster clarifies that, "Kristeva views abjection as conservative, even defensive. 'Edged with the sublime,' the abject is used to test the limits of sublimation, but the task [of the artist] remains to sublimate the abject, to purify it" (Foster 181). If abjection is conservative and defensive, aligned with the Kantian purification of the sublime, then queer theory's romanticization of abjection as the "inarticulable surplus" (Edelman 9) begs for reconsideration, to which my notion of the queer reparative responds.

If, as I note in Chapter 1, Kafka laments the conditions of life as "not death, alas, but the eternal torments of dying" (*Diaries* 302), then I consider the manifestation of the opposite—not dying, thankfully, but death. The last chapter analyzes a narrative that focuses not on the death drive, but on death itself. Because death marks an entrance into mourning, my analysis arrives at a particular vocabulary that lends itself to a new reading strategy, which incorporates such Kleinian terms as remorse, gratitude, responsibility toward the other, recognition, and identification with good objects. If queer theory is to respond to a reparative turn, then how do those Kleinian qualities of reparation facilitate a new way of reading? The "queer reparative" acknowledges and incorporates the necessities of the paranoid processes against coherent intelligibility. The detours the previous chapters take into death-driven narratives, rife with phantasies of omniscience, mark the critical potency of paranoid processes. These processes, however, are prerequisites for the process of letting go—of our part-objects, of our phantasies, of epistemological certainty, of anticipatory defenses.

This chapter investigates the possibilities of reparation in light of *no future*. Simultaneously, the chapter translates a clinical agenda into an aesthetic one. In *Deaths of the Author*, Gallop differentiates two deaths. One death of the author refers to the theoretical slogan attributed to Barthes as a resistance to telos, to the myth of origin, and to patriarchal divinity as our ontological reassurance. The other death refers to the material passing of the author, which brings grief into the process of reading. Bravely, Gallop acknowledges in her reading of Barthes and Sedgwick that, after the author's theoretical and material death, her desire for the author persists. In this last chapter, I want to hold on to Gallop's return to the pleasure of a relation between reader and textual voice, especially in the wake of an ending as irrevocable as death.

Through Sedgwick's death, we can learn a way to return to the life drive. Unexpectedly, a chapter on pedagogy follows Sedgwick's critique of paranoid reading in her collection of essays, *Touching Feeling*, rather than a theoretical explication of reparative practices. Specifically, her book's last chapter is about pedagogy in relation to Buddhism and a reflection on death. Sedgwick works through her impending expiration by drawing a narrative of translation between Eastern and Western epistemologies. That

Sedgwick's turn to the reparative constitutes a return to death and to the failures of pedagogy is peculiar and telling. In her discussion of alternative pedagogy, that is, alternative relations to knowledge, Sedgwick offers a more hopeful view of the compulsion to repeat that has been at the crux of the totalitarian society and the death-driven subject.

The compulsion to repeat, the impetus behind the death drive, is what keeps Humbert fixated on the dead-because-abstracted love object, Lolita, and it is also what keeps the characters and reader trapped within the labyrinth of *House of Leaves*. In *The Wars*, repetition manifests in the narrative compulsion, and its intimacy with the failure to recuperate history offers insight into reparative mourning of the past. In each case, characters and readers struggle with the circularity that structures knowledge and ignorance. Sedgwick offers an alternative way for the thinking subject to regard or articulate circular logic:

> [In Western scholarship,] the hermeneutic tautology is always available as a fulcrum of delegitimization, yet never fully integrated in the practice of any disciplinary protocol . . . In Buddhist pedagogical thought, however, the apparent tautology of learning what you already know does not seem to constitute a paradox, nor an impasse, nor a scandal. It is not even a problem. If anything it is a deliberate and defining practice. (*Touching Feeling* 166–67)

Sedgwick reframes the epistemological failures in which the thinking subject unwittingly returns to the conceptual place she assumed to have "learned out of," or in which, according to Nietzschean critique, knowledge constitutes an eternal return of the same. Following Buddhist thought, Sedgwick differentiates knowing from realizing in the pedagogical process. The acquisition of information is different from its sinking in. She thinks in particular between the knowledge and realization of the experience that is always already foreign to psychic containment: death. Sedgwick identifies the gap between knowing and realizing as the *bardos*, the expansive space between diagnosis and death, particularly with respect to her cancer. The path the speaking subject must traverse in order to complete this kind of experiential repetition of death is a circular one. Circular learning constitutes both repetition and displacement.

Sedgwick's reflections on the displacements of circularity resonate with my discussion in previous chapters about the queer relation to the materiality of the text, which produces an effect not of immediacy but of indeterminable mediation that proliferates temporal ambiguities. As my reading of Bersani concludes, sexualized irony is embedded in the mimetic drive of literature, since something in the repetitive function of the artistic text sends readers to epistemological crisis. Sedgwick's revision of the repetition compulsion introduces another element to the pairing of irony and queer: learning. The tautology of circular logic, to "learn only versions of what you already know," parallels Horkheimer and Adorno's critique of Enlightenment's mastery. The kind of learning Sedgwick articulates in relation to Buddhist pedagogy resembles a pleasurable, if destructive, circularity that resonates with the sexualized reading practice for which this book calls. In this sense, learning constitutes not a phantasy of epistemological progress but a repetitive structure of epistemological crisis.

Kazuo Ishiguro's *Never Let Me Go* traces the *bardos* of the young students, a *bardos* between diagnosis and death that spans almost their entire lives. The narrator, Kathy H., recalls her youth, how she and her peers slowly realize that they are cloned from human citizens, and that their education is a program of containment, which "grows" and prepares them for a series of organ extractions to extend the lives of human beings proper. The emphasis of her story lies in the relationships she develops with other clones and their human teachers at her boarding school, Hailsham. In particular, she focuses on the lifelong love triangle between her and her two friends, Tommy and Ruth. The mundane episodes of their everyday lives take precedence over the horrific condition of their existence. Despite the main characters' efforts to be "good students," complying with the donation program as docilely as possible, they continue to fail necessarily, as knowledge of their deaths does not "sink in" throughout their lives until their final organ donation. Ishiguro's novel is about the difficult, almost impossible, task of learning how to die. Rachel Carroll provides a queer reading of the novel, identifying the clones in contradistinction to heteronormativity and focusing on the textual motifs of "passing": "Ishiguro's clones can be interpreted as embodying a heterosexual identity which is disempowered and marginalised by heteronormativity; as such they reveal the tensions and contradictions at work within and between heterosexuality as an institution and an identity" (60). Although Carroll reflects on Kathy's confusion about having a sexuality that is given no value (66), this reading reproduces a dangerous association between sexuality and reproductive futurism, an association that Edelman critiques in his discussion of the premise of P.D. James's dystopian novel, *The Children of Men.*

Carroll's focus lends itself too easily to a reading of social injustice, in which the investment of moral capital becomes conveniently unambiguous. My chapter's queer reading moves away from explicit manifestations of sexuality toward an interrogation of the relationship between unspeakability and a queer working through. In keeping with Bersani's claim, that art undoes the force of rational argument, this chapter pushes interpretive tendencies with *Never Let Me Go* beyond a social analysis of injustice against marginalized subjectivity, because something in this text is irreducibly sexual. As in the arguments of Chapter 2, which prioritizes Humbert's confession over his physical affair with Lolita, the current chapter explores how the sexual unfolds from the difficulty of thinking rather than diegetic events of sex acts. As in the previous chapters, I emphasize the movement of thought as a quieter but potent expression of sexuality in order to address the issues of futurity that are being taken up within the field of queer theory. I offer here a queer reparative reading of the characters' failure to secure a life of futurity.

II. Mourning Totality

The central question of my book asks how the self can live and love within totality, be it cultural, political, discursive, in a way that is independent but not sealed off from paranoia or negativity. Ishiguro's novel presents a lifelong educational process for a group of characters who, as clones, reflect Edelman's idea of "no future" because they have none. Or, because their lives are predestined, the idea of futurity becomes ironic as their futures become intelligible only when appropriated by aging human beings. The setting presents a totalitarian society whose scientific Enlightenment culminates in a "new barbarism" (Horkheimer and Adorno 25) in which Enlightened humans acquire the mythic power of divine creation in a dialectical collapse of Reason. The death drive reigns among the humans proper, whose incapacity to accept death leads them to project it onto the clones in order to abate a collective anxiety with a phantasy of life's static preservation. The clones' world is economically bound and predetermined. The clones become death-driven subjects only by virtue of their prescribed role as repositories for projection. Yet because of this prescribed role, they occupy a surprisingly privileged position to work through their lives in a process of mourning, while humans proper remain melancholic.

The protagonist, Kathy, immerses the reader gradually into the clones' world. The unnerving queerness about the quarantined children at Hailsham surfaces when Miss Lucy, one of their teachers, or "guardians," makes their purpose in life explicit: "You'll become adults, then before you're old, before you're even middle-aged, you'll start to donate your vital organs. That's what each of you was created to do . . . You were brought into this world for a purpose, and your futures, all of them, have been decided" (Ishiguro 73). The lives of the clones are structured around apprenticeship, mentorship, and institutional support, otherwise known as surveillance. Hailsham is a relatively privileged school within the context of the donation program, a place where the clones receive a humanist education and bear the title of "student." In young adulthood, when the clones begin to donate, they acquire the status, "donor," and receive care from other clones who have yet to begin their donations, named "carers." The fulfillment of their duties in donations marks their "completion," or their death.

The pedagogical circularity that Sedgwick elucidates appears in Ishiguro's novel, beginning with Miss Lucy's well-intentioned "diagnosis" of the clones that initiates their *bardos*. She premises her explication of their life's purpose with an indignant exposure of Hailsham's occlusion of reality: "you've been told and not told. You've been told, but none of you really understand, and I dare say, some people are quite happy to leave it that way. But I'm not. If you're going to have decent lives, then you've got to know and know properly" (Ishiguro 73). But Miss Lucy's pedagogical moment fails, since the knowledge of death does not "sink in" for the clones. Kathy does not tell the reader her immediate emotional reaction to Miss Lucy's statement, but she does suggest a subsequent process of omission in her memory:

> I think that was all she said. When I was discussing it with Ruth a few years ago at the centre in Dover, she claimed Miss Lucy had told us a lot more . . . but I'm pretty sure she didn't. Okay, she probably intended to when she began talking. But my guess is once she'd set off, once she'd seen the puzzled, uncomfortable faces in front of her, she realised the impossibility of completing what she'd started. (Ishiguro 74)

Indeed, Kathy's narrative stops short after Miss Lucy's speech, leaving the reader to speculate on student reactions. If the subject of Miss Lucy's teachings subsequently comes up, the general consensus among the students is to deflect any discussion: "Well so what? We already knew all that" (Ishiguro 74). The students' response to Miss Lucy's conventional pedagogy involves a negation, an affective short circuit by claiming to already know and cancelling out any meaning. While Kathy notes her classmates' negation of the truth, she is complicit in the very same resistance. Miss Lucy fails to educate and instill the reality principle in the students.

The image that the novel presents of a cloned, sterile child, whose future is cut short by the donations of her organs to "immortalized" populations, defamiliarizes the image of the innocent Child, which Edelman critiques as the imaginary benefactor of a better future (*No Future* 12), a benefactor already pregnant with generations to come. The students of Hailsham literalize the image of the Child: one of vulnerable innocence and manufactured meat, whose lifelong preparation results in a slow bodily dissection for the consumptive health of human beings proper. This narrative allegorizes, plays havoc with, Freud's theorization of the death drive in that "the aim of all life is death" (*BPP SE* 46). These clones also literalize the death drive. Yet if the purpose of these children culminates in mere organ farming, then the question arises of why they are subjected to a rigorous program of deferral and detours: acquiring education from an early age; living in Cottages upon graduation; and establishing carer-donor relationships at the end of their lives. In light of the reality of the clones' systematic destruction, an eerie effect—and an eerie affect—lingers around their upbringing. Could there be something more to their lives than their deaths?

Often, on a thematic level, dystopian texts represent the totality of an authoritarian society, or more generally a kind of closed system in which no "outside" exists. The process of reading, however, gets swept up in such a totality as well, so as to exemplify the closed system of signification itself. Ishiguro's novel introduces a strange relationship between subjects and the power network they inhabit. Critics and reviewers attribute the most disturbing aspect of the novel not to the clones' purpose as organ farms but to their generally complacent attitude toward their inhumane treatment. Wai-Chew Sim's chapter on *Never Let Me Go* in his book, *Globalization and Dislocation in the Novels of Kazuo Ishiguro*, notes that "The book is a milieu story because the fatalism of the clones registers an ideological set-up marked by widespread acceptance of neoliberal *doxa*, and the novel takes pains to emphasize that passivity because it seeks to encourage movement beyond that" (261).[1] The clones' complacency or, more critically, their complicity, is perhaps the novel's most perplexing and provocative enigma to which readers attach.

Theories of ideology are pertinent to thinking through the subject as always already proto-authoritarian. In his famous essay "Ideology and Ideological State Apparatuses," Louis Althusser theorizes the concept of ideology to answer the question of how the laborer is compelled to maintain his own subjection to the ruling class. Althusser claims that subjectivation is *totalizing*. Slavoj Žižek's *Sublime Object of Ideology* revises Althusser through a consideration of psychoanalysis and Kafka. His notion of cynicism enhances the totalization of Althusserian ideology. Cynicism refers to the subject's recognition and immediate disavowal of ideology's operation. In the Kafkaesque world, Žižek states that "we all know" that bureaucracy is not all-powerful, but behave *as if* it is (36). Ideology depends on the cynicism of its subjects in order to compound its momentum perpetually. Cynicism renders critique impotent.

Žižek's revision of Althusser underscores the inescapability of interpellation within an ideological totality. Kafka's narratives suggest the limitations of Althusser's claims because the former represent a gap between interpellation and the subject's identification. At the beginning of Kafka's narratives, Žižek argues, the protagonists are subject to an ideological interpellation, entering a social system of signs that alienates them, as they are hailed as "somebody who is *already presumed to know*" (Žižek 181, emphasis in original). The protagonists' struggle involves a search for something in their nonsensical world with which they can identify. Ideology does not necessarily constitute the completeness of the subject, and the subject is not merely an imaginary reflection of himself. Kafka enables Žižek to explore why the ideological subject is not an Imaginary whole but a perpetually inflected subject, fragmented by the discourse of the Other. Ideology becomes associated with a system of signs that produces the subject's intelligibility and yet sends his desire away from his own sense of self and toward the Other, thus sabotaging his ego. The unconscious, emerging only when the subject is introjected into language, accounts for the Kafkaesque gap that ruptures ideological closure, regardless of the subject's cynicism. Ideology, then, is not a false consciousness that escapes or occludes social reality; it is rather a social reality that produces a fantasy in order to escape the Real of one's desire (Žižek 45).

As Žižek observes, totalitarian societies operate on the status of the subject's identification. In *The Trial* (1915), Joseph K.'s efforts to prove his innocence is precisely what makes him always already guilty. The protagonist's journey, as well as the reader's, strives toward mastering the gap between interpellation and identification by reclaiming autonomy, a sense of self, within the system. This autonomy is contingent upon the self-assurance afforded by identification. The desire for identification explains the tendency for readers of *Never Let Me Go* to wonder why the students do not simply run away. Through either the reader's successful or frustrated identifications with the characters, this dystopian text shows that the desire for an autonomous self is precisely what forecloses the totality that traps them. The reader's and the protagonist's desires potentially become the sealing agent in the hermetically closed system.

Unlike Kafka's *The Trial*, George Orwell's *Nineteen Eighty-Four* (1949), or Atwood's *Handmaid's Tale* (1985), Ishiguro's *Never Let Me Go* represents a totalitarian society that does not appeal primarily to the reader's paranoid sensibilities. Readers are uncomfortable with how seamlessly the students integrate themselves into England's ideological framework, in which their identification with their subjection seem complete. Other dystopian texts, such as those of Kafka or Orwell, sustain the protagonist's refusal to identify with an interpellating authoritarian system. Hailsham subjects do not directly confront injustice, nor do they attempt to escape the country once outside the electrified fences of the school, nor, as Shameem Black remarks, do they seem overly troubled by their impending death (791). Placidly, they seem to accept their collective position as a locus into which England projects its death drive.[2] Mark Fisher argues that Hailsham serves as an Ideological State Apparatus (ISA) under the guise of compassionate plea for the humane treatment of the clones. Hailsham is nonetheless an appendage to the organ-farming program. In raising its subjects, Hailsham asserts its power productively over the students, not oppressively like other less progressive schools in this alternative England. Hailsham's productive relation to power is what makes the clones' identification with the system more successful, to such an extent that Kathy and her friends come to love the school that has prepared them so carefully for death.

The novel's focus on the central friendship triangle displaces the obvious yet dominant paranoid critique of dystopia. As Britzman notes about *Never Let Me Go*: "something in these pages cannot be read" ("Slow Reader" 307). Instead of concentrating on the social implications of the novel, this chapter turns toward the psychical. Insofar as the drama unfolds on the level of object relations, Ishiguro's is, more precisely, a very psychoanalytic novel. Kathy's aggression finds its target not in the system that subjugates her but in her best friend, Ruth. This simple, familiar displacement attenuates the enigma of the clones' passivity and gives pause as to why critics do not more readily identify with Kathy's everyday experience. The clones represent the death-driven subject that is unlike the fatalistic, nihilistic figure of twentieth-century fiction. Rather, the clones live with the reality of their death through the way they allow or inhibit their love for one another to develop. If death is their life's purpose, its referent to which all thoughts and actions must lead, then the clones incorporate the lessons of deconstruction into their lives unwittingly by deferring their ultimate referent on detours of signification that make up their constellations of object relations. *Never Let Me Go* demonstrates the ineluctable necessity of the death drive in ways that open up the life drive in acts of signification.

The novel emphasizes psychical life in part through its treatment of the uncanny and the latter's relationship to melancholia and mourning. In his essay on the uncanny, Freud raises the question of whether uncanny aesthetics arise through reader identification. He hypothesizes that the unsettling effect of the juxtaposition between the familiar and the strange emerges when the reader herself feels threatened by an obscure danger in a vicarious experience with the character ("Uncanny" 155–56). Ishiguro provides a unique literary moment when the students decide to play a "trick" on Madame, the central authority figure who evaluates their art for her "gallery." A group of students, including Kathy and Ruth, march out of the school entranceway and, with good timing, force Madame to walk through a line of them, shoulder-to-shoulder, silent and staring. Ishiguro presents the inverse process of realizing that one's self is uncanny for an other:

> Ruth had been right: Madame *was* afraid of us. But she was afraid of us in the same way someone might be afraid of spiders. We hadn't been ready for that. It had never occurred to us to wonder how *we* would feel, being seen like that, being the spiders . . . The first time you glimpse yourself through the eyes of a person like that, it's a cold moment. It's like walking past a mirror you've walked past every day of your life, and suddenly it shows you something else, something troubling and strange. (Ishiguro 32–33, emphasis in original)

Like *House of Leaves*, *Never Let Me Go* presents the queer uncanny through an identification with the uncanny "threat." Both novels present a sympathetic "Minotaur," that monster that becomes the seat of love and shame. The uncanny emerges in the novel in inverse form, an inversion that causes the reader to identify with a mimetic otherness that threatens domestic and normative society. Like *House of Leaves, Never Let Me Go* implicitly evokes inversion. An inverted experience of the uncanny in the latter resonates with Freud's notion of the homosexual as invert (*Three Essays* 2). In this context of the queer uncanny, "inversion" refers to an identification with, not the wrong sex, as Freud would argue, but rather the wrong aesthetic universe.

At this point, the reader does not know that the students are clones. Because Madame's fear is enigmatic, the reader identifies with the clones as queer agents, investing in the aesthetic trope of the uncanny without knowing why. Kathy's simile of the mirror marks an inverse experience of the mirror stage. Instead of encountering an image of a whole self, Kathy confronts a fractured self whose otherness is still unspeakable. The students' collective experience of self-estrangement is one of the first traumatic clues pointing to their difference. For Madame, the absent presence in the mimetic clones is precisely their humanity, their singularity, which dominant society withholds. After the unsettling incident with Madame, Kathy and her friends must negotiate the absent presence within themselves. They attempt a contradictory project: to accept the absence of their humanity while simultaneously learning to express themselves in Hailsham's art program.

The enigma that contradicts the clones' supposed complacency is that their cathectic attachments throughout their lives are strong. Such attachments follow an unconscious logic that bypasses their social injustice. The seat of the clones' sexuality is located not in the sex act, since their sexual activity is not subject to the same system of repression as that of humans proper. Rather, the force of the sexual that leads to psychic pain operates at the level of their "thinking through." Their sexuality unfolds through the difficult task of learning how to die while forming attachments that defy such a lesson. Repeatedly, the sexual brings the clones to epistemological failure as they build and rebuild their conceptual world on their journey to death.

Kathy's struggle to love and to express herself—very human endeavors—appeals to the absent presence of her humanity, which she cannot accept as always already lost. Perhaps her failure prompts readers to consider Ishiguro's novel as a narrative of melancholia. Melancholia is in the service of the death drive, as it involves a fixation on a lost object that perpetuates psychic stasis in the speaking subject. Drawing from Butler, Keith McDonald describes Kathy's incorporation of her friends into her narrative as melancholic. The novel does seem to present itself as a narrative of melancholia; however, the narrative subtly takes an unexpected turn as a process of mourning. According to Freud, the difference between mourning and melancholia hinges on the difference between a lost love object and a love object that was always absent ("Mourning and Melancholia" 164). The Hailsham students would arguably have a melancholic relation to real human life, which they must grieve not because theirs is cut short, but because, by virtue of their social function and status, clones were never granted human life in the first place.

In *The Shell and the Kernel*, Abraham and Torok revise Freud's distinction between mourning and melancholia by differentiating processes of introjection and incorporation. Whether the subject undergoes introjection or incorporation depends on her dialectical negotiations of reality and phantasy. Abraham and Torok define "reality" as either endogenous or exogenous excitation that "affects the psyche by inflicting a topographical shift on it," while "phantasy" denotes "all those representations, beliefs, or bodily states that gravitate toward . . . the preservation of the status quo" (Abraham and Torok 125). Phantasy becomes associated with a narcissistic stasis and occasions the object's incorporation, rendering the absent object unspeakable: "*words* fail to fill the subject's void and hence an imaginary thing is inserted into the mouth in their place" (Abraham and Torok 128–29, emphasis in original). Incorporation entails what Abraham and Torok would call a process of *demetaphorization*, as the object's linguistic representation becomes impossible. The subject "swallows" the unspeakable love object and preserves its ideal state in a psychic tomb, enabling the subject to deny the object's loss. Introjection, on the other hand, describes a process of mourning that is related to the development of language and a "topographical shift" in the ego (Abraham and Torok 125). Introjection begins when the infant experiences an empty mouth simultaneously with the mother's presence. The child's libidinal attachment transfers from breast to words, as the oral pleasures of the moving tongue and the ejection of sound correspond with responses from external reality. Abraham and Torok claim that, as the introjection of the missing breast, language facilitates a healthy development of verbal relationships within the social sphere: "Introjecting a desire, a pain, a situation means channeling them through language into a communion of empty mouths" (Abraham and Torok 128). Introjection enables the mediation of the unconscious in object relations as the ego adjusts to reality accordingly. Through language, the "communion of empty mouths" mourns collectively.[3] In this view of society, the anticipation of how to fill the mouth is less on the side of paranoia than on the side of eroticism, in body and in word.

Fictions about social totality maintain readerly engagement through a melancholic identification with a pre-authoritarian humanity. The method of critique is the best resource readers have to recuperate such a prelapsarian ideal. Given this distinction between mourning and melancholia, however, Kathy's narrative is less a symptom of melancholia than a painful project of mourning. Related to but different from melancholia, the more pleasurable term, nostalgia, mutes the novel's alienating totalitarianism and foregrounds something other than death-driven subjectivity. As opposed to melancholia, nostalgia evokes a memory of a past era, according to the *OED*. In other words, nostalgia recognizes the past as such, as something the subject no longer possesses, albeit emerging as a defense.

Ishiguro defamiliarizes the science fiction plot through a pastoral, largely rural, setting: the secluded boarding school, the Cottages, the abandoned boat beyond the swamp, and the cattle field. Ishiguro's version of the pastoral is hardly idyllic, however, since all of these settings, largely inhospitable, evoke an overwhelming sense of abandonment, neglect, and of a world lost to time. Kathy's confession even takes place in the late 1990s, almost two decades prior to the novel's publication. Whereas the *Handmaid's Tale* and *Nineteen Eighty-Four* posit a wish for the "outside" beyond the bounds of the city, thus eliciting the reader's desire for freedom, Ishigiuro's novel integrates nonurban settings into political totality as a given. If the reader finds anything uncanny in the text, it would be less the clones than the representation of an alternative English countryside. As Earl Ingersoll notes about the author's work as a whole, "Ishiguro is attracted to the comforting deceptions of the familiar, a familiarity that can turn itself inside out to reveal a radical otherness" (42). This setting produces a sense of the familiar (*heimlich*) and unfamiliar (*unheimlich*) through a science fiction conflict that arises out of a heavily nostalgic setting.

Perhaps because of her nostalgia, Kathy warns us immediately that she is an unreliable narrator. The impossibility of finding Hailsham again, she implies, is due to its existence as a memory. She admits: "This was all a long time ago so I might have some of it wrong" (Ishiguro 12). Kathy's temptation to return to Hailsham, which she does through her narrative, also resonates with other returns in the novel. She returns to both Ruth and Tommy at the end of their lives. Also, at the novel's climax, both Tommy and Kathy return to the mundane insight they learned as "students," that their aim in life is death, a death that is now upon them. The return Kathy enacts in her narrative is not a melancholic phantasy of Hailsham, but rather, akin to Sedgwick's pedagogical circularity, a reparative return to the relationships Kathy must mourn and let go of through her act of narration.

For the melancholic subject, time becomes static because her psychic crypt attempts to immortalize her idealized lost object so that it cannot be subject to change. In *Never Let Me Go*, however, the passing of time figures heavily in Kathy's consciousness against the nostalgic backdrop of a timeless England. The novel's structure revolves around several proleptic and analeptic anachronies, which Genette in *Narrative Discourse* defines as a disruption of the story's chronological events by the order of the narrative (40).[4] Kathy's prolepses at times contradict her revisionary analepses. The anachronies both facilitate and disorient identification with Kathy. Kathy introduces herself in her opening remarks: "My name is Kathy H. I'm thirty-one years old, and I've been a carer now for over eleven years. That sounds long enough, I know, but actually they want me to go on for another eight months, until the end of this year. That'll make it almost exactly twelve years" (Ishiguro 3). From this seemingly standard introduction, the reader receives a sense of temporal punctuation. Having a mere initial for a last name, Kathy's public identity is already precarious. Ultimately, we will come to know her on a personal level, but her individuality is, for a reason the reader learns slowly, compromised within her social realm. Indeed, the reader discovers that her public life as a carer, however prominent, remains relegated to the shadowy margins of England. Immediately, Kathy shares with her reader her strong sense of time. Kathy assumes that the reader will agree, a twelve-year career is long, but she does not clarify why. The reader has a sense that Kathy is interpellated as a certain kind of subject, since the disembodied authority she introduces off-handedly as "they" seems to be in charge of her destiny. Tension arises between an unexpected length of experience and, as the reader shall discover, a short life. In any case, the novel's beginning implies a strong sense of an ending.

Despite Kathy's keen awareness of time, her narrative structure does resemble a repetitive circularity. If, for the melancholic, time becomes static, then the compulsion to repeat dominates her psychic life; however, Kathy's prose, as well as her self-conscious framing of her narrative, is a work of mourning. Two similar passages frame the novel. Within the first pages, Kathy invokes her old school, Hailsham, a lost object that she can never retrieve:

> Driving around the country now, I still see things that will remind me of Hailsham. I might pass the corner of a misty field, or see part of a large house in the distance as I come down the side of a valley, even a particular arrangement of poplar trees up on a hillside, and I'll think: 'Maybe that's it! I've found it! This actually *is* Hailsham!' Then I see it's impossible and I go on driving, my thoughts drifting on elsewhere. (Ishiguro 5–6, emphasis in original)

Within the last pages, Kathy repeats herself, alluding to similar images of the first love object that is lost in a rural sea:

> Mind you, though I say I never go looking for Hailsham, what I find is that sometimes, when I'm driving around, I suddenly think I've spotted some bit of it. I see a sports pavilion in the distance and I'm sure it's ours. Or a row of poplars on the horizon next to a big woolly oak, and I'm convinced for a second I'm coming up to the South Playing Field from the other side . . . These moments hit me when I'm least expecting it, when I'm driving with something else entirely in my mind. So maybe at some level, I *am* on the lookout for Hailsham. (Ishiguro 262, emphasis in original)

The two passages above present a number of contradictions. Hailsham is singular in Kathy's mind, but the mundanity of England's countryside—a row of poplars, a misty field—can trigger Kathy's misrecognition. She accompanies her misrecognition with a degree of negation: she claims not to be searching for Hailsham when she sees it everywhere; or she sees it everywhere when she realizes that a return is impossible. Her ghostly sighting of Hailsham opens and closes the novel. The school is a site of their education, their interpellation into organ-donating subjection; but it is also a site where phantasies proliferate, phantasies that unexpectedly disrupt their interpellation. Kathy's repetition compulsion, her return to her love objects, belies both nostalgia and resistance to it. The phantasy of return repeatedly stops short through Kathy's acknowledgment of reality, the reality of her death, of her friends' deaths, and of Hailsham's failure to humanize its subjects within England's social structures.

The two passages are characteristic of Kathy's style, as she often digresses into meandering trains of thought to emphasize a repeated structure of reversal, or negation.[5] Kathy often contradicts herself, either through disavowal, admittance, or a moment of self-denigration in order to convey a single point. The structure of her narrative is based on a series of circular deferrals. As Leona Toker and Daniel Chertoff remark, "This looping narrative movement forces the reader to keep reconsidering earlier sections retrospectively even as new proleptic touches create new informational gaps" (169). Like *House of Leaves*, the narrative in *Never Let Me Go* evokes a spiral structure. Yet the affective resonances do not exacerbate terrifying epistemological anxieties of getting lost through an eternal return of the same. Kathy's repetitive revisionary style revolves around the negation in the title, "Never Let Me Go." Her circular structure resonates with Sedgwick's pedagogical project of learning how to die, to let go of life through its very affirmation. Although the reader bears witness to

Kathy's stubborn attachments to Hailsham, the process of her narrative becomes itself the difficult work of letting go. If the reader considers the imperative statement behind the negation, Kathy's narrative implies the desire, "Let Me Go," as she prepares for her own death and as she lets go of her own objects by introjecting them into language. Her love objects transform into signifiers.

III. Childhood: Objects and Phantasy

At stake in the distinction between melancholia and mourning is the psychical difference between phantasy and reality. Conventionally speaking, phantasy maintains egoic stasis and promotes pleasure, while reality realigns the ego with its surrounding environment, causing a painful change within the ego's structure that is necessary for survival. This difference is contingent on the speaking subject's adaptive relationship to the pleasure principle. In his essay "Two Principles," Freud proposes that motor discharge is in the service of the pleasure principle. The reality principle sublimates motor discharge into thought processes. This sublimation enables the subject to tolerate an increase of tension when interacting with objects in the outside world, while phantasy and daydreaming serve to maintain the static integrity of the ego. Freud states: "Just as the pleasure-ego can do nothing but *wish*, pursue pleasure and avoid unpleasure, so the reality-ego has no other task than to strive for what is *useful* and to protect itself from what is harmful" (417, emphases in original). The effort to maximize pleasure is based on an effort to maintain a sense of constancy, one that begins with biological survival and that extends to epistemological stability.

Freud's two principles can shed some light on the pedagogical process. He locates conventional education in the register of the reality principle: "*Education* can without question be described as an impetus to overcoming the pleasure principle and replacing it with the reality principle; thus it assists the process of development undergone by the ego" ("Two Principles" 418). Education then attempts to facilitate the child's development by transforming her mode of expression from motor activity, or acting out, into the detour of thinking. But he also argues that, "by taking over from the pleasure principle, the reality principle is really just safeguarding it, not deposing it. A momentary pleasure with uncertain consequences is given up, but only in order to obtain, by the new approach, a more secure pleasure later on" ("Two Principles" 417–18). A slippage occurs, then, in Freud's language. On the one hand, he asserts that the reality principle necessarily "replaces" the pleasure principle in the process of development; on the other hand, he expounds that the reality principle serves to safeguard the pleasure principle as opposed to superseding it. Freud implies, of course, that the two principles are not exclusive of one another, that both are the mind's poles, and that the subject can obey them contemporaneously. But he also suggests that, as a disciplinary institution, conventional education may repudiate the pleasure principle in a prioritization of the reality principle.[6]

Given the dialectical conditions of the two principles, Hailsham could be conceived as an education for the clones' sexuality, an education that allows them to negotiate between syncopating *useful* activity under the reality principle with the unavoidable drive to wish, in this case, to wish for the impossible attainment of human viability. In doing so, Hailsham displaces its mimesis of conventional education, thus undermining its own static reality principle as an institutional structure that serves to impart a fixed body of knowledge while administering socialization. Subjection would be much easier for the clones if only they could slough off this drive to wish. The wish manifests the relentlessness of the sexual. Because the drives of life and death push on forever, throughout their lives, the clones must not only think through but also think *with* the wish.

While Kathy's narrative is not melancholic because it marks a painful realization of her reality, phantasy and the pleasure principle have a place in the creative life of the students. Hailsham is a strange institution, because it attempts to prepare its students for their reality of instrumental death while also developing their humanity through an emphasis on the arts. The teachers at Hailsham promote their creativity in a pedagogical structure. Miss Lucy, the renegade teacher, stands for the political desire to instill a clear sense of the social reality in the students, their subjection to bodily exploitation, and the possibility of revolt. By encouraging a sense of phantasy that defers or obscures their reality, the Hailsham project seems to be complicit in producing passive, compliant subjects. Hailsham trains the students to become invested in "useless" activity such as art making, writing, and participating in a capitalist microcosm of Exchanges and Sales, in which objects are created, bartered for, traded, and bought with token currency. As Rebecca Walkowitz also observes, the novel offers us "a collection of bad copies and eccentric interpretations" (224). The clones, copies themselves, lack "intellectual complexity, exceptional artistic abilities, and or even ideas of love that depart from sitcom banality" (Walkowitz 225). The students become interpellated into a simulacral life, one that resembles familiar institutions of education, commodity exchange and, eventually, psychical and medical care. As a product of a cultural repetition compulsion, how can Kathy's world be anything but a melancholic phantasy? Ishiguro's novel begs for a reevaluation of the relation between phantasy and reality and their intersection with melancholia and mourning.

McDonald points out the "poverty of experience" (78) that structures the lives of Hailsham students. Indeed, the students seem completely ignorant of their lack of privilege relative to contemporary bourgeois life. They also seem ignorant of the mimetic nature of the Sales and Exchanges, both of which reproduce the economic basis of identity in the world at large. McDonald critiques the condition that Kathy describes: "how you were regarded at Hailsham, how much you were liked and respected, had to do with how good you were at 'creating'" (Ishiguro 15). In this case, artistic creation serves a system of exchange among the students and, thus, heavily mediates social status and identity.

McDonald misses what the text implies about object relations. Despite their "poverty of experience," the students' relationship to their objects is reminiscent of the child's world. The students' sensitivities to discarded-turned-love objects resonate with their intuitive relationship to their own bodies, which will eventually be dissected, cannibalized, exchanged, and discarded. Through displacement, their "experientially impoverished" world thus becomes heavily cathected with attachments that they find difficult to let go of. Kathy reflects on the irrationality of their excitement at the Sales: "There'd be nothing remotely special and we'd spend our tokens just renewing stuff that was wearing out or broken with more of the same. But the point was, I suppose, we'd all of us in the past found something at a Sale, something that had become special: a jacket, a watch, a pair of craft scissors never used but kept proudly next to a bed" (Ishiguro 38). Here, Kathy's dialectical style of negation and admission manifests as an oscillation between the recognition of reality and the recollection of a phantasy. Phantasy reigns at Hailsham and is the basis of the interpersonal relationships. The young clones can show care toward one another only through the mediation of their collective phantasies that develop from their attachment to objects, from Tommy's polo shirt to a pair of scissors.

Objects—literal mundane objects that are at any given point created, gifted, bought, discarded, and treasured—play a surprisingly large role as conduits for attachment and destruction among the students. Often, Ruth uses objects to extend her own phantasies of omniscience. The pencil case episode—among the many episodes at Hailsham—is a non-cardinal function, in that it is unnecessary for plot development; but as a catalyst, it helps establish the dynamic between Ruth and Kathy.[7] When Kathy notices Ruth with a bright new pencil case, Ruth insinuates that it is a gift from one of their favorite guardians, Miss Geraldine. Ruth becomes the object of fascination, speculation, and envy for the girls in the classroom, while Kathy makes subsequent plans to expose Ruth's manipulative deception. Kathy investigates the list of purchases at the Sales and confirms the origin of the pencil case. When she hints to Ruth that she knows the truth, she regrets her actions:

> Now I saw how upset Ruth was; how for once she was at a complete loss for words, and had turned away on the verge of tears. And suddenly my behaviour seemed to me utterly baffling. All this effort, all this planning, just to upset my dearest friend. So what if she'd fibbed a little about her pencil case? Didn't we all dream from time to time about one guardian or other bending the rules and doing something special for us? A spontaneous hug, a secret letter, a gift? (Ishiguro 55)

Initially, Kathy protests the pencil case as a symbol of Ruth's social superiority, specifically against Ruth's twofold wish: for the capacity to attain intimacy with admired elders, and for the omniscient power to control the desires of her peers. For Ruth, the pencil case replaces her "secret guard" phantasy, in which the most trusted friends of her choice were honored with the duty to protect Miss Geraldine from a conspiratorial abduction into the woods beyond the Hailsham borders. Ruth's new object is an empty and decorative vessel used to house writing utensils: an empty signifier. The pencil case is a signifier of Ruth's perpetuating phantasy, an empty signifier that Kathy exposes as such. Despite Ruth's wish, the pencil case holds no meaning in reality.

Full of regret, Kathy veers away from subjecting Ruth to public exposure and shame. Kathy then obsesses over reparation, to recognize somehow Ruth's rights to her private phantasies. When Midge asks Ruth where her beautiful pencil case went and where it came from, Kathy saves her: "We can't say where it came from . . . a *big* mystery" (Ishiguro 58, emphasis in original). Exposed as an empty signifier, the pencil case becomes a secret that bonds Kathy and Ruth. Throughout the novel, the students experience a central paradox repeatedly, in which a shared encounter with emptiness behind various signifiers negates the absence of meaning. The gratitude that Ruth feels for Kathy drives her desire to reciprocate, again through the mediation of material objects. Kathy observes Ruth's eagerness and ruminates: "It was a good feeling, and I remember even thinking once or twice how it would be better if she didn't get a chance for ages, just so the good feeling between us could go on and on" (Ishiguro 58). The good feeling Kathy identifies in herself, especially because she does not want it to end, can very well be a source of major anxiety in Ruth. Here, the culture of exchange that builds a difficult friendship is based on an economy of power, debt, and envy, as well as a vulnerable reciprocity of gratitude.

Kathy's necessary aggression is much subtler than Ruth's because it is interwoven with the love that unfolds between them. Soon after the pencil case episode, Kathy loses her tape that plays the novel's eponymous song, Judy Bridgewater's "Never Let Me Go." She tries to hide her panic because she feels her attachment to the tape to be a secret: "Maybe all of us at Hailsham had little secrets like that—little private nooks created out of thin air where we could go off alone with our fears and longings" (Ishiguro 67–68). The tape functions as a prompt for Kathy's phantasy about bearing and caring for a child, a phantasy that she dramatizes in play when she is alone. Ruth gives her another tape, having failed to find the original. Ruth's gesture suggests to Kathy a knowledge not of the substantial meaning behind the original tape, but only an acknowledgment that the tape was substantial for Kathy. The continued reciprocity of empty signifiers builds the relationship between them: "Then again, almost immediately, I saw . . . how to Ruth, who didn't know the first thing about music, this tape might easily make up for the one I'd lost. And suddenly I felt the disappointment ebbing away and being replaced by a real happiness" (Ishiguro 69). Again, the tape functions as an exchangeable signifier, a copy void of ontological substance. The importance of the tape's contents diminishes, allowing Kathy to let go of her lost object.

For Kathy, an intimacy with Ruth depends on a mutual identification fueled by mediated communication with material objects. At first, the universe of discarded materials through which the students interact parallels their unconscious knowledge about the scientific exchangeability of bodily contents. But the relationships the students are able to elaborate in their constellation of objects *as signifiers*—not as literal components that are content- and function-specific like organs—differentiate theirs from a world of brutal instrumentality. As Anne Whitehead notes, "Kathy's story seeks to reclaim this 'rubbish,' to assert that these lives cannot simply be disposed of as so much matter or refuse, but claim their own value, have their own dignity and worth" (Whitehead 80). This differentiation is what makes the students' art important: not art's utilitarian potential of ontological evidence, but art as a mode of signification that re-imagines the project to care for and mourn the other and the self. Ishiguro uses the word "carer" as opposed to "caregiver" or "caretaker." According to the *OED*, earlier definitions of care include mental suffering, sorrow, grief, trouble; utterance of sorrow; lamentation, mourning. These definitions evoke the Latin infinitive of the verb *careo*: *carere,* which means to be without, free from; need, miss.[8] In *Never Let Me Go*, care and love are intimately linked to mourning and loss.

Kathy's aggression integrates itself in the structure of her narrative, not only in her desire to maintain the moral upper hand with Ruth, but also in her competition with Ruth for Tommy's affection. The exchange of objects that establishes the intimacy between Ruth and Kathy can serve as a complex narrative deferral, which sets up, ultimately, Kathy's bond with Tommy and the prospect of donation deferrals that dominates the last half of the book. The episodic structure of Kathy's narrative, which Walkowitz describes as aleatory in its vague diction (224), occludes and carries out an unconscious wish: the stories about a growing intimacy with Ruth become mere context for the reader to understand the intimacy between Kathy and Tommy.

In Part II, a small group trip to Norfolk, the "lost corner," revolves around Ruth in her search for her "possible," the original subject from whom she had been cloned and whom Chrissy and Rodney presumably found. While Ruth spends time with the older couple, Tommy and Kathy spend an hour alone together. Tommy admits to Kathy his efforts to find her lost tape years ago: "I really wanted to find it for you. And when it looked in the end like it wasn't going to turn up, I just said to myself, one day I'll go to Norfolk and I'll find it there for her" (Ishiguro 155). This moment is one of the two in the novel's second section in which Tommy and Kathy spend time alone together, and the only one filled with absolute pleasure for Kathy. (The other time is when Tommy questions Kathy's perusal of pornography. Although Kathy finds comfort in Tommy's concern for her, the silence between them at this later moment contributes to their alienation.) The expansive space of a collective search repeats itself, recalling the first time at Hailsham when Ruth rallies all the students together to find Kathy's lost tape. Like the first time, when Kathy expresses the desire for the good feeling with Ruth to last forever, Kathy values the search over the object itself in her moment with Tommy: "When I think of that moment now, standing with Tommy in the little side-street about to begin our search, I feel a warmth welling up through me. Everything suddenly felt perfect: an hour set aside, stretching ahead of us, and there wasn't a better way to spend it" (Ishiguro 157). When Kathy finds another replacement tape, this time with the same content as the lost object, both she and Tommy are disappointed. She admits, "For a second, it even felt like a mistake. The tape had been the perfect excuse for all this fun, and now it had turned up, we'd have to stop" (Ishiguro 157). Both Tommy and Kathy have ambivalent feelings about finding "Never Let Me Go" again in Norfolk—Tommy for having not been the one to find the tape, and Kathy for having found it at all. In this case, desire for the object leads not to the satiation of desire but the mourning of the object.

Both tapes from Ruth and Tommy end up among Kathy's most precious possessions. Walkowitz argues that "In the novel, the preciousness of both tapes is an effect of the social experience—we might say the network—forged by the tapes' circulation" (Walkowitz 228). This claim reinforces Walkowitz's argument that Ishiguro detaches myths of originality or authenticity from the value of art and the human being; however, I would add that the "new contextualization" of circulating objects acquires affective weight only through passions to phantasize and to signify. Upon both discoveries of cassette replacements, Kathy catches herself in an ambivalent reaction. Here, she notes "for a second" it feels like a mistake; when Ruth gives Kathy a replacement, Kathy notes, "Then again, almost immediately," happiness replaces her initial disappointment. The end of each search jars Kathy. The "perfect" feelings or good feelings between Kathy and her best friends occur not in moments when desires are consummated or fulfilled, but in the infinite potential of a search, a shared effort and mutual desire to indulge a secret moment that promises to make up for an irreplaceable loss. The pleasure is located in deferral. If the cassette tapes function as signifiers that bond two people, then the elaborate search for these signifiers functions metaphorically as a mutual endeavor to articulate the relationship that unfolds among the three characters. The "perfect" feeling Kathy repeatedly identifies emerges through the infinite promise of the search for words. When each character finds objects for expression—when Ruth and Tommy each help Kathy replace her lost love object—Kathy finds it difficult to let go of, not the original cassette, but the moment of promise: hence Kathy's need, in her fleeting ambivalence, to mourn the searches in order to recognize the mediated intimacy that grows between them as a result of the signifier's discovery. Kathy's feeling that everything is perfect is a synechdoche of their whole lives: "an hour set aside," paradoxically "stretching ahead" of them. The time the three characters spend together is time aside from their life's purpose, stolen time that is always too short; simultaneously, however, these stolen moments impart an elasticity to time that allows it to fold, expand, contract, even break, through Kathy's narrative.

The pencil case episode's initial status as a non-cardinal function—its role as a narrative unit that is unnecessary to plot development—becomes questionable, due to its role in building an economy of exchange in which the students compensate for each other's lost objects and secret desires. According to Kathy's narrative structure, this economy builds cumulatively and culminates in the attempt at an official donation deferral by two lovers. Kathy's aggression remains incredibly subtle because the episodes of loss and exchange are drawn out, intermingled, subject to narrative jumps and returns, and in themselves elaborate a caring affection between Kathy and Ruth that complicates, even overshadows, their rivalry. This aggression is what makes Kathy an unreliable narrator, because it counters her self-construction as a purely compassionate and patient subject. Her self-image as a reliable, mature "carer," always capable of prioritizing others over herself, is precisely what inhibits identification from readers and critics. Such scholars as Walkowitz are impatient with Kathy's tone, passivity, vagueness, and moral righteousness. Black echoes a reviewer by calling Kathy "a speaking clock" (Black 801) whose simulacral surface obscures more ambiguous characteristics. Yet her subtle aggression provides insight into the transferential complexities of human relations in the face of punctuated life.

IV. Adolescence: Phantasy Theories

The first half of Ishiguro's novel establishes the bond among the three characters with quite literal "object" relations. Their object relations enrich a world of phantasy that serves as a screen for them to defer and perhaps process their impending fates. As they grow older, the three characters begin to depend also on theories that attempt to make sense of their world. While an economy of material objects dominates their time at Hailsham, one of conceptual and speculative objects dominates their time at the Cottages. At Hailsham, the social value of each student depends on the art objects they create. Social status at the Cottages is contingent upon conceptual objects: "In those early months, we'd somehow developed this idea that how well you were settling in at the Cottages—how well you were *coping*—was somehow reflected by how many books you'd read" (Ishiguro 112, emphasis in original). For example, Ruth continues to master the social code aggressively by giving away plots to books. The clones' failure to mimic normal adulthood is due partly to their lack of access to cultural memory and collective practices of the world at large. Under the pretense that the Cottages serve as a site for the students to write their final essay assignment, the clones are waiting for their bodies to mature so that they can begin training to become carers, then donors. The Cottages, then, serve as a site to imagine, to think, to play—precisely to do nothing—while also encouraging the students to perceive Hailsham as the place of childhood. It is a transitional space from a kind of kindergarten to a theoretical life.

In *After-Education*, Britzman challenges the distinction between theory and kindergarten. She explores "theory kindergarten" as a *not quite* experience. She states that theory kindergarten refers "to the difficulty of thinking: the ways the ego structures both itself and the object, and how even if the ego understands the known in terms of its conventions, rules, and traditions, for instance, the ego is not yet prepared to encounter its own thoughts" (*After-Education* 125–26). Theory (kindergarten) attempts to bring knowledge to consciousness. Because much of the subject's knowledge remains latent, the subject encounters difficulty through theory because latent knowledge constantly threatens to dismantle theory's coherence. Britzman questions when theory kindergarten ends and when it begins, suggesting that "theory" and "kindergarten" are inextricably linked. She borrows from Sedgwick's characterization of ignorance as not an absence of knowledge but knowledge's "constitutive and organizing modality" (*After-Education* 126). We have already seen the agency of ignorance in the reading of *House of Leaves* in Chapter 3 and of Felman's *Jacques Lacan and the Adventures of Insight* in Chapter 2. Stemming from the unconscious, ignorance marks the resistance to interpretation that is inassimilable to consciousness. The opposition between education and ignorance becomes undermined. Theory attempts to compensate for the conditions of knowledge that bind it to ignorance. In doing so, however, theory reinforces such a bind. According to Britzman, theory anticipates the object, thereby working as an ego defense, warding off uncertainty or surprise, splitting good and bad objects, integrating anxiety into knowledge and maintaining an "illusion of omnipotence" (*After-Education* 126). Theory holds an ambiguous position, then, between phantasy and reality, stasis and adaptable change. The subject's epistemophilic instinct, her insatiable desire to know, is always cut short by epistemophilic certainty. She desires that which both undoes what she has already made coherent and undermines the illusory prospect of omnipotence. On the one hand, the subject depends on theory to articulate conscious knowledge and to render it applicable to life. On the other hand, the way in which theory necessarily forecloses latent knowledge through its anticipatory stance leads to a subject who is split from the part of herself she is not yet prepared to know. Theory affords a phantasy of certainty that is subject to failure. Metaphorically, theory presents the planar lines that produce a perceptually pleasing sense of depth but are always subject to a vanishing point, where thought unravels for the subject who submits to the allure of phantasy.

Britzman brings Sedgwick and Klein into dialogue in order to articulate the destructive and reparative potentials in theory. She claims that theory must face its own phantasies of love and hate in order for the subject to transition from the paranoid-schizoid position to the depressive position. Whereas the pleasure principle promotes stasis in the ego, reaffirming the conviction of conscious knowledge and protecting the ego from its own anxieties, the reality principle constitutes the moment of educational dialogue, where thinking with the other transforms the ego in a reparative way once the ego divests from its sadistic, epistemophilic instinct to possess and master the object. As Freud reminds his reader, the reality principle safeguards the pleasure principle; this point describes the ways in which educational dialogue and transformation enable love and work, which are in the service of pleasure. Britzman argues: "Kindergarten, after all, also is a fun fair of experiments, thrilling surprises, misrecognitions, near-missed encounters, spectacular mishearings, and phantasies that lead, in the strangest directions, our games of 'let's pretend.' This spirit of bravely or even brazenly entering new kinds of symbolization, of allowing phantasy to become more generous and surprising, are its elaborate and illusive stakes" (*After-Education* 127–28). Theory kindergarten, then, refers to both free play and difficult thinking.

Ishiguro's novel offers a world in which theory and phantasy become indistinguishable as the clones attempt to make their lives bearable and consistent. The time at the Cottages marks a speculative stage that phantasizes their origins and futures. The students would still source their phantasies from objects. Ruth's phantasy about working at an office like her "possible" develops from a withered magazine advertisement she spots on the frosty ground. Kathy's anxieties about the source and intensity of her sex drive lead her to peruse pornographic magazines in search of her "possible." When Tommy catches her breezing through porn, he naïvely explains the sexual operations of scopic drive: "Well, if it's for kicks, you don't do it like that. You've got to look at the pictures much more carefully. It doesn't really work if you go that fast" (Ishiguro 124). Tommy's theory about the deferrals leads to a return to drawing, as if the creation of objects would render his theory true. The clumsy ways in which they attempt an entrance into speculative life indicates their failure to leave their "kindergarten," their lives defined by the institutional structures of Hailsham. Keeping their theoretical objects dear and private, Kathy, Tommy, and Ruth become increasingly vulnerable to the impending necessity of letting each other go.

The alienation between Kathy and Ruth intensifies as the former attempts to maintain the friendship they shared but which the latter seems to want to change. Kathy resists moving on from Hailsham, and she potentially projects her resistance onto all of the Hailsham students: "that picture of us on that first day, huddled together in front of the farmhouse, isn't so incongruous after all . . . Because somewhere underneath, a part of us stayed like that: fearful of the world around us, and . . . unable quite to let each other go" (Ishiguro 109). Kathy has difficulty retaining the image of vulnerability that homogenizes the Hailsham students. Increasingly, her reluctance to let go becomes a lonely and singular experience. She remains keen to write her final essay, even though no final evaluation would follow, intuiting that its gravity expresses the bond among the Hailsham students. When Ruth finds a church in order to be alone and read, Kathy "hadn't at first been too keen on this development, remembering how the previous summer [they'd] all sat around together in the grass right outside the Cottages" (Ishiguro 176). The reader's identification with the narrator may encourage less sympathy for Ruth; but Kathy could also seem emotionally regressive. In different ways, both characters struggle between moving toward their fates and wanting things to stay the same. Kathy's struggles to cope with Ruth's aggressive attempts at independence lead Kathy to psychically split her objects into good and bad: "In those first months at the Cottages, our friendship had stayed intact because, on my side at least, I'd had this notion there were two quite separate Ruths" (Ishiguro 117). That Kathy expects the public, aggressive Ruth never to merge with the private, intimate Ruth exemplifies the difficulty to see the other as an autonomous whole. Kathy cherishes their nightly routine together: "however much we might have fallen out during the day, come bed-time, Ruth and I would still find ourselves sitting side by side on my mattress, sipping our hot drinks, exchanging our deepest feelings about our new life like nothing had ever come between us" (Ishiguro 115). Despite moments such as these, as well as moments in which Ruth attempts to hold on to Kathy, they both must learn that neither of them is theirs to keep.

Kathy identifies Ruth as the first graduate of their year to occupy the role of an adult. Retrospectively and reparatively, Kathy rationalizes Ruth's sadistic exploitation of her and Tommy: "Sometimes, as I said, she did things to impress the veterans at our expense. But it seems to me Ruth believed, at some level, she was doing all this *on behalf of us all* . . . She was struggling to become someone else, and maybe felt the pressure more than the rest of us because, as I say, she'd somehow taken on the responsibility for all of us" (Ishiguro 118, emphasis in original). Kathy's repetitive claim of Ruth's responsibility suggests the former's attempt to convince herself to justify the latter's motivations. Right before Part II begins, when Ruth decides to get back together with Tommy, she declares confidently, "We're adults now" (96), as if to assert the beginning of more mature object relations. For Ruth, adulthood means letting go of childhood relationships, building new ones, and, at the same time, taking care of people for whom she feels responsible. This process becomes mimetic, however, in moments when Ruth has trouble letting go of childhood bonds and compensates with a phantasy of omniscience.

The phantasies that reinforce Ruth's sense of self elicit a claim to knowledge that produces a possessive and controlling power over Kathy and Tommy. Ruth's performance of "precocious" knowledge keeps Kathy and Tommy apart and Ruth herself at the central apex of their love triangle. Her search for her "possible" in Norfolk entertains phantasies about her origins or her future, working in a clean office. Ruth's phantasy of escape defers her predetermined future of completing as a donor. She cannot maintain that phantasy when her curiosity about her "possible" leads the group of friends to follow a stranger who turns out to be obviously different from Ruth. With the exception of this moment, Ruth's "epistemophilic instinct" does not allow for ambiguity and keeps her curiosity inhibited; she is the one who always already "knows." She forcibly forecloses the "unthought known" (Bollas 4) that incessantly threatens conscious knowledge, and is therefore unresponsive to Tommy's theories about their futures. For Ruth, adulthood means to occupy a paranoid-schizoid position, an aggressive and possessive approach to knowledge that accelerates Ruth's linear development.

Ruth's condescension toward Tommy reaches a peak when he shares with her his theory about art, Madame's gallery, love, and deferral. Tommy is the question-child of the three friends.[9] He is often slow to catch on to Ruth's truth claims and so unwittingly sabotages her illusory omnipotence. He challenges Ruth's claim to know about the opportunity for Hailsham students to defer their donations. Tommy's last temper tantrum in the cattle fields mirrors his behavior at the beginning of the novel, and Kathy offers insight to Tommy's unconscious knowledge: "back then, at Hailsham, when you used to go bonkers like that . . . I was thinking maybe the reason you used to get like that was because at some level you always *knew*" (Ishiguro 252, emphasis in original). Kathy here refers to the truth about the students' conditions of existence, that no escape exists. Like the question-child, Tommy's latent knowledge about their purpose disrupts everyday life at Hailsham. Governed by his unconscious, he acts out through motor discharge.

In his late adolescence, Tommy brings together everything that had previously baffled him: the need to produce good art; the reason behind Madame's gallery; Miss Lucy's behavior toward the students; and the rumor of the possibility to defer donations if two Hailsham students could prove their love as true. He resolves these mysteries into a detailed, coherent theory:

> Suppose some special arrangement *has* been made for Hailsham students. Suppose two people say they're truly in love, and they want extra time to be together. Then you see, Kath, there has to be a way to judge if they're really telling the truth . . . But the point is, whoever decides, Madame or whoever it is, *they need something to go on* . . . Madame's got a gallery somewhere filled with stuff by students from when they were tiny. Suppose two people come up and say they're in love. She can find the art they've done over years and years. She can see if they go. If they match. Don't forget, Kath, what she's got reveals our souls. She could decide for herself what's a good match and what's just a stupid crush . . . The thing about being from Hailsham was that you had this special chance. And if you didn't get stuff into Madame's gallery, then you were as good as throwing that chance away. (Ishiguro 160–61, emphases in original)

Tommy's theory reads like an infantile phantasy. But the framing of the novel—a nostalgic, rustic, rural setting juxtaposed against a science fiction plot—allows a suspension of disbelief. The reader's judgment becomes disoriented through an evaluation of what is possible in the diegetic world, so identification with the characters readily allows room for phantasy in a realm that forecloses life.

The route that Tommy takes to arrive at his theory follows a decoding similar to the process of reading. He uses his imagination to organize a series of clues into a coherent narrative. Tommy tries to make sense out of the affectively charged fragments of their everyday lives. His theoretical formula requires a number of variables: a love object (in his case, Kathy), a big Other (Madame), a series of signs (the artwork), and the subject's transparent authenticity (meaning). Tommy postulates meaning out of fragmentary experience. He finds a way to justify the cultural value of the artwork at Hailsham, as well as the collective activities surrounding its production, both of which alienate Tommy. The justification of the art in turn justifies Tommy's inexplicable anxiety and sense of lack: he has yet to catch up with his peers in the activity of producing, perhaps exhibiting, his identity. This phantasy also affords Tommy a degree of omniscience. The assumption that the content of the art "reveals" the artists' souls depends on a mutual agreement between sign and referent. Art, in this case, does not signify but rather transubstantiates its subject. Synchronicity between two "soul mates" would then be readily transparent to the designated authoritative reader. The Other, Madame, is the one presumed to know: she gains access to exclusive knowledge about her subjects, knowledge from which the subjects themselves are barred. Should the subject's work be worthy, and should that work mirror another worthy subject's work, the Other can grant life.

Tommy's theory reaffirms his guilt at his lack of identification with the Hailsham art project, thus explaining his social isolation. In this way, Tommy is the novel's closest resemblance to a Kafkaesque character trapped within social totality. The theory obscures his unconscious knowledge of the reality that art, for all practical purposes, does not matter. Although Tommy has been Ruth's boyfriend for much of their young lives, Tommy shares his theory first with Kathy as an indication that he has something to live for: a love for Kathy that he has already failed to prove, a love that overshadows their impending death and which finds signification through Tommy's phantasy theory. Tommy's theory dominates the action in the second half of the novel. It reaffirms all of his anxieties about his shortcomings, his relationships, and his death.

Ruth's sadistic dynamic with Tommy allows her, on discovery of his theory, to humiliate and betray him while manipulating Kathy into complicity: "It's not the *theory* people will find funny, sweety gums. They might well buy the theory, right enough. But the idea that you'll swing it by showing Madame your little animals . . . It's not just me sweetie. Kathy here finds your animals a complete hoot" (178, emphasis in original). Because Ruth directly rejects not Tommy's theory but his art, she ultimately attacks the soul he postulates within himself, the soul unworthy of matching up with either woman in his life, but especially Kathy. Ruth exacts revenge on both of them. She attempts to make reparations for her destructive behavior at the end of the novel by urging Tommy and Kathy to apply for the elusive deferral. Her intention to repair the damages for which she is responsible fails, since she invests in a theory that is not much more than a phantasy because its truth depends on the absent referent of the soul.

For all of Ruth's efforts to "grow up," to behave like an adult with evolving constellations of relationships, and to move on from Hailsham, she displaces her own resistance to letting her childhood go onto an aggressive sabotage of Tommy and Kathy's growing intimacy in order to keep them the way they always were for herself. Each of their ontological speculations, ones that give each character's life meaning, merge and provoke Kathy's decision to leave the Cottages: Ruth's theory of the "possible" as indicative of one's character and inherent potential; Tommy's theory about art revealing what one is like inside; and Kathy's theory about her origins as a *Playboy* model to rationalize her sex drive. Ruth's manipulations are particularly violent because she uses to her advantage Tommy's and Kathy's private phantasy theories, which attempt to contain what they are each ashamed of in themselves, namely, Tommy's art and Kathy's sexual urges. Ruth is successful in alienating Kathy from Tommy, first, by implicating Kathy in Ruth's humiliation of Tommy, and second, by telling Kathy that, even though Tommy and Ruth "might not be a couple for ever . . . Tommy doesn't like girls who've been with . . . well, you know, with this person and that" (Ishiguro 183). Ruth's lie exploits Kathy's confusion and shame about her sex drive. As a result, Kathy and Tommy's relationship as silent and reciprocal protectors unravels.

V. Childhood Redux: Art and the Thinking Subject

At the climax's revelatory moment, Kathy and Tommy find Madame, the driving force behind the institutional imperative to make good art. As Toker and Chertoff observe, this interview is consistent with such dystopian novels as *Brave New World* and *Nineteen Eighty-Four*: the narrative path culminates in an explanation by the rulers of the mechanics by which their society operates (175). Kathy and Tommy's hopes shatter as they confront a sardonic and patronizing Madame:

> 'And this is why you think I gathered all those things of yours. My *gallery*, as all of you always called it . . . Why would my gallery help in telling which of you were really in love?'
>
> 'Because it would help show you what we were like,' Tommy said, 'Because . . .'
>
> 'Because of course'—Madame cut in suddenly—'your art will reveal your inner selves! That's it, isn't it? Because your art will display your *souls*!' (Ishiguro 232, emphasis in original)

That Madame mocks Tommy's theory almost verbatim before he enunciates it suggests her position as omnipotent authority, reminding Tommy and Kathy that no matter how old they get (they are nearing 30 at this point) they will be nothing more than children. She also mocks the clichéd interpretation of art. In this passage, the repetition of the causal conjunction "because" marks Tommy's stumble over his own logic, thus accentuating the absence of original cause or substantiating evidence of something so ethereal and abstract as love. Particularly, the repetitive stumble on the word "because" is an unconscious acknowledgment of the soul's irrelevance. Tommy's theory establishes an institution, the gallery, in order to construct a hermeneutical relationship to their art production at Hailsham.

Tommy and Kathy's tragedy is neither that they are not really in love nor that art is not a mimetic reflection of souls; their tragedy is that their souls, their love, and their art never really mattered, regardless of their relation to truth. In this way, Tommy and Kathy's love is not unlike queer love and society's historical disavowal of it. Reduced to phantasy and mere child's play, Tommy's hopes resonate with Edelman's dictum, that the future is kid stuff. Edelman points out the mutual reinforcement between the ideological investment in ideal futurity and the image of the ideal Child. As an uncanny repetition and displacement of this image of Child/futurity, Tommy shatters the phantasy of a socially viable life. Like Edelman's queer figure, as a mere projection of England's death drive, Tommy fails to redeem a humanity for himself, and in doing so he exposes it as a melancholic phantasy in the Other. This climactic exposure of reality and a resulting paranoid position sends Tommy to thrash about on the grounds of the English countryside. His regressive tantrum is a reaction not to the injustice of his subjectivation, but rather to the mundanity of the knowledge about one's death, and the impossibility to realize any promissory identity.

Tommy and Kathy's revelation at the end of the novel is completely unremarkable. Their epistemological failure is located less in realization that their theory was wrong than the disappointing repetition of learning what they already knew. Neither of them learns anything more than what Miss Lucy had told them in their childhoods: "'So what you're saying, Miss,' Tommy said, 'is that everything we did, all the lessons, everything. It was all about what you just told us? There was nothing more to it than that?'" (Ishiguro 243). The mundanity he reveals about their lessons renders their application for deferral as mere child's play. He encounters the painfully obvious given that no education is so miraculous that it can cheat death. Yet the negation in his statement, "nothing more," suggests an excess to the knowledge they held all along and learned again. Ishiguro's characters follow Sedgwick's movement away from the question of whether a particular piece of knowledge is true. Instead, like Sedgwick, they must ask: "What does knowledge *do?*—the pursuit of it, the having and exposing of it, the receiving again of knowledge of what one already knows? *How*, in short, is knowledge performative?" (*Touching Feeling* 124). While the students' education and their subsequent phantasies about their futures are useless, their approach toward love and death marks a disruptive return of the repressed. That the students persist and thrive creatively underscores a latent knowledge of the violence inflicted on an entire population of people for the sake of production, a latency that haunts England invisibly and repulses the guardians who must face the ones they teach.

The role of visual art, however, can still tell us something about the way subjects arrive at knowledge. Shameem Black productively differentiates two kinds of art in *Never Let Me Go*, each of which evokes divergent kinds of empathy. She argues for the aesthetics of "inhuman" art, one that supersedes the humanist art that Hailsham fosters. Black critiques the Romantic ideal of artistic self-expression and its supposed link with moral action, claiming that this ideal becomes "horrifyingly literal in the act of organ donation," revealing the "dystopian potential of such an aesthetic" (790). Behind Miss Emily and Madame's project lies the assumption that art inspires identification and bolsters the urge for humane consideration by shareholders. This assumption compounds the teachers' complicity with the organ-farming operation and exacerbates a counterproductive effect of student art production. Art at Hailsham functions to interpellate the students: "As the students become more and more emotionally bound to each other through the exchange of art, they gradually lose their ability to imagine themselves outside the system that governs their collective lives. As a result, they find it difficult to consider independent action"

(Black 795). On the one hand, humanist art at Hailsham serves to prove to society at large the status of the clones as human beings. On the other hand, as Black argues, humanist art keeps the students unconscious of their own biomechanical condition, leading them to their predetermined fates through processes of disavowal.

The inhuman art that Black identifies in *Never Let Me Go* becomes established toward the novel's conclusion in Tommy's animal drawings. Although based on his imagination, Tommy's art is, according to Black, the most realist in the novel. Kathy notes her reaction when a nervous Tommy first shows her his sketchbook: "The first impression was like one you'd get if you took the back off a radio set: tiny canals, weaving tendons, miniature screws and wheels were all drawn with obsessive precision, and only when you held the page away could you see it was some kind of armadillo, say, or a bird" (Ishiguro 171). Tommy's drawings represent the death-driven, automatized subject, where the organic and mechanical combine. Such dialectical visions are effects of totalitarianism, visions in which the drives culminate in an all-consuming system that incorporates organic life in a formulaic machinery.[10]

Tommy presents something much more vulnerable than the totalitarian subject-machine: a frog, an armadillo, or a bird, all put together with an intricate and precariously balanced network of inorganic parts. Later, as Tommy prepares for the deferral application, Kathy expresses concern about the art: "Something was definitely gone, and they looked laboured, almost like they'd been copied" (Ishiguro 221). Black notes insightfully that Tommy's art reflects the absence of his three organs, and the labored quality is evidence of his physical hardship as a result. I would add that, at this point, the labored and copied quality of his art indicates a desperation stemming from a knowledge he shares with Kathy, that they are applying too late, and that the unconscious purpose of his art—to prepare for death—is inconsistent with their intended purpose for deferral. Black concludes:

> Tommy's drawings of imaginary animals reveal 'the soul' to be an illusion; if we open up the animal, we find only the workings of an intricate form of machinery . . . This inhuman art, which marries the animal with the automatic, provides an alternative to the destructive visions of soul-based humanity that the novel critiques. Art that exposes soullessness, not soulfulness, offers the truer vision of Tommy's simulated life. (Black 801)

Puchner's suggestion of a posthuman becoming agrees with Black's call for inhuman art. He observes that the clones are uncanny not because of a deficiency that forecloses them from the status of normal human, but "because Ishiguro has profoundly unsettled what it means to imitate and be imitated, and therefore what it means to be human" (Puchner 45). Puchner reinforces my argument about Ishiguro's inversion of the uncanny, in which the reader's compassionate identification with the novel's unsettling otherness invokes a reevaluation of pre-established egoic structures.

In Chapter 3 I noted how the visual aspects in the *House of Leaves* emerge at a crisis of knowledge, in the face of absolute darkness. In *Never Let Me Go*, a dependence on the visual also develops, not only as a tool for Tommy to resolve the enigmatic minutiae of his life, but also for the Hailsham project to prove the clones' status as humans. In both Danielewski's and Ishiguro's novels, the visual image attempts to close the gap between unknown referent and material sign. In both novels, the visual marks a failure for the characters and reader. Visual art fails to save Tommy and Kathy from the epistemological crisis of death, as Madame and Miss Emily reduce the image back to mere empty signifier. But what Kathy and Tommy have in the wake of the image is precisely a series of signifiers, a set of stories that find materialization only through remnant objects, through traces, of everyday life. The novel's climax marks the end of another search, another end of a promising moment that stretches time and bonds the three friends. What Tommy and Kathy mourn in the cattle fields together is not the value of art, nor even their status as human subjects, but rather the inevitable end to a phantasy that all three characters elaborate together, as in the cassette search. In the novel, the process of the search for signification constitutes an eventual necessity of letting go once the signifiers are found. This process elucidates the human drive to signify through and beyond epistemological crises. The exceptional situation of the clones takes to an illustrative extreme the condition that, in the ever-unfolding process of signification, the subject mourns.

The circular structure of the novel, the movement between the exchange of objects and the continual search for signifiers, does not end within the diegetic world. As Whitehead notes, "Ishiguro stages the act of reading itself as an event, so that the reader's experience of finishing the book powerfully reenacts Kathy's own closing action of moving on and leaving the past behind" (58). Unlike the *House of Leaves*, in which the narrative becomes literally disrupted by a visual transmission of horror's essence, *Never Let Me Go* prioritizes narrative for the reader, over and over again. Kathy's return to her past through narrative recollection parallels Felman's notion of the repetition compulsion: "what is repeated in the text is not the content of a fantasy but the symbolic displacement of a signifier through the insistence of a signifying chain; repetition is not of *sameness* but of *difference*, not of independent terms or of analogous themes but of a structure of differential interrelationships, in which what *returns* is always *other*" (Felman 44, emphases in original). In other words, the circular learning that the reader participates in with Kathy and Tommy opens up the unconscious through the circulation of signifiers. Britzman concludes her article with an argument for slow reading: "Psychoanalytic reading teaches us a lesson we already know, that we cannot let go of affected life, we are always reading between the lines, wagering meaning and deferring it. Here is where we find that our constructs fail" ("Slow Reader" 317). The narrative *return* occasions the transformative possibilities of symbolized life and a repeated encounter with failure.

Madame's farewell to Kathy and Tommy leaves an affective void. Her final statement to her students, however, gestures toward the transformative potential of pedagogical experience for both student and teacher. Madame admits: "Your stories this evening, they touched me . . . Poor creatures. I wish I could help you. But now you're by yourselves" (Ishiguro 249). At the end of the novel, the reader learns that Kathy is alone and is about to become a donor. In *After-Education,* Britzman explores loneliness as an effect of the contact with the incoherent and as the condition of possibility for reparative thinking. This process of "difficult learning" marks a flirtation with the Real in a way that resembles but necessarily displaces the paranoid imperative's enthusiasm for a queer death drive. In his 1911 essay, Freud initially differentiates between the pleasure principle and reality principle. The former is dominated by a world of phantasy while the latter soberly acknowledges external conditions. By the time Freud is speculating about the drives in 1920, the pleasure principle and reality principle are closer on the spectrum than he had first conceptualized. Ishiguro's novel reflects Britzman's argument that what follows phantasy is not reality but loneliness, remorse, and mourning in the encounter with the unknown. In terms of the drives, then, object relations take on a subtler formulation. The death drive perpetuates a universe of part objects that the subject phantasizes and enjoys. The life drive facilitates the painful process that lets go of phantasy for the experience of deep absence in the signifier. Far from dichotomous and exclusive, the drives operate simultaneously, in blends and rhythms that send the self toward provisional and innumerable proximities with the other.

What fails in Tommy's theory, then, is the phantasy that love defines itself through a mutual projective identification between self and other, a paranoid-schizoid "match" that reinforces one's ontological existence through a kind of mirrored repetition. In the wake of this conceptual failure, however, Tommy and Kathy unwittingly discover another way to experience love. Tommy would be trapped in a melancholic attachment had his belief in art's transubstantiating properties remained. But after the revelation he continues his art as a private activity that excludes Kathy; the function of art changes for Tommy from proof of ontological existence to the ongoing act of signification. His love for his animals defines a binding love for the signifier in the wake of a world of part objects that has come undone. Whitehead contrasts the horrific care the "normals" institutionalize with Tommy's "compassionate release" of Kathy, illustrating a care that allows him to "let go" of the one he loves (Whitehead 79). In a depressive position, Tommy's decision to replace Kathy with a different carer before his death marks a desire to be alone in the presence of love. Kathy's loneliness culminates in the act of her own narration. She thus purges her anger against Ruth, whose possessiveness keeps Tommy and Kathy apart throughout their lives. Her narrative of remembering is a reparative reading of her relationship with Ruth, Tommy, and Hailsham. Unlike Ruth's desperate omnipotence and Tommy's erroneous theory of deferral, both of which fail to master their future deaths, Kathy's lonely closure with these relationships finally allows her to die in her own way.

Insofar as Tommy celebrates the manufactured condition of his existence, insofar as Kathy closes her narrative on the brink of donor status, insofar as their love fails to save them, insofar as their signification forecloses viable identity, these clones illustrate the claim that the death-driven subject is a queer subject. The dynamics that play out among the dying characters draw our attention again to the paranoid imperative and queer reparative. The former insists on a critical omnipotence invested in an exposure of meaning. But paranoid reading nonetheless rejects the postulation of hidden, static meaning. This position aligns itself implicitly with Sedgwick's call—which I introduce in my first chapter and will reiterate here—for a subsequent *depressive* position to repair "part-objects into something like a whole—though . . . *not necessarily like any preexisting whole*" (*Touching Feeling* 128, emphasis in original). This point corresponds to Phillips's clarification of the death drive in *Darwin's Worms*, also referenced in the first chapter and which returns at the end of this last analysis. According to Phillips, death as the aim of life marks a wish to die in freedom, from within, after a struggle to satisfy oneself in life, to die in one's own way. The performative force of Kathy's narration allows her to appropriate her own life from the powers that mechanically produced it and reassemble her subjectivity unlike any prescribed one. Her lonely closure of these relationships resonates with Sedgwick's working through in preparation for her own death.

VI. Conclusion

The one thing that remains certain throughout the novel is the inevitability of organ donations, which Kathy and Tommy cannot accept for the majority of their lives. Rather, they build a weave of phantasies that attach their epistemological certainties elsewhere in life, to phantasies that are bound to fail. The sexual occasions epistemological crises at the vanishing point of signification. In other words, the force of the sexual sends the self rhythmically to its non-referential expression through the repetitive displacements of thought. This movement indicates how both drives are sexual in their implication of attachment and destruction. The repetition of both economic and dynamic binding and unbinding describes the experience of pausing in the pleasure of stasis and silence, investing in certainty to the point at which it unravels, breaking the peace of reified knowledge, and putting the remnants together with new signifiers in the face of a yawning absence. Through difficult thinking, Kathy and Tommy slip in and out of phantasies they create, as well as the system of humanist phantasies that Hailsham establishes for them. Because both characters are determined to see these theories through, all of these phantasies are subject to conceptual vanishing points. Even when the clone is assured the monolithic certainty of death, she chooses to wander through a matrix of epistemological failures. This curious detour is an expression of sexuality, where the death and the life drives blend to produce an oscillation between a series of breaking points and a passion for new, albeit provisional, significations.

Kathy's love resonates with but is ultimately different from the final passages of *Nineteen Eighty-Four*, in which the protagonist, Winston Smith, comes to love Big Br[O]ther in the moment when his long *bardos* ends with the generous bestowal of his execution. While Smith loves the Big Br[O]ther because it grants him his death, Kathy and her friends love Hailsham because, through a series of misunderstandings, deferrals, displacements, experimentations, and unprecedented outcomes, it is able to grant them lives. Certainly, this condition speaks to the Foucauldian problematics of biopower, in which modern power defines itself productively by regulating life as opposed to punishing through death. The mode of expression both Kathy and Tommy find at the end of their lives as clones, however, surpasses Hailsham's naïve humanist project. While springing from the institutional framework of Hailsham, Tommy's and Kathy's art celebrates a passion for signification that allows them to experience a singular freedom independent from the circumscribed life the institutional structures afford. Their creative play holds no ambitions to overthrow the diegetic totality in a romanticized revolution, nor is it an escape to an idealized "outside." Rather, Kathy and Tommy's creativity is quiet, slow, and works through the necessities of their drives.

Ultimately, the Elysian deferral that Kathy and Tommy search for only "too late" manifests in the supposed non-cardinal functions of Kathy's narrative: in other words, in narrative deferrals. Tangents like the pencil case episode make Kathy's story not about death but about life, and implied in Kathy's story is the insight that "life" is creative only in its intimate relation to rather than maniacal denial of an ending. As they grow up, the three main characters exchange objects instead of words. Through this silent system of exchange, they collaborate to maintain, destroy, and renew each other's private phantasies, away from the public realm of discourse and from the panoptic space of Hailsham, in order to build a weave of attachments among one another that they must, in the end, dismantle with linguistic introjection in order to mourn each other. *Never Let Me Go* reminds us of the difference that Winnicott elucidates between object-relating and object-usage. Both processes are necessary in creative life. As the three main characters grow up, the mode of their relationships develops from an exchange of material objects, ones into which they project parts of themselves and give one another, to an exchange of words that allows them to mourn and work through the destruction that takes place among them as they prepare for death.

Conclusion

> Our curiosity depends upon a receding horizon.
>
> —Adam Phillips, *The Beast in the Nursery*, 17

Benjamin's Angel of History is not "man enough" to blast through the discards of history, but as a figure for longing he may lead us to a "good enough" relationship with phantasy that we-the-close-readers can nonetheless work through. The theory of reading that I develop indulges the desire for both aesthetic distance and tactile omniscience as a means to foster erotic vulnerability in the self. The paranoid imperative and queer reparative embrace the tumult of both drives and allow the histories of their theoretical application to seep into the pages of the text. Literature offers a unique space in which we can complete our phantasies in order to let them go so that, in the social sphere, we can imagine a future that remains unknown yet negotiable. An elaborative relationship to literary texts allows the self, at least, to negotiate with the other, and at best, to negotiate the other with pleasure.

The productive confusion between the economic and dynamic modes of binding accounts for the ambivalence between, on the one hand, the impetus behind identity politics and, on the other hand, an undoing of identity. These seemingly contradictory impetuses do not come from any single drive but are products of how both drives play out together. The attraction to radical, politicized modes of undoing formations of identity comes from a detour into the death drive. A breaking of the peace (*BPP SE* 77), a shattering of reified thinking, occurs as subjects, enthralled by literary pleasures, traverse planar lines of conceptual categories up to their point of failure. Throughout the chapters of this book, the metaphor of the vanishing point illustrates a three-dimensional phantasy of conceptual depth on a two-dimensional plane. Such a lure attracts subjects to where only the eye can see but the self cannot go. The self-shattering for which Bersani calls is a necessary function of the drives, but operates through aesthetic sublimation.

The drives send the subject in and out of epistemological crises, which result not simply from the condition of not knowing, but from the outcome of a process that exhausts knowledge. Psychical exhaustion manifests in the movement of the sexual. There is a sexual relation. It emerges in the compulsion to repeat a curious engagement with the object of inquiry. Psychical exhaustion develops from the compulsion to reduce the object through a phantasy of omniscience, only to realize again and again that the phantasy glosses over conceptual rupture. A repeated engagement with the object wears away at phantasy to expose the self to unknowable otherness. The repetition of epistemological crisis involves the binding of conceptual sublimation and the unbinding of the unconscious in both language and artistic representation.

The queer theory that my book offers has departed from the romanticized project of undoing the "congealments of identity" (*No Future* 17). The paranoid imperative of queer theory belies an ambivalence about a desire for subversion and the impossibility of calling for an active, revolutionary politics. The desire for political subversion reacts to the history of discriminatory injustice against queers. Yet voices for political subversion recognize that no "outside" exists beyond the confines of social intelligibility. The social totality of signification predetermines formations of identity. In this case, the deployment of language is performative; language itself is a series of performative statements that have direct, material effects on how subjects live within the social.

Indeed, perhaps due to Foucault's association between discourse and subjectivity, much of queer theory's struggle stems from the homogenization of language and identity, of intelligibility and conceptual categories with which the subject can identify. Contrary to the agendas of queer scholars, the current split in queer theory between the anti-social thesis of radical undoing and the reparative turn toward affect reinforces the reductive question of undoing identity and identity politics. My wish for the reparative turn in queer theory is for scholars not to abandon the negative as a necessary precondition for creative life. Bound to the negative is the fight for life. The readings of the central texts by Nabokov, Danielewski, Findley, and Ishiguro push the deconstructive cleverness of repetition and displacement to its limit. Even though language exerts a performative force, it is not synonymous with identity. Because its method involves the synthesis between language and encounters with the unknown, psychoanalysis offers an alternative approach to intelligibility that does not resort to the reductions of identity and the question of whether to undo or reinforce it. I invite thinkers to engage with the paranoid imperative and queer reparative as a dialectical pair of epistemological *positions* that enjoy projective identification, splitting, and, ultimately, letting go of omniscience over a universe of part objects once the self experiences the pain of conceptual failure.

I began this project with the attempt to reconcile the pleasure of the text with the ineluctability of semiotic totalities. While Kristeva's position on the "schizoid manifestations" in avant-garde art strikes me as reactionary, it is perhaps symptomatic that the novels I analyzed are not avant-garde in terms of formal technique: that is, they are not conceptually difficult, abstract works of art that celebrate the incoherent on a manifest level. The novels that I analyze are beautiful, in the Kantian sense of the spontaneous but independent agreement between the subject's Imagination and Understanding, which renders the object as aesthetically *bound* (Kant 101–102). The event of beholding the beautiful is, at least at first, pleasurable, comforting, and self-affirming because the subject can comprehend what he or she perceives. Simply put, these novels not only make denotative sense; they also appeal to aesthetic sensibilities of pleasure. As insensitive as Humbert is to the external world, his prose combines pleasurable linguistic rhythms with the good timing of humor. As an artifact, a material object, *House of Leaves* is beautiful in its visual innovation. The seamless transference of Ross's story from one narrative figure to the next resembles the momentum of a dream that tempts a passive consumption of the text. Ishiguro's world presents a muted pastoral beauty, with characters that recall the Romantic tabula rasa.

If, aesthetically speaking, beauty and the sublime in the postwar era are equated with fascism, then the subject's attachment to the work of art becomes consistently suspect. The beauty in these novels could not be reducible to Benjamin's thesis that fascism aestheticizes politics ("Work of Art" 242). Conceptually, there was something incredibly difficult in these novels, despite, or perhaps because of, the aesthetic pleasures they afford. Close readings proved that the conceptual difficulty of the text is not behind its aesthetic pleasures but very much bound up with it. The metaphor of the vanishing point illustrates how difficult thinking can still spring from the pleasures of beauty. The allure of the vanishing point lies in its power to draw in and direct the eye, even before critical thinking becomes activated. Keeping the metaphor of the vanishing point in mind, the close readings worked to identify the conceptual difficulty in these aesthetically seductive texts. The readings facilitated a way to reconcile the necessity of the drive both beyond the pleasure principle and a return to pleasure.

Despite beauty, destruction and catastrophe figure heavily in these aesthetic objects. The attachment to catastrophe, whose death-driven comfort my reading attempted to slough off, potentially contradicts the assertion that the life drive is reparative in its activation of the signifier. Language is the vehicle for both the death-driven vanishing point of conceptual thought and reparative practices of new signification, because aesthetic sublimation requires both drives. Bersani identifies a designifying mobility in the text that seduces readers to engage with and attach to words. The anaclitic character of the drives—the drive's propping on and perversion of biological instincts—resonates with the function of language. Insofar as language can also be described as a propping on and perversion of its referents, language is also, in a way, anaclitic. Through language, the drives express themselves. The act of signification leads the speaking subject to a place in which one lets go of omniscience, entering into a proliferative if uncertain and provisional relation to the other.

Unlike the critical position that laments one's own subjectivity within social totality (in terms of literary analysis, the most paranoid elementary category of narrative conflict, self versus society), my book took object relations into consideration. Once the critical reader gains a sense of omniscience about the networks of power that determine biopolitical life, language again becomes transformative through art even as it arises from the discourses of political containment. Art allows the intimate articulation of the self in relation to the unknowable other within the ineluctable backdrop of social and semiotic totality. Insofar as the other is always already unknowable, such a question is distinctly a creative one.

Through acts of reading queerly, the self opens up to a vulnerable, sexualized curiosity that does not panic in the grip of the anxiety of not knowing, nor does she foreclose the potentials of such curiosity with anticipatory phantasies of certainty. Rather, the self enjoys the rhythmic flow in and out of provisional ego identifications and subsequent epistemophilic frustrations. I ended up with a mode of queer reading that celebrates a thorough love of the other that neither resorts to the nice scruples of repression nor abandons self and other to nihilistic destruction. Rather, repression and destruction—or to put it more accurately, binding and unbinding—become part of a creative process of sublimation that marks the transition from object-relating to object-usage, from a search for signifiers to a process of mourning.

The life drive is loud. It breaks the quiet peace of deadened stasis. It makes the "task of living more difficult" (*BPP SE* 77). Yet, ultimately, the life drive is not destructive because it occasions new syntheses between subject and object, particularly through the process of signification. It fosters new links through associative chains that make up the structures of the articulable world. The oscillation between the paranoid imperative and queer reparative alters engagements with literary texts by slowing down the process of attachment. Identification is an entrance into the literary text, but in order to move beside identity politics, such identifications cannot provide the final instance in literary interpretation. As the field of literary studies repeatedly proves, there are many ways to investigate modes of identification. This book presents one way in which the reader can perform such an exploration, and in doing so it also provides an opportunity to think about sexuality, how it pervades intelligibility—directs it, disrupts it, excites it. In thinking about how one reads, one does not simply come up with the answer of identifying sexual object-choice: rather, it allows one to articulate the conditions and limits of erotic attachments.

Like Kathy and Tommy, I, too, return to some mundane, incredibly disappointing insights that I hoped to have learned out of: the human subject is often complicit in dominant modes of power; the desire for omniscience underlies the pursuit of meaning; art is important to human subjectivity, but not in any useful way. Yet a more stimulating discovery is that this question of subjectivity, while worth raising, becomes more productive upon letting go of the phantasy of an answer. The desire for an absolute answer is what leads the paranoid imperative to romanticize the death drive, a position that refuses the world of promissory, empty signifiers with which narratives of progress have left human subjectivity. In the wake of the dead referent, the subject's erotic attachment to the aesthetic artifact persists. The desire to determine the answer to whether or not human subjects are trapped in a totality of their own creation is a reaction to an anxiety stemming from an implacable human aggression. Paranoid readings in practices of critique are vital for dialectical thinking processes but become subject to stasis as a goal in itself. As a mode of working through object relations, the search for signifiers is an erotic process. Human intimacy accumulates in the search itself—in the deferrals and detours and loud silences.

Notes

Introduction

1. Although sometimes interchangeable with "fantasy," phantasy is psychoanalytically specific. Jean Laplanche and J.B. Pontalis divide the term according to its German and French roots. While the French term for fantasy refers to specific imaginary production (conscious daydreams), the German term for phantasy refers to the world of phantasy that is unconscious and structures the perception of reality and of the subject's identity (314). As Eve Sedgwick clarifies in her posthumously published collection of essays, *The Weather in Proust,* Melanie Klein offers a "literal-minded animism" to object relations: it is Klein "who put the objects in object relations. In her concept of phantasy-with-a-*ph*, human mental life becomes populated, not with ideas, representations, knowledges, urges, and repressions, but with *things*, things with physical properties, including people and hacked-off bits of people" (*Weather* 126).

2. One text that addresses the politically ambivalent figure of the "angel of history" in relation to queer theory is Heather Love's *Feeling Backward.* In her Epilogue, Love points out the dangers and potentials for change in what Wendy Brown calls "Left Melancholy" for which the Angel stands. In his essay "Ever After" Lee Edelman also invokes the Angel of History in relation to what he has called the "sinthomosexual" (117).

3. Berlant defines cruel optimism as an attachment to the "moral-intimate-economic" fantasy of "the good life" (2). Cruel optimism differs from Michael Snediker's *Queer Optimism* in that, while the former considers optimism an object of critique, the latter finds in optimism a possibility for positive celebration. Berlant clarifies that cruel optimism is "a relation of attachment to compromised conditions of possibility whose realization is discovered either to be *im*possible, sheer fantasy, or *too* possible, and toxic . . . Cruel optimism is the condition of maintaining an attachment to a significantly problematic object" (*Cruel Optimism,* 24, emphases in original).

4. Often in her article, Kristeva writes about technology in tandem with religious fundamentalism. Rhetorically, her conflation critiques the dialectical collapse between myth and reason that traces back to Horkheimer and Adorno's

Dialectic of Enlightenment. In contradistinction to Kristeva's resistance, the emergent field of the digital humanities is an example of collective creative thinking. Digital humanities explicates and works through the anxiety about technology in the neoliberal era, as well as its effects on subjectivity and reading practices. For example, in her new work, *Habitual New Media,* Wendy Hui Kyong Chun calls for active engagement with new media as a text that begs for new reading/writing practices. Her book argues the inextricability between digital media and human subjectivity. She contends that "through habits we become our machines: we stream, update, capture, upload, share, grind, link, verify, map, save, trash and troll. Repetition breeds expertise, even as it breeds boredom" (n.p. 2016). Chun imagines new relationalities with big data in her call to fight for the right to "loiter" in the digital realm: that is, to indulge online habits free from the fear of becoming managed by them.

5. The relationship between omniscience, totality, the drives, and fascist subjectivity has been a concern spanning modernist and contemporary literary scholarship. See Žižek's reading of Kafka in *Sublime Object of Ideology*, which I address in my last chapter. See also Tyrus Miller's thematization of the interwar period in his book, *Late Modernism*.

6. Mitchell claims that "modern thought has reoriented itself around visual paradigms that seem to threaten and overwhelm any possibility of discursive mastery" (9).

7. See D.A. Miller's article "Hitchcock's Hidden Pictures" for a close reading in which he invokes the viewer to explore the problematics of visual literalization in Hitchcock's films. His use of "visual literalization" (Miller 125) is more general that my psychoanalytic conception of the term in Chapter 3.

8. The edited volume *After Sex?* addresses the precarious link between queer theory and talk about sex. On the topic of queer theory's relationship to sex (and good writing), the Fall 2015 issue of *American Literary History* volume 27 includes Tim Dean's review of *Sex, or the Unbearable* and a heated exchange with its authors, Berlant and Edelman.

9. See Judith (Jack) Halberstam's *The Queer Art of Failure* and José Muñoz's *Cruising Utopia* for examples of this contradictory struggle between anti-identitarian and minority positions.

10. See Jane Gallop's *Deaths of the Author* (2011) and Tim Dean's *Beyond Sexuality* (2000) and *Unlimited Intimacy* (2009) for different examples of theorizing the concept of "queer."

11. Carla Freccero's article "Queer Times" "queers" an otherwise linear sense of temporality.

12. For examples of influential texts on affect, see Ann Cvetkovich's *The Archive of Feeling*, Berlant's *Cruel Optimism*, Love's *Feeling Backward*, and Berlant and Edelman's *Sex, or the Unbearable.*

13. Derrida's essay in *Without Alibi*, "Psychoanalysis Searches for the States of its Soul," illustrates the asymmetry of the drives. He marks the drive for the cruelty of destruction as the "irreducible thing in the life of the animate being"

(239). At the same time, he qualifies this irreducibility by positing "the ruse of the detour" as the "antagonistic force of Eros, love and the love of life, against the death drive" (272). Although Derrida reinforces the strength of the death drive, he also attributes "radical discontinuity, a heterogeneity, a leap into the ethical" (273) to the life drive, describing the latter as the "difficult concept" (272).

14. Snediker aligns Butler with negativity in his reading of her work, which sees melancholia as a permanent condition (6). See Bersani's "Is the Rectum a Grave?," Dean's *Beyond Sexuality* and *Unlimited Intimacy,* as well as de Lauretis's *The Practice of Love* (1994) and *Freud's Drive* (2010) for readings that align queer with negativity.

15. Part of the reparative turn addresses the crisis of the humanities. A question has persisted about the status of futurity: whether institutional futurity is possible for queer theory. Debates about futurity have taken place in conferences and symposia (such as the panel on queer futurity at the 2010 ACCUTE conference), but few studies offer an analysis of these debates as indicative of our dilemmas with reading. Snediker's book *Queer Optimism* works similarly to Donald E. Hall's *Reading Sexualities* (2009) in that both critique Butler, Bersani, and Edelman directly in a repudiation of the relationship between queerness and negativity. Although Snediker offers a psychoanalytically invested conception of queer optimism, his theory requires an unequivocal rejection of the death drive. Snediker's approach reads as a disavowal of the negative rather than an intimate engagement with, historicization, and evaluation of why queer and the negative have come together. Implied in both Snediker's and Hall's critiques is the assumption that the negative and futurity are mutually exclusive. In this sense, they both agree with Edelman's thesis despite themselves. In contrast, Gallop's book *The Deaths of the Author* offers an exemplary engagement in close reading within a queer framework. In her article "Precocious *Jouissance,*" Gallop connects queer theory with the question of sexual dysfunction, as authors deal with their inevitably aging bodies, a more material kind of failure that manifests symptomatically in the theoretical text. Gallop states that, "in its opposition to plaisir, [jouissance] is on the side of the perverted versus the normative, the shocking versus the legitimated; jouissance is on the side of queer" ("Precocious *Jouissance*" 566).

16. Like *Sex, or the Unbearable,* another book structured on conversational dialogue is Leo Bersani and Adam Phillips's *Intimacies*, which Chapter 4 discusses. In light of such theory, my analyses in each chapter show how intimacy has less to do with an experience of relational immediacy than with linguistic mediation.

17. See Winnicott's essay "Transitional Object and Transitional Phenomena" in the collection *Playing and Reality*. He describes transitional phenomena as an "intermediate area of experience" (2), designating objects that are "not part of the infant's body yet are not fully recognized as belonging to external reality" (3). According to Winnicott, the transitional object, such as a toy bear or a blanket, marks the "use of the first 'not-me' possession" (2). By extension in adult life, objects—even linguistic or aesthetic ones—that mediate relations between self and other and that facilitate thinking can serve as transitional objects.

18. In "After Male Sex," Richard Rambuss thinks through the exclusionary tendencies of gay male sexuality, a sexuality connected to the drive, or more particularly to the cock or the male ass. He considers traces of misogyny and/or transphobia in androcentric queer theory. Andrew McLean also addresses uncomfortable gender politics in his critique of trans-misogyny. Butler and Cvetkovich prioritize lesbian sexuality and keep feminism and social change as their agenda.

19. Michael Hames-García and Ernesto Javier Martínez's volume, *Gay Latino Studies: A Critical Reader* (2011), and Fran Martin's volume, *Asiapacifiqueer* (2008), focus on the relationship between queer subjectivity and decolonization. The project in Lisa Downing and Robert Gillet's *Queer in Europe* (2011) involves the "Europeanization of queer theory" and the "queering of Europe." For these scholars, queer theory enables a rethinking of Europe as liminal borderland.

20. Besides de Lauretis's *Freud's Drive*, another exception thus far is Whitney Davis's *Queer Beauty* (2010), an interdisciplinary engagement of queer aesthetics as it intersects with Continental philosophy, psychoanalysis, and the writings of Michel Foucault.

21. See Carla Freccero's "Queer Times" and Madhavi Menon's edited volume *Shakesqueer* (2011) for Foucauldian approaches to queer histories. See Tim Dean's "Bareback Times" in *Queer Times, Queer Becomings* (2011) as he discusses the role of *Nachträglichkeit* in sexuality.

22. See Beatriz Preciado's *Testo-Junkie* for an "updated" Foucauldian formulation of gender based on addiction, the pharmaceutical industry, plastics, and industrial warfare.

23. For examples, see *Queering Paradigms, ShakesQueer,* and Gallop's *Deaths of the Author.*

24. See Hongwei Bao's essay in *Queering Paradigms* (2010).

25. Eugenie Brinkema's *The Form of the Affects* (2014) offers a stellar redefinition of affect in relation to textual form and to psychoanalytic concepts of mourning and melancholia. Hers is a uniquely reparative approach that considers discourses of affect and psychoanalysis together.

26. Love differentiates her agenda from Edelman's: "I am ultimately less interested in accounts of same-sex desire as antisocial or asocial than I am in instances of ruined or failed sociality" (22). Such failed sociality often crystallizes around a singular nonheteronormative figure in her work in order to sustain, similarly to Edelman, an "engagement with the stubborn negativity of the past" (147). Unlike Edelman, Love calls not for no future but for a "backward future" that resists the reproductive imperative, optimism, and redemption (147). Berlant, Edelman, and Love enter into similar projects of implicating the work of the negative into affect theory.

27. Some new reading practices that are not based in queer theory still engage the negative. Recently, in his unpublished paper presented at Congress 2015, Peter Schwenger proposes reading for what he calls the Zero Effect in relation to the Zen concept of Mu, or nothing. He claims that "the text that ends with a zero effect does not give you anything: it takes away. The initial

sensation is one of Mu: a blankness that robs one of all words . . . There is no click as things fall into place, nor a place for them to fall. Rather there is a sort of fraying out into emptiness." (2015). His reading practice parallels the work of the negative that infuses queer critical practice.

28. While the definition of "surface reading" is multifaceted, associated with materiality, formal attentiveness, description, affect, and ethics, it ultimately offers alternatives to paranoid forms of reading. Felski attempts to get outside the "orbit" of the hermeneutics of suspicion, while Best and Marcus argue that psychoanalytic reading practices "took meaning to be hidden, repressed, deep, and in need of detection and disclosure by an interpreter" (Best and Marcus 1).

29. In her article, "Precocious *Jouissance*," Gallop addresses *The Pleasure of the Text* as a problematic of sexual dysfunction, that of an orgasm that has bad timing, either premature or delayed, which is why, she explains, the book's end comes too quickly. For her, Barthes proposes "a radically antinormative sexual theory. As liberating as his celebration of perversion is, it is this moment where he moves beyond perversion to valorize sexual dysfunction that I find truly stunning, particularly brave and valuable" ("Precocious *Jouissance*" 570).

Chapter One

1. See my Chapter 4 for an extensive discussion of Rose's ideas about epistemological failure.

2. Ambivalence arises from the two major translations of Freud: the *Standard Edition,* translated by James Strachey, and the New Penguin addition, translated by John Reddick and edited by Adam Phillips. Reddick's translation is generally freer from scientistic wording, which Strachey injected into Freud's work when psychoanalysis was still trying to establish itself as a science (see Sander Gilman's 1991 article, "Reading Freud in English"). Most notably, Reddick translates *Trieb* and *Instinkt* separately into "drive" and "instinct," unlike Strachey, who homogenizes both German words into the English translation of "instinct" in order to emphasize a biological vocabulary. The difference between drive and instinct is central to my argument, and the *Standard Edition* has caused similar problems for theorists like de Lauretis when working with the drives. But, as I indicate in major moments of my argument, the *Standard Edition* emphasizes striking imagery in *Beyond the Pleasure Principle.* While I predominantly employ the *Standard Edition,* I follow Reddick and mark moments when *Trieb* in the original text ought to be translated into "drive" as opposed to "instinct."

3. In the *Standard Edition*, Strachey translates the original German *durchgebrannt* (*Jenseits* 23) into "baked through" (*BPP SE* 29) when describing the cortical layer. Reddick's translation in the Penguin edition uses the word "tempered" (65). For metaphorical purposes, I prioritize Strachey's translation to retain the imagery of what I translate as the organism's outer *bark* (*eine Rinde*) as *burnt through* (*durchgebrannt*) with stimuli. Indeed, bark is neither impermeable nor dead matter.

Also, the fire imagery in this passage invokes a mobile energy: to be "fired up" or to burn with desire. Such potential contradictions speak to the mobility of the drives that Freud struggles with when he employs biological metaphors to illustrate how the drives operate.

4. Freud analogizes the principle of constancy in his discussion about his grandson Ernst, who invented the "Fort-da" game. When playing with his wooden spool attached to a string, the boy would throw it over the edge of his curtained cot and say "ooo," for the German word "fort," or "gone." Upon retrieving it, he would exclaim "da," or "there." Freud concludes that the game "was related to the child's great cultural achievement [in successfully abnegating his drives] . . . which he had made in allowing his mother to go away without protesting" (*BPP SE* 14). The wooden spool becomes the manipulable substitute for the love object upon which the boy can exact a kind of active revenge in the form of repeated rejection and summoning. In turn, he maintains great attachment to his mother. The overwhelming unpleasurable experience—the absence of the mother—becomes a detour that leads ultimately to pleasure through the function of repetition. Following the reality principle, the "Fort-da" game illustrates a compulsion to repeat that serves sublimation. Repetition is fundamental to the structure of signification itself.

5. Though radical, the concept of the death drive is far from cynical for Freud. He seeks consolation in the concept: "Perhaps we have adopted the belief because there is some comfort in it. If we are to die ourselves, and first to lose in death those who are dearest to us, it is easier to submit to a remorseless law of nature, the sublime . . . [Necessity], than to a chance which might perhaps have been escaped" (*BPP SE* 53). In *Darwin's Worms,* Phillips clarifies Freud's assertion that life's aim is death, expounding that Freud's wish was to die in freedom from Nazi persecution: that is, "to die in one's own way" (9). The death drive allows for an illusion of mastery over one's own death, a measure of control over a singular experience that is the subject's alone but that she cannot be present to possess.

6. Throughout my book, the term *melancholia* is used in association with the death drive, indicating a kind of attachment that denies the absence of the love-object and is marked by a refusal of signification. Chapter 3 discusses melancholia in relation to visual pleasure, and Chapter 5 engages a theoretical discussion of melancholia in relation to mourning.

7. See Klein's essay "The Importance of Symbol Formation in the Development of the Ego" for an explanation of the paranoid position and the reparative position.

8. Laplanche and Pontalis's work maintains the link between the death drive and unbinding, which denotes the following: release of unpleasure; release of pleasure; sexual release of excitation; release of affect; release of anxiety (51). An economic contradiction arises when the same term, unbinding, applies to both the release of unpleasure and pleasure, the increase and decrease in tension. At the time of *Beyond the Pleasure Principle,* Freud has not yet decided how binding and unbinding relates to the changes of the ego's energy quantities, whether

homeostasis refers to an optimal level of energy or zero energy. Laplanche and Pontalis clarify that if ego is a mass of neurones full of bound energy, "every release of primary-process energy—no matter whether it tends to increase or to diminish the *absolute* level of tension—poses a threat to the ego's relatively constant level" (51, emphasis in original). The ego moderates the quantity of excitation, and either an increase or a decrease in the *net* quantity would result in an unbinding. This clarification of unbinding would be consistent with Freud's conclusions in later texts that if the aim is zero cathexis, the death drive operates through a *dynamic* unbinding.

9. Reddick more directly translates *Störenfriede* as "troublemakers" (102). Again, Strachey's perhaps more dramatic translation, "breakers of the peace," is provocative and resonates as an image throughout the book.

10. Laplanche and Pontalis's characterization of the death drive as the "daemonic" force differs from my reading of *Beyond the Pleasure Principle,* in which Freud at first attributes that character to the death drive but later implies that it is (also) an attribute of the life drives as the breakers of the peace.

11. In "Global High Culture in the Era of Neo-Liberalism: The Case of Documenta11," Karyn Ball links the Freudian image of the monad to cultural production, drawing from psychoanalytic theories of reification and the Frankfurt School's critique of "affirmative culture" in her reading of Documenta11, an exhibition of modern and contemporary art.

12. In *Intimacies,* Bersani applies the concept of sameness differently in queer narcissism, redefining it as a potential for new relationalities between self and other.

13. In an interview, Sedgwick defines queer as epistemological crisis, which developed in relation to the socio-historical problem of the AIDS crisis (Barber and Clark 1). Dominant discourse conflated and relegated AIDS and queers to the unknown, which continually threatens the fabric of civil society with an infectious death. Because its emergence was precisely a social emergency, queer theory works from epistemological urgency, one that is ongoing.

14. A detailed explication of Lacanian psychoanalysis and its relationship to queer theory is beyond the scope of this book. For a thorough and nuanced, always self-reflexively provisional understanding of Lacan, as well as a convincing argument about how Edelman and Butler misapply Lacan for the purposes of queer theory, see Dean's *Beyond Sexuality.* Because a thorough discussion of Lacan inevitably implies entering into a highly specific and contentious debate, and because the aim of this particular analysis is to trace the relation between binding and the drives, my reading restricts itself to Edelman's text.

15. Here, Edelman depends on the cleverness of deconstruction, as he upholds queer identity in order to undo identity as such. Edelman's neologism, *Sinthom*osexuality, is a play on the Lacanian concept of the *sinthome.* Edelman defines the *sinthome* as "stupid enjoyment, as the node of senseless compulsion on which the subject's singularity depends" (*No Future* 38). The *sinthome* structures *jouissance,* which connects us to the unrepresentable Real, that tear embedded within the fabric of the Symbolic. Jacques Lacan explains his concept of the

sinthome in his seminar, *Le Sinthome* (1975–76). See Slavoj Žižek's *The Sublime Object of Ideology* for an exploration of the relations between the symptom, the *sinthome*, and ideological interpellation.

16. See Dean's *Beyond Sexuality* and Snediker for explorations of these contradictions.

17. Halberstam's book *The Queer Art of Failure* (2011) is one of the first to explore thoroughly the theoretical link between queer and failure, focusing on low theory, marginalized groups, popular culture, the poor student. Halberstam's approach is based on a critique of exclusionary logic that differentiates self from other through value judgment: some fail, others do not. My approach differs as it incorporates psychoanalytic considerations of the unconscious, focusing on the necessary, universal failure of intelligibility and institutional discourse themselves.

18. See Felman's *Jacques Lacan and the Adventures of Insight* (1987) for a reading of Klein's session with Dick.

19. See also Mari Ruti's *A World of Fragile Things.* Ruti argues that the autonomous self and relational self are not mutually exclusive. The notion of the autonomous subject is different from the sovereign subject, which emerges at the level of power and fantasies of coherence.

20. I suggest that we need transitional objects to elaborate love. We need our cultural objects—literature, art, ideas—because they are both partly inside and partly outside. They are both immediate and mediated. But like any transitional object, narratives cannot emerge out of thin air, nor can a narrative exist without it being shared with another. Winnicott notes that "talking *to oneself* does not reflect back . . . [the talk must be] reflected back by *someone not oneself*" (*Playing and Reality* 85, emphases in original). Creative potentiality bears fruit when the search for the self is reflected back by the other. Winnicott also emphasizes that the transitional object exists prior to the baby's finding of it, that finding something to attach to is a creative act.

Chapter Two

1. Eric Naiman's queer reading of Nabokov is similar to mine in his move away from character-centered sexuality. In his ideas of "hermenteutic arousal" and "hermophobia," Naiman identifies a reading performance of Nabokov as a sexual performance, fraught with anxiety about earning the approval of the Master (Nabokov) through rigorously proven omniscience, the mark of a good reader. My reading process is different from Naiman's in that mine does not revolve around the Master's approval. For me, "misreadings" occur not because they are unsanctioned by the author, as Naiman claims, but because narratives of certainty are necessary pathways toward conceptual crisis.

2. In the 1979 special issue of *Modern Fiction Studies* on Nabokov, Ross notes that "modern theorists invariably offer allegories, often psychological or sociological, to rationalize Humbert's desire for nymphets" (Ross 514). By 1979, the allegorical readings of Lolita were well established, including the notion that

the nymphet symbolizes America in the hands of a middle-aged Europe (Ross 523). Allegory rationalizes the perversion of the novel and keeps reading safe. On the other hand, critics such as Lionel Trilling have controversially proposed that *Lolita* is the greatest love story of the century, and that the reader should refrain from moralistic judgment in order to identify with Humbert's human desires to be authentic. The question remains whether readers ought to take Humbert's pedophilia at face value and, if so, what its implications are. While criticism of *Lolita* since 1979 has expanded from positions of the allegorical, the text continues to exert uncomfortable pressure on critical interpretation.

3. Stockton marks lateral displacements of queer from child to animal or to images of vehicles in motion. She explores the sexuality of the child as queer, as arising either in deferral or belatedly. These "lateral" temporalities reposition Lolita as a queer sexual agent. In his chapter "Sentimentality, Desire, and Aestheticism in *Lolita*," Kevin Ohi explores the negating violence of Humbert's confession against Lolita's character, marking an erasure of her sexual pleasures, but I am more interested in Humbert's relationship to the reader.

4. See criticism by Alan Wilde, Frederic Jameson, and Linda Hutcheon for a more general exploration of the relationship between irony and parody.

5. For an extensive discussion about the debates on Foucault and Freud in queer theory, see Dean and Lane's edited volume, *Homosexuality and Psychoanalysis*.

6. See Stephen Mitchell and Margaret Black's *Freud and Beyond: A History of Modern Psychoanalytic Thought* (1995) for a discussion of the historical controversies in psychoanalysis.

7. See Britzman's *After-Education* for an explanation of the Freud-Klein controversies.

8. Stephen H. Blackwell (2009) states that Nabokov's investment in science had to do with its tremendous advances at the time in zoology, psychology, and physics (Blackwell 4). According to Blackwell's description of these fields, science proper seems to be abstracted from issues of sexuality altogether. As Blackwell implies, psychoanalysis is among those supposed sciences that "pervert" the discourse with an "over-application of nonempirical (un- or undersubstantiated) theory [that] contributed to a myth of the perfectibility of scientific knowledge in various spheres" (Blackwell 11). Blackwell's dichotomization of myth and science comes into question in light of Horkheimer and Adorno's critique of Enlightenment, in which the phantasy of progress, abstraction, and mastery in reason supposedly replaced the fantasy in myth.

9. Appel points out that Humbert pokes fun at Alfred Kinsey, suggesting that sexual science in general is subject to mocking (*Annotated Lolita* 324). Maurice Couturier claims that Nabokov battled only against "pseudo-scientific hermeneutics" (19). David Andrews is among the few who critique Freud as a strict scientist, whose theories, unlike Nabokov's art, depend on a "physical determinism" (9) of infantile and early childhood development in adult psychic life.

10. Goldman reads Nabokov as sympathetic to Kinsey's project in that both challenge the notion of "deviance" by producing evidence of its ubiquity in American populations: "both Kinsey and Nabokov essentially challenged myths

about the presumed 'innocence,' or sexual naïveté, of American women" (Goldman 87). Goldman still dichotomizes science and myth in the presumption that the contamination of science by myth allows unethical acts to be justified, such as the case in both Freudian "myth" and Humbert's mythification of Lolita. Goldman claims that science allows the reader to see Lolita's sexuality as part of normal development, while myth allows Humbert to place Lolita in a position of power and himself in one of passive victimhood.

11. See Chapter 1 for a discussion on Laplanche's outline of the drive [*Trieb*].

12. In his article, Frederick Whiting offers a Foucauldian historicization of *Lolita* in relation to Cold War ideologies that surrounded the publication of the novel. Whiting connects the proliferation of sexual subjectivity with legal discourse, pointing out that the publication of *Lolita* coincided with an epidemic of child molestation. Laws between 1937 and 1955—such as the legal codification of homosexuality and pedophilia—distinguished sex crimes on the basis of the psychological profile of the criminal.

13. Geoffrey Green's book *Freud and Nabokov* (1988) applies Freud's more literary essays to Nabokov's practice as a writer in general. In *Disenfranchised from America* (2009), Melissa Lam explores Nabokov's defamiliarization of America through Humbert's uncanny perspective. Couturier offers insightful and detailed psychoanalytic readings of Humbert's character, but while he acknowledges the author's position on Freud and the narrator's resistances to psychoanalysis, he disregards them for the most part. Couturier sees a Lacanian articulation of the death drive in Humbert's search for sexual satisfaction in the face of his waning desire. Couturier's point about the death drive supports my argument that the pleasure Humbert takes from Lolita pales in comparison to the pleasures of confession.

14. In the last address, as Appel points out, Humbert refers to Charles Baudelaire's famous hail of the reader in *Les Fleurs du Mal*: "*Hypocrite lecteur,—mon semblable,—mon frère!*" (quoted in *Annotated Lolita* 436). Baudelaire's poem exposes the complicity bound up in the process of reading, a complicity that counters the reader's desire to distance him- or herself from the modern condition with aesthetic contemplation. The poetic voice elicits an identification by the reader through a shared complicity. Humbert's parodic citation of Baudelaire, I argue, has the opposite effect, accentuating a failed identification between reader and text.

15. See Chapter 5 for a discussion of interpellation and ideology.

16. In *Why War?*, Rose argues: "Mourning appears here almost as a metaphor for psychoanalysis itself, or at least for the mental processes it describes . . . More important, the thought provoked by mourning takes the form of a dissociation. It is not thought as assured knowledge, but a form of thinking unable, in any single or singular way, to own or possess itself" (19–20).

17. In "The Unconscious," Freud describes how different parts of the psychic topography, the Pre-Conscious, the Unconscious, and the Conscious, communicate with one another, through processes of *phantasy-formation* and *substitution-formation* (138). He states: "all the associations in the neighbourhood of the substitutive idea become endowed with a peculiar intensity of cathexis, so

that they may display a high degree of sensibility to excitation" ("Unconscious" 131). In a dream reconstructed in analysis, the associative links that make up the scene take on this hyper-cathexis. See de Lauretis's reading of Freud's essay "A Child is Being Beaten" in *The Practice of Love*. Freud's essay delineates three phases of the beating fantasy common among those afflicted by hysteria or compulsive neurosis: "*The father is beating the child*"; "*I am being beaten by my father*"; and a child is being beaten, with the subject probably watching among many children ("Child" 287, emphasis in original). De Lauretis reads the progression of these stages as a process of desubjectivation in which the masochistic pleasures become increasingly disembodied, as the subject dissolves into the scene itself.

18. Green and Andrews recognize that the authorial voice of Nabokov is still very much a construction: "Through his interviews Nabokov was constructing a fictive version of himself" (Green 38). Gene H. Bell-Villada, on the other hand, stumbles over the authorial voice, since Nabokov's interviews offend him and interrupt his attachment to the prose. Regardless of whether or not critics use Nabokov's interviews in their interpretations, Nabokov's persona is so alluring and vociferous that it is almost impossible to resist measuring his fiction against his "real" views.

19. As an aesthetic that is related to but different from "queer," camp is another multifaceted and evolving "vanishing point." An elaboration of the camp aesthetic is beyond the scope of this book. As Fabio Cleto (1999) indicates that camp's theoretical complexity involves the allure of aesthetic desires and failures. In a general sense, Eric Savoy defines camp as "a speech act that inverts the customary hierarchy of the serious and the trivial in order to show their interlinearity, that confounds the boundaries between figurative and literal language" ("Jamesian Thing" 272).

20. Ferger's 2004 article "Who's Who in the Sublimelight" enters into one of the more recent critical debates, which began in 1995, between Julian Connolly, Alexander Dolinin, and Boyd on the status of the novel's last scenes, which an inconsistency of recorded dates places into question. According to the revisionist reading, Humbert fantasizes Quilty's murder and his last meeting with Lolita. Tekiner asserts that in light of this discrepancy, Humbert is in prison for his crimes against Lolita, not his murder of Quilty, and "the last nine chapters of the novel are entirely the products of his imagination" (469). According to this argument, Humbert's "pure solipsistic art" takes precedence over the sexual crime, since his confession takes on a life of its own and displaces the actual events that transpired. The implications of Tekiner's argument, that the pleasures of writing exceed the bodily pleasures of the sex act, correspond with other critics' views, such as Couturier's, that Humbert's sexual relation with Lolita is subject to a death-driven decline. Boyd counters the revisionist reading, however, in his conclusion that Nabokov simply made an error in dating the sequence of events accurately. Based on an evaluation of Humbert's enduring incompetence and a rigorous tracing of Dr. John Ray's name throughout the text, Ferger posits Ray as the textual referent and argues that the doctor heavily edited Humbert's prose and constructed the ending as a forced "moral apotheosis."

Chapter Three

1. Hayles identifies two accomplishments of the novel: "First, it extends the claims of the print book by showing what print can be in a digital age; second, it recuperates the vitality of the novel as a genre by recovering, *through the processes of remediation*, subjectivities coherent enough to become the foci of the sustained narration that remains the hallmark of the print novel" (781, emphasis in original).

2. As Neil Badmington remarks, "The boundaries that ought to fall into line with common sense, the laws of science and the land, turn out to be far more uncertain" (19).

3. See Chapter 1 on dynamic binding and the difference between signification and symbolization.

4. Hayles associates the problem of knowledge with "highly energized inversion:" "The labyrinth thus becomes a trope for incomplete knowledge as well as a site where paradoxical inversions become highly energized as absence flips into presence, the contained stretches far beyond its container, and outside becomes inside becomes outside" (792). Implicitly, Hayles describes a kind of "highly energized" queer failure.

5. The floating signifier, "house," appears in blue throughout the book, regardless of its referent, whether or not it appears as part of a compound word. Martin Brick identifies the blue text as a citation and disruption of authoritative medieval manuscripts (n.p.). Hansen investigates this referential void in his essay "Digital Topography." Hansen identifies the blue signifier as an image of a hyperlink. In book form, the hyperlink mocks the function of digital media, suggesting that beyond the signifier there lies a whole world of information that, because the reader cannot click on it, remains inaccessible. Hansen's point implies that the Internet is an apt metaphor for the unconscious. The hyperlink is a wish fulfillment to manifest as immediately accessible all of the repressed free associations that render any given signifier overdetermined.

6. See Paul Auster's *The New York Trilogy* for an example of a canonical novel that exploits readerly anxiety through its narrative unfolding.

7. Nele Bemong's article "Exploration #6: The Uncanny" provides a thorough tracing of the *unheimlich*, but, because the novel presents its own totality, Zampanò's footnotes explain the concept for the reader according to Freud, Lacan, and Martin Heidegger. The *unheimlich* is not overtly threatening, but disturbs domestic safety, associated with homely comforts but ultimately signifying "not-at-home" (Danielewski 24). The slippage between *heimlich* and *unheimlich* occurs due to a repetition compulsion that renders the familiar strange and thus produces anxiety.

8. In *Powers of Horror*, Kristeva defines abjection as the constitutive outside, including contaminants such as menstrual blood, vomit, feces, decay, all of which must be expropriated from the body in efforts to maintain the integrity of ego. Internal to but inassimilable by the body, the abject is a non-object: "That is, of rampancy, boundlessness, the unthinkable, the untenable, the unsymbolizable. But

what is it? Unless it be the untiring repetition of a drive, which, propelled by an initial loss, does not cease wandering, unsated, deceived, warped, until it finds its only stable object—death" (*Horror* 23).

9. In "Law of Genre," Jacques Derrida exhibits how categories of genre and *genre* (gender in French) become subject to "degenerescence" upon the repetition of an utterance (226). He questions the structural sustainability of literary genre. His writing in this essay becomes subject to "invagination, an internal pocket larger than the whole" ("Genre" 228). One could say that, as a solipsistic, invaginating force, *House of Leaves* invaginates its readers in turn, another queer function of the text.

10. Bemong argues that the repetitious structure of the uncanny in the text indeed points to the death drive, citing Zampanò's reference to Freud (Danielewski 359).

11. Hayles's observation about what lies at the center of this book corresponds to my description of it as a vanishing point, something that directs the eye toward a visual collapse: "The absence at the center of this space is not merely nothing. It is so commanding and absolute that it paradoxically becomes an especially intense kind of presence, violent in its impossibility and impossible to ignore" (788).

12. Martin Brick notes the text's awareness of its own "physical manifestation of word matter" (Jan 2004). Hayles coins the term "technotext" to characterize texts like *House of Leaves* that "display a heightened sense of their materiality . . . technotexts construct their materialities so as to foreground the inscription technologies that produced them" (794).

13. More precisely, Abraham and Torok describe when the subject literalizes the lost love objects as *demetaphorization* (126), in order to indicate a regression by which the subject can no longer replace the love object with words. Because the root word, "metaphor," is a loaded term in literary studies, I prefer the term *literalization* to describe the same psychical process. Abraham and Torok's text also figures in my last chapter's discussion of mourning and melancholia.

14. The cinematic and photographic effects that Danielewski's text acquires lead Hansen to characterize *House of Leaves* not as a postmodern, angst-ridden celebration of simulation, but rather as a critique of orthography, of the exact repetition of experience through technological mediation (627). For other examples of visual literalization similar to Danielewski's text, but specific to the notion of inscription and the racialized body, see the innovative work of Theresa Cha in *Dictee* (1982) and Salvador Plascencia in *People of Paper* (2005).

15. As Hayles observes, "Whether excruciatingly slow or amazingly fast, the time it takes to read a page functions as a remediation of the narrative action in the life-world of the reader, linking real-time decoding with the intensity and pacing of the represented events in a correlation that itself is a remediation of eye-tracking in cinematic action" (797).

16. Hayles reflects on the paradox of looking through a page while looking at a page, which emphasizes the materiality of the novel by denying the transparency it promises (792–94).

17. See Roman Jakobson's essay "Two Aspects of Language" for a discussion on the function of metonymy in nineteenth-century realism.

18. See Natalie Hamilton's article "The A-Mazing House" for an extensive discussion of *House of Leaves* and its homage to Jorge Luis Borges's conceptualizations of the labyrinth.

19. Hamilton divides the experience of a labyrinth into two modes: synchronic and diachronic (13). The latter describes the arduous process of treading through the labyrinth, while the former describes Daedalus's aerial view of the entire design, a kind of divine omniscience. A synchronic experience of the *House of Leaves* is impossible. Brian Chanen's article "Surfing the Text" provides an impressive, synchronic map of the footnotes in the monstrous Chapter 9 in order to illustrate the chapter's resemblance to a network of hyperlinks, as well as the pleasures and contingencies of "surfing" through the footnotes arbitrarily (Chanen 170). His construction of an abstracted web, however, defeats the purpose of the house as narrative enigma and, in the end, does not contribute to a decoding of meaning. A synchronic experience is an unattainable object of desire that seduces the reader, again and again, into a diachronic experience of getting lost.

20. My last chapter discusses further the ways in which interpellation functions with the drives.

21. As Hansen notes, "the impossibility of an external, first-order observation of the entire system functions to ennoble second-order observations that take this very impossibility—always from their singular standpoint within the system—as their content. No wonder, then, that Ruby Dahl, Zampanò's invented expert on space, 'fails to consider why the house never opens into what is necessarily outside of itself'" (628).

22. See Felman's *Jacques Lacan and the Adventures of Insight* for an elucidation of the structural role ignorance plays in knowledge production, as well as my discussion of her text in Chapter 2.

23. For a theoretical discussion about the performative contradiction of censorship, see Judith Butler's article "Ruled Out: Vocabularies of the Censor" in Robert C. Post's edited volume, *Censorship and Silencing: Practices of Cultural Regulation*.

24. See Gérard Genette's *Narrative Discourse*, which defines analepsis as a subcategory of anachrony. The latter marks a discordance between two temporal orders of story and narrative: "any evocation after the fact of an event that took place earlier than the point in the story where we are at any given moment" (40).

25. See Katherine Cox's article, "What Has Made Me? Locating the Mother in the Textual Labyrinth of Mark Danielewski's *House of Leaves*," for a reading of Truant's relationship to his mother as a structural necessity of the text.

26. For a discussion on queer temporality, see Elizabeth Freeman's "Still After." See Hayles's "Saving the Subject" on the temporality of remediation in *House of Leaves*.

Chapter Four

1. Central texts that engage this debate include David L. Eng's and David Kazanjian's edited volume, *Loss: The Politics of Mourning*. See also Dominick LaCapra's chapter, "Canons, Texts, and Contexts," in his book *Representing the Holocaust: History, Theory, Trauma* for an exploration of how the process of canonization forecloses the possibility of mourning by closing over the wounds of a traumatic past (23). See also Eugenie Brinkema's critique of the romanticization of melancholia and the conceptual difficulty of mourning in her book, *The Forms of the Affect*.

2. All of Ross's acts of killing—the horse on the ship, the German soldier at the crater—are carried out against his will or in panic.

3. Remediation in this case describes the textual representation of objects displaced by their representation in other media, such as film, photography, newspapers, and voice recordings. See the previous chapter on remediation in the *House of Leaves*.

4. See *Sublime Object* for Žižek's reading of identification in Kafka. See also my fifth chapter for a discussion on literary representations of interpellation in systems of totality.

Chapter Five

1. See also articles by Mark Jerng, Martin Puchner, and Nancy Fraser, all of whom address the lack of the desire to rebel. Mark Fisher also notes the relentless fatalism in the film adaptation.

2. Much of the scholarship on *Never Let Me Go* considers the symptomatic enigma of the clones' passivity, their intellectual limitations, Kathy's flat style of narration, the social injustice of organ farming, and the ethical impact of reproductive cloning within a posthuman realm. The clones' passivity about their fate is often the departure point for criticism. This kind of reading focuses on the social implications of the novel. Such scholars as Sim, Henriette Roos, Gabriele Griffin, Jerng, Leona Toker, and Daniel Chertoff use the novel's premise of cloning to consider burgeoning technologies in the United States and United Kingdom at the millennial turn. Matthew Eatough uses the novel to discuss affective complexities in end-of-life care. Robbie Goh provides a "post-clone-nial" reading of the clones as bodies subjected to technologically induced racialization.

3. Incorporation differs from Klein's notion of projective identification. Both result from the problem of what cannot be seen inside the subject. But, for Klein, projective identification produces a phantasy of seeing what is inside in the outside world: it bears the seeds for phantasy and thus for, not the perpetual stasis of melancholia, but a creative life.

4. Prolepsis evokes events that will occur in the future, a narrative strategy that is anticipatory. Analepsis evokes events that already occurred, a strategy marked by belatedness (Genette 40).

5. See Freud's essay "Negation," in which he concludes that any answer in the negative indicates a disavowal and a preference for repression: "during analysis we never find a 'no' in the unconscious, and recognition of the unconscious by the ego is always expressed in negative formulations" (99).

6. Britzman deals with the two principles of mental functioning at length in her book *Freud and Education*, in which she states: "The two formulations of the pleasure and reality principles, sketchy as they are, represent the psyche's objections, objects, and obstacles to learning. However, they may also be considered as principles of knowledge creating our relations to life and death, to imagination and duty, and to our relations with and responsibilities to the world on offer. If the pleasure principle belongs to narcissism, the reality principle will be constituted through loss of the object" (142). The process of learning, then, involves the dialectical oscillation between the two principles. Later in this chapter, I consider how these principles interact with the forces of drive.

7. See Roland Barthes's book, *Introduction to the Structural Analysis of Narrative* for a structuralist theorization of narrative into a series of narrative units: cardinal functions, catalysts, indexes proper, and informants.

8. I am grateful to Bernice Neal for pointing out the Latin variations of "care."

9. The subject of theory kindergarten, the question-child, is a figure of deferral, someone who desires to satisfy her curiosity about the world but whose resistances reject conventional truths of adulthood. For all the anxiety the question-child faces, she is governed predominantly by the pleasure principle, something that the conventional educator attempts to replace with the reality of known truths. But the child's insistence on questioning, as well as her resistance to enlightenment, brings the adult's knowledge into question in turn, dismantles the phantasy of the adult's coherence, and pulls the adult back into theory kindergarten with the child. This situation facilitates dialogue between educator and student that initiates mutual transformation. See Britzman's *After-Education* for a thorough discussion of the question-child.

10. Tiffany Tsao offers a refreshing interpretation of *Never Let Me Go* as a theological novel about creation. She applies to *Never Let Me Go* the medieval question in *Paradise Lost* of whether purposeful creation is inherently problematic, concluding that the drive toward a sense of purpose in both religion and biotechnology is "terrifyingly reductive and devoid of freedom" (223). Tsao suggests that biotechnological creation should continue *for no practical reason* in order to acquire more ethical practices. Like Black, Tsao differentiates Hailsham's humanist art production to which Tommy is resistant and the art he creates at the end of his life: "Tommy's art not only manages to move beyond practical motives, but also the need to be aesthetically pleasing or innovative . . . Unlike the artworks they created at Hailsham, which had to meet certain aesthetic requirements set

by the guardians . . . Tommy's art has no expectations set on it" (Tsao 228). See also Myra Seaman's article about posthuman becoming, which asserts the difference between two possible results from technological processes: on the one hand, the nightmare posthuman benefactor of the donation program, and on the other, the posthuman clone who, through her working through, is able to enhance the capacity for creativity, love, and vulnerability. In this technological dystopia, creative excess flourishes in ways that Horkheimer and Adorno do not anticipate.

Bibliography

Abraham, Nicolas, and Maria Torok. *The Shell and the Kernel.* Ed. & Trans. Nicholas T. Rand. Chicago: U of Chicago P, 1994. Print.

Althusser, Louis. "Ideology and Ideological State Apparatuses." Leitch 1483–1509.

Andrews, David. "Varieties of Determinism: Nabokov among Rorty, Freud, and Sartre." *Nabokov Studies* 6 (2000/2001): 1–33. Print.

Appel, Alfred Jr. "'Lolita': The Springboard of Parody." *Contemporary Literature* 8.2 (1967): 204–41. Print.

Atwood, Margaret. *The Handmaid's Tale.* Toronto: M&S, 2006. Print.

Auster, Paul. *The New York Trilogy.* London: Faber and Faber, 1987. Print.

Badmington, Neil. "Theorizing Posthumanism." *Cultural Critique* 53 (2003): 10–27. Print.

Ball, Karyn. "Global High Culture in the Era of Neo-Liberalism: The Case of Documenta11." *Research in Political Economy* 21 (2004): 121–40. Print.

Bao, Hongwei. "People's Park: The Politics of Naming and the Rights to the City." In Scherer and Ball, 115–32. Print.

Barber, Stephen, and David L. Clark. *Regarding Sedgwick: Essays on Queer Culture and Critical Theory.* Eds. Stephen Barber and David L. Clark. New York: Routledge, 2002. Print.

Barnes, Djuna. *Nightwood.* New York: New Directions Books, 1937. Print.

Barthes, Roland. *Camera Lucida.* Trans. Richard Howard. New York: Hill and Wang, 1981. Print.

———. *Introduction to the Structural Analysis of the Narrative.* Birmingham: Centre for Contemporary Cultural Studies, University of Birmingham, 1970. Print.

———. *The Pleasure of the Text.* Trans. Richard Miller. New York: Hill and Wang, 1975. Print.

———. *S/Z.* Trans. Richard Miller. New York: Hill and Wang, 1970. Print.

Bell-Villada, Gene H. "On the Cold War American Aestheticism, the Nabokov Problem, and Me." In *Art and Life in Aestheticism: De-Humanizing and Re-Humanizing Art.* Ed. Kelly Comfort. New York: Palgrave Macmillan, 2008. Print.

Bemong, Nele. "Exploration # 6: The Uncanny in Mark Z. Danielewski's *House of Leaves.*" *Image and Narrative.* Jan 2003. Web. 20 June 2011.

Benjamin, Walter. "Theses on the Philosophy of History." *Illuminations*. Ed. Hannah Arendt. Trans. Harry Zohn. New York: Schocken Books, 1968. 253–64. Print.

———. "The Work of Art in the Age of Mechanical Reproduction." *Illuminations*. Ed. Hannah Arendt. Trans. Harry Zohn. New York: Schocken Books, 1968. 217–52. Print.

Benveniste, Émile. *Problems in General Linguistics*. Trans. Mary Elizabeth Meek. Coral Gables: U of Miami P, 1971. Print.

Berlant, Lauren. *Cruel Optimism*. Durham, NC: Duke UP, 2011. Print.

———. "Starved." Halley and Parker 79–90.

Berlant, Lauren and Lee Edelman. *Sex, or the Unbearable*. Durham, NC: Duke UP, 2014. Print.

———. "Reading, Sex, and the Unbearable: A Response to Tim Dean." *American Literary History* 27.3 (2015): 625–29. Print.

Bersani, Leo. *The Freudian Body*. New York: Columbia UP, 1986. Print.

———. "Is the Rectum a Grave?" *October* 43 (1987): 197–222. Print.

———. "Shame on You." Halley and Parker 91–109.

Bersani, Leo, and Adam Phillips. *Intimacies*. Chicago: U of Chicago P, 2008. Print.

Best, Stephen, and Sharon Marcus. "'Surface Reading: An Introduction." *Representations* 108.1 (2009): 1–21. Print.

Black, Shameem. "Ishiguro's Inhuman Aesthetics." *Modern Fiction Studies*. 55.4 (2009): 785–807. Print.

Blackwell, Stephen H. *The Quill and the Scalpel: Nabokov's Art and the Worlds of Science*. Columbus: Ohio State UP, 2009. Print.

Bollas, Christopher. *The Shadow of the Object: Psychoanalysis of the Unthought Known*. New York: Columbia UP, 1987. Print.

Boyd, Brian. *Stalking Nabokov: Selected Essays*. New York: Columbia UP, 2011. Print.

Brady, Anita. "'How Could it Hurt you When it Looks so Good?': Commodity Culture and Queer Authenticity." In Scherer and Ball, 13–28. Print.

Brick, Martin. "Blueprint(s): Rubric for a Deconstructed Age in *House of Leaves*." *Philament: An Online Journal of the Arts and Culture*. Jan. 2004. Web. 15 July 2010.

Brinkema, Eugenie. *The Forms of the Affects*. Durham, NC: Duke UP, 2014. Print.

Britzman, Deborah. *After-Education: Anna Freud, Melanie Klein, and Psychoanalytic Histories of Learning*. Albany, NY: SUNY Press, 2003. Print.

———. "Difficulties in the Study, Research, and Pedagogy of Sexuality: Problems of Origin, Discourse, and Vulnerability." Facultad de Filosofia y Letras-Universidad de Buenos Aires. November 2011. Address.

———. *Freud and Education*. New York: Routledge, 2011. Print.

———. "On Being a Slow Reader: Psychoanalytic Reading Problems in Ishiguro's *Never Let Me Go*." *Changing English: Studies in Culture and Education* 13.3 (2006): 307–18. Print.

———. "Queer Pedagogy and Its Strange Techniques." *Lost Objects, Contested Subjects*. Albany, NY: SUNY Press, 1998. Chapter 4. Print.

Britzman, Deborah, et al. "Affective Equality: Love, Care, and Injustice." *British Journal of Sociology of Education* 30.6 (2009): 773–87. Print.

Bruhm, Steven. "On Stephen King's Phallus: Or the Postmodern Gothic." *Narrative* 4.1 (1996): 55–73. Print.

Brydon, Diana. "A Devotion to Fragility: Timothy Findley's *The Wars*." *World Literature Written in English* 26.1 (1986): 75–84. Print.

Burroughs, William S. *Naked Lunch*. Eds. James Grauerholz and Barry Miles. New York: Grove Press, 2001. Print.

Butler, Judith. *Bodies that Matter: On the Discursive Limits of Sex*. New York: Routledge, 1993. Print.

———. *Gender Trouble*. New York: Routledge, 2006. Print.

———. *The Psychic Life of Power: Theories in Subjection*. Stanford, CA: Stanford UP, 1997. Print.

———. "Ruled Out: Vocabularies of the Censor." *Censorship and Silencing: Practices of Cultural Regulation*. Ed. Robert C. Post. Getty Research Institute, 1998. 247–59. Print.

———. *Undoing Gender*. New York: Routledge, 2004. Print.

Carroll, Rachel. "Imitation of Life: Cloning, Heterosexuality and the Human in Kazuo Ishiguro's Never Let Me Go." *Journal of Gender Studies* 19.1 (2010): 59–71. Print.

Caserio, Robert, et al. "The Antisocial Thesis in Queer Theory." *PMLA* 121.3 (2006): 819–36. Print.

Cha, Theresa Hak Kyung. *Dictee*. Berkeley: U of California P, 2001. Print.

Chanen, Brian. "Surfing the Text." *European Journal of English Studies* 11.2 (2007): 163–76. Print.

Chun, Wendy Hui Kyong. *Habitual New Media*. Cambridge: MIT Press, 2016. Print.

Cleto, Fabio, ed. *Camp: Queer Aesthetics and the Performing Subject: A Reader*. Ann Arbor: U of Michigan P, 1999. Print.

Cobb, Michael. "A Little Like Reading: Preference, *Facebook*, and Overwhelmed Interpretations." *PMLA* 28.1 (2013): 201–206. Print.

———. "Lonely." Halley and Parker 207–20.

Cobley, Evelyn. "Postmodernist War Fiction: Findley's *The Wars*." *Canadian Literature* 147 (1995): 98–124. Print.

Connolly, Julian. "'Nature's Reality' or Humbert's 'Fancy': Scenes of Reunion and Murder in Lolita." *Nabokov Studies* 2 (1995): 41–61. Print.

Couturier, Maurice. "Narcissism and Demand in Lolita." *Nabokov Studies* 9 (2005): 19–46. Print.

Cox, Katherine. "What Has Made Me? Locating the Mother in the Textual Labyrinth of Mark Danielewski's *House of Leaves*." *Critical Survey* 18.2 (2006): 4–15. Print.

Cvetkovich, Ann. *The Archive of Feelings: Trauma, Sexuality, and Lesbian Public Cultures*. Durham, NC: Duke UP, 2003. Print.

———. "Public Feelings." In Halley and Parker, 169–179. Print.

De Lauretis, Teresa. *Freud's Drive: Psychoanalysis, Literature and Film*. New York: Palgrave Macmillan, 2010. Print.

———. *The Practice of Love: Lesbian Sexuality and Perverse Desire*. Bloomington: Indiana UP, 1994. Print.

De Man, Paul. "The Rhetoric of Temporality." *Blindness and Insight: Essays in the Rhetoric of Contemporary Criticism*. Minneapolis: U of Minnesota P, 1971. 187–228. Print.

Danielewski, Mark. *House of Leaves*. New York: Pantheon Books, 2000. Print.

Davis, Whitney. *Queer Beauty: Sexuality and Aesthetics from Winckelmann to Freud and Beyond*. New York: Columbia UP, 2010. Print.

Dean, Tim. "Bareback Times." *Queer Times, Queer Becomings*. Albany, NY: SUNY, 2011. 75–100. Print.

———. *Beyond Sexuality*. Chicago: U of Chicago P, 2000. Print.

———. "Clear and Sonorous: A Reply to Lauren Berlant and Lee Edelman." *American Literary History* 27.3 (2015): 630–33. Print.

———. "The Erotics of Transgression." In Stevens, 65–80. Print.

———. "No Sex, Please, We're American." *American Literary History* 27.3 (2015): 630–33. Print.

———. *Unlimited Intimacy: Reflections on the Subculture of Barebacking*. Chicago: U of Chicago P, 2009. Print.

Dean, Tim, and Christopher Lane, eds. *Homosexuality and Psychoanalysis*. Chicago: U of Chicago Press, 2001. Print.

Derrida, Jacques. "Différance." *Margins of Philosophy*. Chicago: U of Chicago P, 1982. 1–28. Print.

———. "Law of Genre." *Acts of Literature*. Ed. Derek Attridge. New York: Routledge, 1992. 221–52. Print.

———. *Without Alibi*. Trans. Peggy Kamuf. Stanford, CA: Stanford UP, 2002. Print.

Dolinin, Alexander. "Nabokov's Time Doubling: From The Gift to Lolita." *Nabokov Studies* 2 (1995): 3–40. Print.

Dollimore, Jonathan. "Post/Modern: On the Gay Sensibility, or the Pervert's Revenge on Authenticity—Wilde, Genet, Orton, and Others." *Sexual Dissidence: Augustine to Wilde, Freud to Foucault*. Oxford: Oxford UP, 1991. 307–28. Print.

Downing, Lisa, and Robert Gillett, eds. *Queer in Europe*. Farnham: Ashgate, 2011. Print.

Eatough, Matthew. "The Time that Remains: Organ Donation, Temporal Duration, and Bildung in Kazuo Ishiguro's Never Let Me Go." *Literature and Medicine* 29.1 (2011): 132–60. Print.

Edelman, Lee. *Homographesis: Essays in Gay Literary and Cultural Theory*. New York: Routledge, 1994. Print.

———. "Ever After: History, Negativity, and the Social." In Halley and Parker, 110–118. Print.

———. *No Future: Queer Theory and the Death Drive*. Durham, NC: Duke UP, 2004. Print.

Ellis, Havelock. *The Psychology of Sex: A Manual for Students*. London: William Heinemann (Medical Books), 1933. Print.

Eng, David L., and David Kazanjian, eds. *Loss: The Politics of Mourning*. Los Angeles: U of California P, 2003. Print.

Felman, Shoshana. *Jacques Lacan and the Adventures of Insight*. Cambridge: Harvard UP, 1987. Print.

Felski, Rita. *Limits of Critique*. Chicago: U of Chicago P, 2015. Print.

Ferger, George. "Who's Who in the Sublimelight: 'Suave John Ray' and Lolita's 'Secret Points.'" *Nabokov Studies* 8 (2004): 137–98. Print.

Fincher, Max. *Queering the Gothic in the Romantic Age: The Penetrating Eye*. Basingstoke: Palgrave Macmillan, 2007. Print.

Findley, Timothy. *The Wars*. Toronto: Penguin, 1977. Print.

Fisher, Mark. "Precarious Dystopias: The Hunger Games, in Time, and Never Let Me Go." *Film Quarterly* 65.4 (2011): 27–33. Print.

Foer, Jonathan Safran. *Extremely Loud and Incredibly Close*. Boston: Houghton Mifflin Company, 2005. Print.

Foster, Hal. "Obscene, Abject, Traumatic (1996)." *October Files 6: Cindy Sherman*. Ed. Johanna Burton. Cambridge: MIT Press, 2006. 193–216. Print.

Foucault, Michel. *History of Sexuality: Volume 1*. Trans. Robert Hurley. New York: Random House, 1978. Print.

Fraser, Nancy. "On Justice: Lessons from Plato, Rawls and Ishiguro." *New Left Review* 74 (2012): 41–51. Print.

Freccero, Carla. "Queer Times." In Halley and Parker, 17–26. Print.

Freeman, Elizabeth. "Still After." In Halley and Parker, 27–33. Print.

Freud, Sigmund. *Beyond the Pleasure Principle*. Standard Edition. Ed. and Trans. James Strachey. New York: W. W. Norton & Company, 1961. Print.

———. *Beyond the Pleasure Principle and Other Writings*. Trans. John Reddick. London: Penguin, 2003. Print.

———. "A Child is Being Beaten." *The Psychology of Love*. Trans. Shaun Whiteside. London: Penguin, 2006. 279–306. Print.

———. *Civilization and Its Discontents*. Trans. David McLintock. London: Penguin, 2002. Print.

———. "Formulations on Two Principles of Psychic Functioning." *The Penguin Freud Reader*. Ed. Adam Phillips. Trans. Graham Frankland. London: Penguin, 2006. 414–21. Print.

———. *Inhibitions, Symptoms, Anxiety*. Trans. Alix Strachey. London: Hogarth, 1936. Print.

———. *Jenseits des Lustprinzips*. Leipzig, Wein, und Zurich: Internationaler Psychoanalytischer Verlag, G.M.B.H., 1921. Print.

———. *The Joke and Its Relation to the Unconscious*. Trans. Joyce Crick. London: Penguin, 2002. Print.

———. "On the Mechanism of Paranoia." *General Psychological Theory*. Ed. Philip Rieff. New York: Macmillan, 1963. 29–48. Print.

———. "Mourning and Melancholia." Trans. Joan Riviere. *General Psychological Theory*. Ed. Philip Rieff. New York: MacMillan, 1963. 164–79. Print.

———. "Negation." Trans. Joan Riviere. *General Psychological Theory*. Ed. Philip Rieff. New York: MacMillan, 1963. 213–17. Print.

———. "A Note Upon the 'Mystic Writing Pad.'" Trans. James Strachey. *General Psychological Theory*. Ed. Philip Rieff. New York: MacMillan, 1963. 207–12. Print.

———. "An Outline of Psychoanalysis." *The Penguin Freud Reader*. Ed. Adam Phillips. London: Penguin, 2006. 1–63. Print.

———. *Three Essays on the Theory of Sexuality*. Trans. James Strachey. New York: Basic Books, 2000. Print.

———. *The Uncanny*. Trans. David McLintock. London: Penguin, 2003. Print.

———. "The Unconscious." Trans. Cecil M. Baines. *General Psychological Theory*. Ed. Philip Rieff. New York: Macmillan, 1963. 116–50. Print.

Gallop, Jane. *The Deaths of the Author: Reading and Writing in Time*. Durham and London: Duke UP, 2011. Print.

———. "Precocious *Jouissance*: Roland Barthes, Amatory Maladjustment, and Emotion." *New Literary History* 43.3 (2012):565–82. Print.

Genette, Gérard. *Narrative Discourse: An Essay in Method*. Trans. Jane E. Lewin. Ithaca, NY: Cornell UP, 1980. Print.

Gilman, Sander. "Reading Freud in English." *International Review of Psychoanalysis* 18 (1991): 331–344. Print.

Goh, Robbie. "The Postclone-nial in Kazuo Ishiguro's Never Let Me Go and Amitav Ghosh's the Calcutta Chromosome: Science and the Body in the Asian Diaspora." *Ariel-a Review of International English Literature* 41.3–4 (2010): 45–71. Print.

Goldie, Terry. *Pink Snow: Homotextual Possibilities in Canadian Fiction*. Peterborough: Broadview P, 2003. Print.

Goldman, Eric. "'Knowing' Lolita: Sexual Deviance and Normality in Nabokov's Lolita." *Nabokov Studies* 8 (2004): 87–104. Print.

Green, Geoffrey. *Freud and Nabokov*. Lincoln: U of Nebraska P, 1988. Print.

Griffin, Gabriele. "Science and the Cultural Imaginary: The Case of Kazuo Ishiguro's Never Let Me Go." *Textual Practice* 23.4 (2009): 645–63. Print.

Halberstam, Judith. *The Queer Art of Failure*. Durham and London: Duke UP, 2011. Print.

———. *Skin Shows*. Durham, NC and London: Duke UP, 1995. Print.

Hall, Donald E. *Reading Sexualities: Hermeneutic Theory and the Future of Queer Studies*. New York: Routledge, 2009. Print.

Halley, Janet, and Andrew Parker. Introduction. In Halley and Parker, 1–16. Print.

Halley, Janet, and Andrew Parker, eds. *After Sex? Writing Since Queer Theory*. Durham, NC and London: Duke UP, 2011. Print.

Halperin, David. *Saint Foucault: Toward a Gay Hagiography*. Oxford: Oxford UP, 1999. Print.

Hames-García, Michael, and Ernesto Javier Martínez, eds. *Gay Latino Studies: A Critical Reader*. Durham, NC and London: Duke UP, 2011. Print.

Hamilton, Natalie. "The A-Mazing House: The Labyrinth as Theme and Form in Mark Z. Danielewski's *House of Leaves*." *Critique* 50.1 (2008): 3–15. Print.

Hansen, Mark. "The Digital Topography in Mark Z. Danielewski's *House of Leaves*." *Contemporary Literature* 45.4 (2004): 597–636. Print.

Haraway, Donna. "A Cyborg Manifesto: Science Technology, and Socialist-Feminism in the Late Twentieth Century." *Simians, Cyborgs and Women: The Reinvention of Nature*. New York: Routledge, 1991. 149–82. Print.

Hatch, R.B. "Narrative Development in the Canadian Historical Novel." *Canadian Literature* 110 (1986): 79–96. Print.

Hawke, Shé, and Baden Offord. "Queer(y)ing Pedagogy and Cultural Studies: Critical Reflections on Teaching Sexuality." In Scherer and Ball, 191. Print.

Hayles, Katherine. "Saving the Subject: (Re)Mediation in *House of Leaves*." *American Literature* 74.4 (2002): 779–806. Print.

Hennelly, Mark. "Framing the Gothic: From Pillar to Post-Structuralism." *College Literature* 28.3 (2001): 67–87. Print.

Herbold, Sarah. "'(I have camouflaged everything, my love)': Lolita and the Woman Reader." *Nabokov Studies* 5 (1998/9): 71–98. Print.

Horkheimer, Max, and Theodor Adorno. *Dialectic of Enlightenment*. Ed. Gunzelin Schmid Noerr. Trans. Edmund Jephcott. Stanford, CA: Stanford UP, 2002. Print.

Hughes, William, and Andrew Smith, eds. *Queering the Gothic*. New York: Manchester UP, 2009. Print.

Hutcheon, Linda. *Irony's Edge: The Theory and Politics of Irony*. London and New York: Routledge, 1994. Print.

Ingersoll, Earl. "Taking Off into the Realm of Metaphor: Kazuo Ishiguro's Never Let Me Go." *Studies in the Humanities* 34.1 (2007): 40–59. Print.

Ingham, David. "Bashing the Fascists: The Moral Dimensions of Findley's Fiction." *Studies in Canadian Literature* 15.2 (1990): 33–54. Print.

Ishiguro, Kazuo. *Never Let Me Go*. Toronto: Vintage, 2005. Print.

Jakobson, Roman. "Two Aspects of Language." Leitch. 1265–69.

Jameson, Frederic. *Postmodernism: The Cultural Logic of Late Capitalism*. Durham: Duke UP, 1991. Print.

Jerng, Mark. "Giving Form to Life: Cloning and Narrative Expectations of the Human." *Partial Answers: Journal of Literature and the History of Ideas* 6 (2008): 369–93. Print.

Kafka, Franz. *Diaries*. Ed. Max Brod. Schocken Books, 1948. Print.

———. *The Trial*. Ed. George Steiner. Trans. Willa and Edwin Muir. New York: Schocken Books, 1992. Print.

Kant, Immanuel. *The Critique of Judgment.* Trans. J.H. Bernard. New York: Prometheus, 2000. Print.

Kinsey, Alfed C. *Sexual Behaviour in the Human Male.* Philadelphia and London: W.B. Saunders Company, 1948. Print.

Klein, Melanie. "A Contribution to the Psycho-Genesis of Manic-Depressive States." In *The Selected Melanie Klein.* Ed. Juliet Mitchell. New York: The Free Press, 1986. 115–45. Print.

———. "The Importance of Symbol-Formation in the Development of the Ego." *The Selected Melanie Klein.* Ed. Juliet Mitchell. New York: The Free Press, 1986. 95–114. Print.

Kristeva, Julia. *Melanie Klein.* Trans. Ross Guberman. New York: Columbia UP, 2001. Print.

———. *The Powers of Horror: An Essay on Abjection.* New York: Columbia UP, 1982. Print.

———. "Thinking in Dark Times." *Profession* (2006): 13–21. Print.

Kröller, Eva-Marie. "Exploding the Frame: Uses of Photography in Timothy Findley's *The Wars.*" *Journal of Canadian Studies* 16.3 (1981): 68–74. Print.

Kundera, Milan. *The Unbearable Lightness of Being.* Trans. Michael Henry Heim. New York: HarperCollins, 1991. Print.

Lacan, Jacques. *Ecrits.* Trans. Bruce Fink. New York: Norton, 1966. Print.

———. *Le Sinthome.* University of Texas. Austin. 1975–76. Seminar 23. Print.

LaCapra, Dominick. *Representing the Holocaust: History, Theory, Trauma.* New York: Cornell UP, 1994. Print.

Lam, Melissa. *Disenfranchised From America: Reinventing Language and Love in Pynchon and Nabokov.* Lanham, MD: UP of America, 2009. Print.

Laplanche, Jean. *Life and Death in Psychoanalysis.* Trans. Jeffrey Mehlman. Baltimore and London: Johns Hopkins UP, 1976. Print.

Laplanche, Jean, and J.B. Pontalis. *The Language of Psychoanalysis.* Trans. Donald Nicholson-Smith. New York and London: W.W. Norton & Co. 1973. Print.

Leitch, Vincent B., ed. *The Norton Anthology of Theory and Criticism.* New York: Norton, 2001. Print.

Levine, Robert T., "'My Ultraviolet Darling': The Loss of Lolita's Childhood." *Modern Fiction Studies* 25.3 (1979): 471–79. Print.

Love, Heather. *Feeling Backward: Loss and the Politics of Queer History.* Cambridge: Harvard UP, 2007. Print.

———. "Queers____This." In Halley and Parker, 180–191. Print.

———. "Transgender Fiction and Politics." In Stevens, 148–164. Print.

———. "Truth and Consequences: On Paranoid Reading and Reparative Reading." *Criticism* 52.2 (2010): 235–41. Print.

Martin, Fran, et al., eds. *AsiapacifiQueer: Rethinking Genders and Sexualities.* Chicago: U of Illinois P, 2008. Print.

McDonald, Keith. "Days of Past Futures: Kazuo Ishiguro's Never Let Me Go as 'Speculative Memoir.'" *Biography: An Interdisciplinary Quarterly* 30 (2007): 74–83. Print.

McLean, Andrew. "'I Don't Hate "Real" Women:' Gay Men and 'Trans-misogyny.'" In Scherer and Ball, 83–98. Print.

Medd, Jodie. "Encountering the Past in Recent Lesbian and Gay Fiction." In Stevens 167–84. Print.

Menon, Madhavi. Introduction. *ShakesQueer: A Queer Companion to the Complete Works of Shakespeare*. 1–27. Durham, NC: Duke UP, 2011. Print.

Merrill, Robert. "Nabokov and Fictional Artifice." *Modern Fiction Studies* 25.3 (1979): 439–62. Print.

Miller, D. A. "Hitchcock's Hidden Pictures." *Critical Inquiry* 37.1 (2010): 106–30. Print.

Miller, Tyrus. *Late Modernism: Politics, Fiction, and the Arts Between the World Wars*. Berkeley: U of California P, 1999. Print.

Mitchell, Stephen, and Margaret Black. *Freud and Beyond: A History of Modern Psychoanalytic Thought*. New York: Basic Books, 1995. Print.

Mitchell, W.J.G. *Picture Theory: Essays on Verbal and Visual Representation*. Chicago: U of Chicago P, 1994. Print.

Mulvey, Laura. "Visual Pleasure and Narrative Cinema" Leitch 2181–92.

Naiman, Eric. "Hermophobia (On Sexual Orientation and Reading Nabokov." *Representations* 101 (2008): 116–43. Print.

Nabokov, Vladimir. *The Annotated Lolita*. 1955. Ed. Alfred Appel, Jr. New York: Vintage, 1991. Print.

———. *Speak, Memory*. 1966. New York: Vintage, 1989. Print.

———. *Strong Opinions*. New York: Vintage, 1990. Print.

OED Online. "care, n.1." March 2013. Oxford UP. Web. 24 April 2013.

OED Online. "fix, v." March 2013. Oxford UP. Web. 25 April 2013.

OED Online. "nostalgia, n." March 2013. Oxford UP. Web. 28 April 2013.

OED Online. "omniscience, n." May 2015. Oxford UP. Web. 25 April 2013.

Ohi, Kevin. *Innocence and Rapture: The Erotic Child in Pater, Wilde, James, and Nabokov*. New York: Palgrave Macmillan, 2005. Print.

Orwell, George. *Nineteen Eighty-Four*. London: Penguin, 1954. Print.

Palmer, Paulina. *The Queer Uncanny: New Perspectives on the Gothic*. Cardiff: U of Wales P, 2012. Print.

Pennee, Donna Palmateer. "Imagined Innocence, Endlessley Mourned: Postcolonial Nationalism and Cultural Expression in Timothy Findley's *The Wars*." *ESC: English Studies in Canada* 32.2–3 (2006): 89–113. Print.

Phillips, Adam. *The Beast in the Nursery: On Curiosity and Other Appetites*. New York: Random House, 1998. Print.

———. *Darwin's Worms: On Life Stories and Death Stories*. New York: Basic Books, 2000. Print.

———. Introduction. *The Penguin Freud Reader*. Ed. Adam Phillips. London: Penguin, 2006. vii–xv. Print.

———. *Missing Out: In Praise of the Unlived Life*. New York: Farrar, Straus and Giroux, 2012. Print.

Plascencia, Salvador. *The People of Paper*. Orlando, FL: Harcourt, 2005. Print.

Poe, Edgar Allan. *Annabel Lee.* 1849. *Literature Online.* Web. 15 May 2013.

Pomeroy, Wardell. *Dr. Kinsey and the Institute for Sex Research.* New York: Harper and Row, 1972. Print.

Preciado, Beatriz. *Testo Junkie: Sex, Drugs, and Biopolitics in the Pharmacopornographic Era.* Bruce Benderson. New York: Feminist Press, 2013. Print.

Prince, Gerald. "Introduction to the Study of the Narratee." *Reader-Response Criticism: From Formalism to Post-structuralism.* Ed. Jane P. Tomkins. Baltimore: Johns Hopkins UP, 1980. 7–25. Print.

Puchner, Martin. "When We Were Clones." *Raritan-a Quarterly Review* 27.4 (2008): 34–49. Print.

Rambuss, Richard. "After Male Sex." Halley and Parker 192–206.

Rampton, David. *Vladimir Nabokov.* New York: St Martin's Press, 1993. Print.

Rand, Erica. "After Sex?!" In Halley and Parker, 270–282. Print.

Rhodes, Shane. "Buggering with History: Sexual Warfare and Historical Reconstruction in Timothy Findley's *The Wars.*" *Canadian Literature* (159) 1998: 38–53. Print.

Rodgers: "Queers Doing Theory: Australian Queer Student Activist Print Media's Representations of Capitalism." In Scherer and Ball, 29–46. Print.

Roos, Henriette. "'Not Properly Human': Literary and Cinematic Narratives about Human Harvesting." *Journal of Literary Studies/Tydskrif vir Literatuurwetenskap* 24.3 (2008): 40–53. Print.

Rose, Jacqueline. *Sexuality in the Field of Vision.* London: Verso, 1986. Print.

——. *Why War? Psychoanalysis, Politics, and the Return to Melanie Klein.* Oxford: Blackwell, 1993. Print.

Ross, Charles S. "Nabokov's Mistress/Muse Metaphor: Some Recent Books (Book Review)." *Modern Fiction Studies* 25.3 (1979): 514–24. Print.

Ruti, Mari. *A World of Fragile Things: Psychoanalysis and the Art of Living.* Albany, NY: SUNY P, 2008. Print.

Savoy, Eric. "A Jamesian Thing." *The Henry James Review* 22.3 (2001): 268–77. Print.

Scherer, Burkhard, and Matthew Ball, eds. *Queering Paradigms II: Interrogating Agendas.* Bern: Peter Lang, 2010. Print.

Schwenger, Peter. "The Zero Effect." Congress. Ottawa University, 75 Laurier Ave E, 31 May 2015. Conference Proceeding.

Seaman, Myra. "Becoming More (than) Human: Affective Posthumanisms, Past and Future." *Journal of Narrative Theory* 37 (2007): 246–75. Print.

Sebald, W.G. *Austerlitz.* Trans. Anthea Bell. New York: Modern Library, 2001. Print.

Sedgwick, Eve Kosofksy. *Epistemology of the Closet.* Berkeley: U of California P, 1990. Print.

———. "Melanie Klein and the Difference Affect Makes." In Halley and Parker, 283–302. Print.

———. *Touching Feeling.* Durham, NC: Duke UP, 2003. Print.

———. *The Weather in Proust.* Ed. Jonathan Goldberg. Durham, NC & London: Duke UP, 2011. Print.

Sim, Wai-Chew. *Globalization and Dislocation in the Novels of Kazuo Ishiguro*. Lewiston, NY: Edwin Mellen Press, 2006. Print.

Snediker, Michael D. *Queer Optimism: Lyric Personhood and Other Felicitous Persuasions*. Minneapolis: U of Minnesota P, 2009. Print.

Stevens, Hugh, ed. *Cambridge Companion to Gay and Lesbian Writing*. Cambridge: Cambridge UP 2011. Print.

Stockton, Kathryn Bond. *The Queer Child, Or Growing Sideways in the Twentieth Century*. Durham, NC and London: Duke UP 2009. Print.

———. "The Queerness of Race and Same-sex Desire." In Stevens, 116–131. Print.

Tekiner, Christina. "Time in Lolita." *Moden Fiction Studies* 25.3 (1979): 463–69. Print.

Thomas, Kate. "Post Sex: On Being Too Slow, Too Stupid, Too Soon." In Halley and Parker, 66–78. Print.

Toker, Leona, and Daniel Chertoff. "Reader Response and the Recycling of Topoi in Kazuo Ishiguro's Never Let Me Go." *Partial Answers-Journal of Literature and the History of Ideas* 6.1 (2008): 163–80. Print.

Trilling, Lionel. "The Last Lover." *Encounter* 4 (1958): 9–19. Print.

Tsao, Tiffany. "The Tyranny of Purpose: Religion and Biotechnology in Ishiguro's Never Let Me Go." *Literature and Theology* 26.2 (2012): 214–32. Print.

Tweedie, James. "Lolita's Loose Ends: Nabokov and the Boundless Novel." *Twentieth Century Literature* 46.2 (2000): 150–70. Print.

Walkowitz, Rebecca. "Unimaginable Largeness: Kazuo Ishiguro, Translation, and the New World Literature." *Novel: A Forum on Fiction* 40 (2007): 216–39. Print.

Webber, Andrew. "Psychoanalysis, Homosexuality, and Modernism." Stevens 34–49.

Whitehead, Anne. "Writing with Care: Kazuo Ishiguro's Never Let Me Go." *Contemporary Literature* 52.1 (2011): 54–83. Print.

Whiting, Frederick. "'The Strange Particularity of the Lover's Preference': Pedophilia, Pornography, and the Anatomy of Monstrosity in Lolita" *American Literature* 70.4 (1998): 833–62. Print.

Wilde, Alan. *Horizons of Assent: Modernism, Postmodernism, and the Ironic Imagination*. Philadelphia: U of Pennsylvania P, 1987. Print.

Winnicott, D.W. *Playing and Reality*. New York: Routledge, 2005. Print.

Wyile, Herb. "It's Just a Story: Postmodernism, Politics and Findley's Italics." *Journal of Canadian Studies* 33.4 (1998–99): 63–74. Print.

York, Lorraine. "A Shout of Recognition: Likeness and the Art of Recognition in Timothy Findley's *The Wars*." *English Studies in Canada* 11.2 (1985): 223–30. Print.

———. "'Violent Stillness': Photography and Postmodernism in Canadian Fiction." *Mosaic* 21.2 (1988): 193–201. Print.

Žižek, Slavoj. *The Sublime Object of Ideology*. London: Verso, 1989. Print.

Index